Aspects of
Interstate Rendition
and
International Extradition

I0505724

James Biser Whiskcr
and
Kevin R. Spiker

Heritage House, 2021

This book is respectfully dedicated to

Royal Clarence Gilkey, Ph.D. (1919-2014)

Major, U. S. Army Air Corps
World War II veteran

Professor of Political Science
West Virginia University
beloved teacher
accomplished researcher

Denied *Emeritus* status
by vindictive and jealous colleagues

James B Whisker is professor emeritus from West Virginia University where he taught for over 37 years. He was adviser to the WVU College Republicans during most of his tenure. He received his B.S. From Mount St. Mary's College; masters degrees in history and philosophy from Niagara University; and Ph. D. in 1969 from the University of Maryland. He is author or co-author of books on gunsmiths and arms makers of eighteen states. He co-authored books on clockmakers and silversmiths of Pennsylvania, Virginia, West Virginia, and Maryland. His book on West Virginia arms makers has gone through four editions. His five volume study of the colonial American Militia won the Adele Mellon Prize. He recently published a book on the armorers of the U. S. Arsenal at Harpers Ferry. Among his other books are *Command Responsibility; The Militia; The Right to Hunt; Capital Punishment in American Courts; Capital Punishment in Traditional Thought; The Citizen-Soldier and U.S. Military Policy, Our Vanishing Freedom: The Right to Keep and Bear Arms,* and the *Rise and Decline of the American Militia System.* Most recently Sage Publications accepted both his *The Alien Tort Claims Act* and *The Just War in Traditional Catholic Thought.* He currently resides in Everett with his wife of 51 years, the former Sheila Elaine Bailey.

Kevin R. Spiker Is a graduate of Bedfprd High School, the Pennsylvania State University, and West Virginia University where he earned his Ph.D. He has taught political science at West Virginia University, Frostburg State Univerity and is currently associate professor at Ohio University. With Professor Whisker he has co-authored a series on Bedford County, Pennsylvania, history; *The Pennsylvania Coloial Militia; The Alien Tort Statute,* and *Command Responsibility.* They are currently working on additional publications on the death penalty. His teaching areas include areas of American political institutiions and the American presidency. He is currently preparing a book on presidentiual clemency.

Contents

Introduction

When I was teaching international law at West Virginia University, extradition was among the several subjects that took more than one lecture. Conversely, when I and others were teaching American national, state, and local government we rarely spent any time at all on interstate rendition. Indeed, in lectures and textbooks little was said of rendition as an idea, with extradition being the mistakenly preferred term. So it has also emerged in the various media to the exclusion of the term rendition.[1]

Extradition has evolved considerably within my lifetime, especially with the emergence of the refoulement doctrine in opposition to the long established non-inquiry rule. In and of itself, the non-inquiry is, at one and the same time, both necessary and illogical. A less civilized nation is far less likely to extradite if it realizes the requesting nation looks down upon its system of justice. But inequality in all aspects of the justice system is an absolute unquestioned fact.

Too, most of the Western Democracies have rejected capital punishment as appropriate for certain heinous crimes, and so may refuse extradition, despite the existence of treaties, to the United States and other nations where executions of convicted criminals is still possible. Other nations which oppose capital punishment may agree to extradition only if the requesting nation agrees not to seek execution as punishment should the subject be convicted. That condition is hard, if not impossible, to deal with in the United States simply because all diplomacy is conducted by the national government which cannot dictate to the states how and under what conditions they may choose to prosecute. In one incident, the U. S. State Department agreed that a fugitive hiding in Canada would not be prosecuted for a capital crime. When he was returned the state chose to prosecute for a capital crime. Nothing of course could be done, although there was a heated exchange of diplomatic notes. And that prosecution made it mire difficult to effect extradition the next time. A few nations have taken a middle course: they will extradite a person for possible execution, excepting only if the subject is a citizen of the host state.

Regarding interstate rendition, the only change of any significance to laymen is the U.S. Supreme Court's ruling that it is a manda-

---

1   Scott, James A. *The Law of Interstate Rendition Erroneously Referred to as Interstate Extradition: A Treatise*. Chicago: Sherman Hight, 1917.

tory, not a discretionary, duty of the executive offices within the fifty states and also in American territories. Most of the earlier cases of refusal to render up an escaped or fleeing subject had involved vast regional differences in treatment, beginning with slavery. Northern officials who were scrupulously opposed to that human bondage often refused to return escaped slaves, even after the Fugitive Slave Act of 1793, and especially the later legislation of the same name enacted in 1850. Related to that same reasoning were various anti-miscegenation laws and prohibitions against inter-racial marriages. Once the federal Constitution prohibited slavery, so-called chain gangs made up of convicted criminals appeared. Many Northern states were outraged by not only the use of chain gangs, but in the treatment of the prisoners.

The law of rendition is covered by the U. S. Constitution, Article IV, section 2, clause 2, as interpreted and illuminated by decisions of the U. S. Supreme Court. Because the federal government acts as the superior judging authority, and not as an equal party, it can order how, when, and why extradition is to occur and then supervise the full and correct execution of its order.

The law of extradition is made by treaties among two or more sovereign states, and each treaty may be quite unique regarding what offenses are subject to extradition, how the arrest and transfer are made, and many other conditions. But there are two eual and sovereign powers, with the one having not greater authority than the other. To suggest that some international tribunal which is superior to be parties may settle disputes regarding treaty requirements is premature. Most states, upon losing their cases, frequently ignore the international court which then has no power to back its judgments.

If sovereign states, for whatever reason, refuse extradition, the requesting state may choose to kidnap the subject. Many states have accepted the abduction of a fleeing person but only if the taking outside the sovereign state's own jurisdiction is accomplished by persons not directly associated with the state. Once the kidnapped person is brought within the jurisdiction of the requesting state, officials may take custody and remand the prisoner to the justice system. The bold kidnapping of Nazi fugitive Adolf Eichmann by Israeli state secret police while he was living in Argentina not only brought strong condemnation from Argentine officials, it offended the sense of justice in other states. Can one do a good thing (prosecution of a war criminal) by illegal means (kidnapping)? The outrage was largely connected with the clear violation of Argentine territorial sovereignty. Under the traditional law of nations, any and all abduction, in lieu of formal extradition, is illegal. The practice of nations has proved to be otherwise. It would be hard, if not impossible, to construct a legal argument that would allow for kidnapping.

Since the end of World War II, modern democratic nations have sought to ensure basic human rights for all humanity. Various pronouncements, such as the Universal Declaration of Human Rights (UDHR) of 10 December 1948, have brought human rights concerns to the forefront of international debate and concern. When a nation requests the extradition of one of its citizens, is it because of a real crime or is it from advocacy of human rights? Many rights activists flee from persecution, often asking for asylum. One of the most difficult questions for states is how to differentiate between criminal acts and civil rights activities. Simple request asylum is not a guarantee of innocent behavior, nor is a state demand for return of a purported criminal a guarantee of his having committed an actual crime.

James B. Whisker
Professor Emeritus
West Virginia University

Extradition and Rendition

The Articles of Confederation contained a strong Extradition Clause which made clear a distinction between domestic interstate rendition and international extradition. The Northwest Ordinance of July 1787 contained a provision which said that slaves "may be lawfully reclaimed" from free states and territories. Soon after, a fugitive slave clause, specifically Article IV, Section 2, was incorporated into the new federal Constitution. That provision was sponsored by the Southern delegation at Philadelphia. Delegate Charles Pinckney of South Carolina wrote that, "We have obtained a right to recover our slaves in whatever part of America they may take refuge, which is a right we had not before."

Technically the term extradition applies to a process of returning a fugitive from one country to another. This process is governed by treaty agreements between the two countries. The process between two states is one of rendering the fugitive by one state to another, or *interstate rendition*. The rendition process is governed by the US Constitution, federal statute and state statues. International extradition procedure differs significantly from interstate rendition. Despite the differences, the procedure between the states is commonly referred to as *extradition*.[2]

James Alexander Scott (1848-1915), a century ago, was unable to convince scholars and judges, as well as his fellow attorneys, to use the correct term rendition instead of extradition. It is therefore most unlikely that this tome will have the slightest impact on the legal lexicon. We shall surrender early on and fall into the common usage, *extradition*.

Rendition

Interstate Rendition is the right of one state to demand from the asylum state the surrender of a fugitive from justice from the demanding state when the fugitive is found in the asylum state. Rendition means to surrender or handing over of a person or property,

---

2 Scott, James Alexander *The law of interstate rendition erroneously referred to as interstate extradition; a treatise on the arrest and surrender of fugitives from the justice of one state to another; the removal of federal prisoners from one district to another; and the exemption of persons from service of civil process; with an appendix of the statutes of the states and territories on fugitives from justice.* (1917). Reprint by Hardpress, 2013.

particularly from one jurisdiction to another. Interstate rendition clause refers to a clause in the U. S. Constitution that provides for the extradition of a criminal back to the state where s/he has committed a crime. Rendition in common parlance means the surrender or handing over of a person or property, particularly from one jurisdiction to another. The asylum state is where the fugitive or defendant is found and the demanding state is the state which seeks to extradite the fugitive. Extraditable Offense refers to any criminal offense, felony or misdemeanor, in the demanding state regardless of whether the offense is a crime in the asylum state. Interstate rendition refers to the surrender by one state or country of a person charged with a crime in another state or country. Formally, the request of the state, usually through the Governor's office, claiming the right to prosecute is made to the Governor of the state in which the accused is present. Occasionally a Governor will refuse to render up a person if that governor is satisfied that the prosecution is not warranted, despite a constitutional mandate that "on demand of the Executive authority of the State from which a fugitive from justice fled, be delivered up, to be removed to the State having jurisdiction of the crime." The defendant may "waive extradition" and allow himself/herself to be taken into custody and returned to the state where charges are pending.[3]

Rendition means to surrender or handing over of a person or property, particularly from one jurisdiction to another. Interstate rendition clause refers to a clause in the U.S. Constitution that provides for the extradition of a criminal back to the state where s/he has committed a crime. Rendition in common parlance means the surrender or handing over of a person or property, particularly from one jurisdiction to another. In the U.S. Constitution, there is a provision for interstate rendition.[4] This provision of the constitution reads as "A Person charged in any State with Treason, Felony, or other Crime, who shall flee from Justice, and be found in another State, shall on Demand of the executive Authority of the State from which he fled, be delivered up, to be removed to the State having Jurisdiction of the Crime". Each state has a presumptive duty to render the suspects on the request of another state. This clause is also known as extradition clause.

---

3   U.S.Legal.com. See also "Interstate Rendition: Executive Practices and the Effects of Discretion," *Yale Law Journal*, 66: 1 (1956), pp. 97-120; . Zimmerman, Joseph F., "Dimensions of Interstate Relations," *Publius,* 24: 4 (1994), pp. 1-11.
4   USCS Const. Art. IV, § 2, Cl 2.

The Interstate Rendition Clause derives from similar language in the Articles of Confederation, but the principle of extradition between governments dates to antiquity. The Framers' purpose was to foster comity between states and to prevent criminals from evading law enforcement. Despite its classical roots, the Framers regarded interstate rendition as distinct from international extradition. In 1793, Congress passed the first rendition act because it suspected that the clause would not be viewed legally as self-executing. That early statute governed rendition from territories as well as states. Although there is no express power granted to Congress to govern rendition, Justice Joseph Story regarded it as implied from the moral duty of Congress to carry into execution the duties imposed on the federal government by the Constitution.[5]

The Interstate Rendition Clause has certain requirements: (A) a facially valid criminal charge in a demanding state, (B) a flight to an asylum state, and (C) an executive demand for return. The Framers specified the words "Treason" and "Felony" to show that political crimes warrant rendition, as well as "other Crimes" to comprehend all crimes, regardless of gravity.[6] Exempted from the scope of the clause are civil liabilities and private debts. As to what constitutes a criminal charge, the 1793 act requires indictment or affidavit, but does not mention the criminal information. This omission arguably was deliberate, as such information was a known device abused by the British. The meaning of *charged* remains unresolved in this respect.

The Interstate Rendition Clause apparently assumes that deliberate flight has occurred. Early writers speculated, for example, that a person involuntarily removed from one state to a second state could not be rendered back to the first state. Neither could that person be rendered forward to a third state. Considering the purpose of the clause as an assist to enforcement of the law, flight has been construed without regard to intent, requiring only that the person sought be alleged to have been physically present in the demanding state so as to commit an overt act in furtherance of a crime there.[7] The fact that a fugitive is present in an asylum state before the indictment is issued does not insulate him from rendition.[8]

---

5   *Prigg v. Pennsylvania*, 41 U. S. 539 (1842).

6   *Taylor v. Taintor*, 83 U. S. 366 (1872); *Kentucky v. Dennison,* 65 U. S. 66 (1860).

7   *Strassheim v. Daily* 221 U. S. 280 (1911); *Appleyard v. Massachusetts, 203 U. S. 222* (1906).

8   *Roberts v. Reilly,* 116 U. S. 80 (1885).

In the period before the U.S. Civil War, some Northern governors refused to return fugitives charged with slavery-related crimes to
Southern states. As we shall see, since the Civil War, the U. S.
Supreme Court has limited the scope of the executive power in the
asylum state to decline rendition. An executive wishing to decline
may only determine whether the person sought is charged with a
crime under the law of the state's making the request. He may also determine whether that person is truly a fugitive, meaning that the person was actually present in state making the request when the alleged
overt act occurred.[9]

However, other question, for example, guilt or innocence, sufficiency of evidence, construction of state law, or adequacy of justice
can be determined only in the state making the request for interstate
rendition, not in the asylum state.[10] As we shall see, in 1987, the
Supreme Court removed the last vestige of antebellum choice, ruling
that federal courts may compel state executives to render fugitives so
long as the request is properly framed.[11]

The details and complexities of the Interstate Rendition Clause
particulars are controlled by the Uniform Extradition and Rendition
Act, adopted in some form in every state. State rendition laws have
been upheld insofar as they are consistent with the Constitution and
federal statute. Furthermore, the states today provide for rendition
outside the scope of the clause. For example, states may agree to render subpoenaed witnesses and charged persons who were never
present in the demanding state. It is unclear whether these ancillary
agreements in any way offend the original conception of the Interstate
Rendition Clause as an exclusive process. For example, an agreement
between two states to allow rendition even if there are procedural de-
ficiencies in the demand for rendition may contravene the Due
Process Clause of the Fourteenth Amendment.

Rendition concerns a fugitive from justice. To be included
within the meaning of this clause, it is necessary that, in the regular
course of judicial proceedings, one has been charged with a crime. It
is not necessary that one has left the state after having been charged. It
is sufficient that, having been charged with a crime in one state, one is

---

9   *Munsey v. Clough*, 196 U. S. 364 (1905)
10 *New Mexico ex rel. Ortiz v. Reed*, 524 U.S. 151 (1998); *Lascelles v. Georgia*,
     148 U. S. 547 (1893).
11 *Puerto Rico v. Branstad*, 483 U. S. 219 (1987)

found in another state.[12] And the motive that induced the flight is of no interest to the courts.[13] Even if a fugitive was to be brought involuntarily into the state where found by requisition from another state, he may still be surrendered to a third state upon an extradition warrant.[14] A person indicted a second time for the same offense is nonetheless a fugitive from justice by reason of the fact that after dismissal of the first indictment, on which he was originally indicted, he left the state with the knowledge of, or without objection by, state authorities.[15] But a defendant cannot be extradited if he was only constructively present in the demanding state at the time of the commission of the crime charged.[16] For the purpose of determining who is a fugitive from justice, the words "treason, felony or other crime" embrace every act forbidden and made punishable by a law of a state, including misdemeanors.[17]

Only after a person has been charged with a crime in normal judicial proceedings is the governor of a state allowed to demand for a fugitive's return from another state. The requesting executive must produce a copy of an indictment found or an affidavit made before a magistrate of any State or Territory. The requesting executive must produce a copy of an indictment found or an affidavit made before a magistrate of any State or Territory. That document must charge the fugitive demanded with having committed treason, felony, or other crime. The document must be certified as authentic by the governor or chief magistrate of the state or territory from whence the person so charged has fled. [18] The executive receiving the request must then cause the fugitive to be arrested and secured, and notify the requesting executive authority or agent to receive the fugitive. An agent of the executive of the State demanding extradition must appear to receive the prisoner, which must occur within thirty days from time of arrest or the prisoner may be released. The fugitive has no constitutional

---

12 *Roberts v. Reilly,* 116 U.S. 80, 95 (1885). See also *Strassheim v. Daily,* 221 U.S. 280 (1911); *Appleyard v. Massachusetts,* 203 U.S. 222 (1906); *Ex parte Reggel,* 114 U.S. 642, 650 (1885).

13 *Drew v. Thaw,* 235 U.S. 432 (1914).

14 *Innes v. Tobin,* 240 U.S. 127 (1916).

15 *Bassing v. Cady,* 208 U.S. 386 (1908).

16 *Hyatt v. People ex rel. Corkran,* 188 U.S. 691 (1903).

17 *Kentucky v. Dennison,* 65 U.S. (24 How.) 66, 103 (1861).

18 *Kentucky v. Dennison,* 65 U.S. (24 How.) 66, 104 (1861); *Pierce v. Creecy,* 210 U.S. 387 (1908). See also *Matter of Strauss,* 197 U.S. 324, 325 (1905); *Marbles v. Creecy,* 215 U.S. 63 (1909); *Strassheim v. Daily,* 221 U.S. 280 (1911).

right to be heard before the governor of the state to which he has fled on the question whether he has been substantially charged with crime and is truly a fugitive.[19] The constitutionally required surrender is not to be interrupted by a *habeas corpus* centering on speculations as to what might be the result of a trial.[20] Neither is it proper thereby to inquire concerning the motives controlling the actions of the governors of the respective states.[21] Matters that might be used by the defense, such as the statute of limitations,[22] or the contention that continued confinement in the prison of the demanding state would amount to cruel and unjust punishment,[23] also cannot be heard on *habeas corpus* but should be tested in the courts of the demanding state, where all parties may be heard, where all pertinent testimony will be readily available. There alone appropriate relief, if any is appropriate, may be fashioned. A defendant must be discharged on *habeas corpus* if he can show, by clear and satisfactory evidence, that he was not inside the demanding state at the time of the crime.[24] If, however, the evidence is conflicting, *habeas corpus* is not a proper proceeding to try the question of alibi. The concern of the *habeas court* is quite limited.[25]

The Uniform Criminal Extradition Act has been adopted by 48 of the 50 states, the exceptions being South Carolina and Missouri. The Act sets forth the process by which a state may request surrender of a wanted individual and the manner in which that individual is surrendered. While there are some variances among the Act as adopted by the states, the principal requirements for extradition are as follows: There must be a valid arrest warrant issued by the demanding state. The executive authority, usually the state's governor must make a formal dean for the person's return. A judicial hearing in the state having custody of the wanted person follows. The subject may waive extradition. If he chooses to reject extradition there will be a hearing that will determine whether the request follows all legal requirements. As-

---

19 *Munsey v. Clough,* 196 U.S. 364 (1905); *Pettibone v. Nichols*, 203 U.S. 192 (1906).

20 *Drew v. Thaw,* 235 U.S. 432 (1914).

21 *Pettibone v. Nichols*, 203 U.S. 192 (1906).

22 *Biddinger v. Commissioner of Police*, 245 U.S. 128 (1917). See also *Rodman v. Pothier,* 264 U.S. 399 (1924).

23 *Sweeney v. Woodall*, 344 U.S. 86 (1952).

24 *Hyatt v. People ex rel. Corkran*, 188 U.S. 691 (1903). See also *South Carolina v. Bailey*, 289 U.S. 412 (1933).

25 Munsey v. Clough, 196 U.S. 364 at 375 (1905).

suming that extradition is granted or the right to the hearing is waived, the state which requested rendition must take custody within thirty days. If the demanding state does not take custody within 30 days, the prisoner may be discharged..[26]

Fugitive from Justice

Soon after the ratification of the U. S. Constitution, Congress adopted legislation in effect enacting the non-self-executing provision of interstate rendition of fugitives from justice. Congress ordered that governors of all states be willing to render up fugitives, but that duty is not absolute. To understand the executive duty we must first understand what legally a fugitive from justice is.[27]

To be a fugitive from justice within the meaning of the interstate rendition clause of the U. S. Constitution, it is necessary that, in the regular course of judicial proceedings, one have been charged with a crime, but it is not necessary that one have left the state after having been charged. It is sufficient that, having been charged with a crime in one state, one is found in another state.[28] During the era (1864-1873) when Chief Justice Salmon P. Chase (1808-1873) led the Supreme Court, Congress had stripped the Court of the authority to hear appeals from *habeas* petitions in the circuit courts, but Congress subsequently restored that power. In *Roberts v. Reilly* (1885), the Supreme Court under Chief Justice Morrison Waite (1816-1888) affirmed a denial of *habeas corpus* on the merits, but held that it had jurisdiction to consider such appeals under the Extradition Act.

It is immaterial what the motive was which had induced the subject to flee.[29] Because the Constitution requires that, upon proper demand, the person charged with crime shall be delivered up to be removed to the state having jurisdiction of the crime, there is no discretion allowed, nor any inquiry permitted, into motives. Nothing is to be said in regard to *habeas corpus,* and the technical sufficiency of the

---

26 Black, Forrest Revere," Interstate Rendition as Applied to a Person Brought Involuntarily into the Surrendering State," 29 *American Institute of Criminal Law & Criminology* 309 (1938-1939)

27 "Scope of Inquiry on *Habeas Corpus* by Fugitive from Justice in Interstate Rendition" *Columbia Law Review,* 21: 7 (1921), pp. 709-11.

28 *Roberts v. Reilly,* 116 U.S. 80, 95 (1885). See also *Strassheim v. Daily,* 221 U.S. 280 (1911); *Appleyard v. Massachusetts,* 203 U.S. 222 (1906); *Ex parte Reggel,* 114 U.S. 642, 650 (1885).

29 *Drew v. Thaw,* 235 U.S. 432, 439 (1914).

indictment is not open. Questions as to the sufficiency of an indictment charging an admittedly insane person, as was the case here, with having committed a crime are for the courts of the state having jurisdiction of the crime to determine according to the law of that state. They cannot be determined by the courts of another state on *habeas corpus* proceedings in interstate rendition. The constitutionally required surrender of an identified fugitive from justice on a demand made in due form is not to be interfered with by the summary process of *habeas corpus* upon speculation as to what ought to be the result of a trial in the place where the Constitution provides for its taking place. The case of *Drew v. Thaw* held that "A party to a crime who afterwards leaves the State is a fugitive from justice; and, for the purposes of interstate rendition, it does not matter what motive induced the departure." going." The Supreme Court ruled that "A party to a crime who afterwards leaves the State is a fugitive from justice; and, for the purposes of interstate rendition, it does not matter what motive induced the departure."

Even if a fugitive were brought involuntarily into the state where found by requisition from another state, he may be surrendered to a third state upon an extradition warrant.[30] The *Innes* case involved three states. The governor of Oregon had honored a requisition made by the governor of Texas for the delivery of the plaintiff in error for removal to Texas as a fugitive from the justice of that state. The accused was taken to Texas, tried for murder and a conspiracy to comit murder, as stated in the Texas extradition request, but she was acquitted. She was not released from custody because the governor of Georgia had requested extradition to that state, to be held as a fugitive from justice. The doctrine of asylum applicable under international law by which a person extradited from a foreign country cannot be tried for an offense other than the one for which the extradition was asked does not apply to interstate rendition. The Supreme Court held:

> An Act of Congress which leaves a subject with which Congress has power to deal under the Constitution unprovided for does not necessarily take the matters within the unprovided area out of any possible state action, and so held that the exclusive character of § 5278 Revised Statutes. does not relate to the rendition between criminals found in, but who had not fled to, the surrendering state but had been involuntarily brought therein. In construing an Act of Congress, this Court will not presume

---

30 *Innes v. Tobin*, 240 U.S. 127 (1916).

that, because its provisions were not coterminous with the power granted by Congress, it was so framed for the purpose of leaving the subject, so far as unprovided for, beyond the operation of any legal authority whatever, state or national.

In July 1907 the governor of Rhode Island issued a warrant of arrest based upon information that had been communicated to him by the governor of New York that Jacob Bassing had been charged with the crime of grand larceny in New York, and was a fugitive from the justice of the latter state, and was supposed to be then in Rhode Island. Bassing claimed that he had previously been extradited from Rhode Island in March 1907 on the same change, tried, and released in New York. The Supreme Court, however, ruled that Bassing was a fugitive from justice insofar as the governor of Rhode Island was concerned and thus had been lawfully taken into custody. Therefore, a person indicted a second time for the same offense is nonetheless a fugitive from justice by reason of the fact that after dismissal of the first indictment, on which he was originally indicted, he left the state with the knowledge of, or without objection by, state authorities. In *Bassing v. Cady* the high court held that "One charged with crime and who was in the place where, and at the time when, the crime was committed, and who thereafter leaves the State, no matter for what reason, is a fugitive from justice within the meaning of the interstate rendition proceedings of the Constitution . . . and this none the less if he leaves the State with the knowledge and without the objection of its authorities."[31]

However, person for whose delivery a demand has been made by executive authority of one state upon the executive authority of another state, and who can show conclusively, based upon conceded facts, that he was not within the demanding state at the time stated in the indictment, nor at any time when the acts were, if ever, committed, is not a fugitive from justice according to the federal statute upon the subject of interstate extradition and rendition. A defendant cannot be extradited if he was only constructively present in the demanding state at the time of the commission of the crime charged.[32]

For the purpose of determining who is a fugitive from justice, the words "treason, felony or other crime" embrace every act forbid-

---

31 *Bassing v. Cady,* 208 U.S. 386 (1908).
32 *Hyatt v. People ex rel. Corkran,* 188 U.S. 691 (1903).

den and made punishable by a law of a state,[33] including misdemeanors.[34]

Extradition Defined

As the first circuit, U. S. Court of Appeals[35] viewed extradition,
one must begin with the plain meaning and derivations of the words
extradite and *extradition*. The dictionary definition of "extradite" is,
"To deliver up, as to another state or nation."[36] Extradition is alternatively defined in dictionaries as, "The surrender of an accused person
by a government to the justice of another government, or of a prisoner
by one authority to another," id., as "the surrender of an alleged fugitive from justice or criminal by one state, nation, or authority to another."[37] A third definition reads, "The surrender or delivery of an
alleged criminal usu[ually] under the provisions of a treaty or statute
by one country, state, or other power to another having jurisdiction to
try the charge."[38] Legal usage has followed the word's plain meaning.
Online dictionary.com defines extradition as "the procedure by which
a state or nation, upon receipt of a formal request by another state or
nation, turns over to that second jurisdiction an individual charged
with or convicted of a crime in that jurisdiction."[39] Another dictionary
on the worldwide net defines extradition as "the transfer of an accused
from one state or country to another state or country that seeks to
place the accused on trial.[40] *Black's Law Dictionary*[41] defines "extradition" by closely paraphrasing the formula given in the *Terlinden* decision, wherein the Supreme Court defined "[e]xtradition" as "the
surrender by one nation to another of an individual accused or convicted of an offence outside its own territory, and within the territorial
jurisdiction of the other, which, being competent to try and to punish

---

33 *Kentucky v. Dennison*, 65 U.S. (24 How.) 66, 103 (1861).
34 *Taylor v. Taintor*, 83 U.S. (16 Wall.) 366, 375 (1873).
35 *United States v Lui Kin-Hong,* also known as Lerry lui, 83 F. 3rd 523 (1996),
    First Circuit.
36 Funk & Wagnalls *New Comprehensive International Dictionary of the English
    Language* 450 (1978)
37 The Random House *Dictionary of the English Language* 685 (2d ed.1987)
38 Webster's *Third International Dictionary* 806 (1986).
39 https://www.dictionary.com/browse/extradition
40 https://legal-dictionary.thefreedictionary.com/Extradition+treaty
41 *Black's Law Dictionary* 526 (5th ed.1979) (replacing the word "nation" with
    "state or country").

him, demands the surrender."[42]

Reference is always made to the U. S. Supreme Court's seminal decision on extradition, rendered in 1902, and cited as *Terlinden v. Ames*[43] In *Terlinden*, the Court explained that a state requesting a relator's extradition must be "competent to try and to punish him." The Supreme Court in Terlinden was asked to determine whether the German Empire could successfully request a relator's extradition on the basis of a treaty between the United States and the Kingdom of Prussia, where the two sovereigns, King and Emperor, were one and the same. The Court concluded that the Kingdom of Prussia, although part of the subsequently formed German Empire, continued to enjoy "its identity as such," and treaties that it had entered could still be performed "either in the name of its King or that of the Emperor." In making its determination, the Court explained that "the question whether power remains in a foreign State to carry out its treaty obligations is in its nature political and not judicial, and that the courts ought not to interfere with the conclusions of the political department in that regard." In *Terlinden*, the question was whether or not the Kingdom of Prussia continued to have an independent existence and whether its treaty obligations could be exercised in the name of its King notwithstanding the fact that he had subsequently acquired "the title of German Emperor."

Extradition Among Nations

There is no international obligation to extradite in the absence of a treaty. The United States, therefore, has entered into extradition agreements with more than eighty nations. Most of the current treaties contain clauses expressly setting forth the specialty principle in one form or another. These clauses, however, vary greatly in scope and are either vague or silent on the respective rights of the surrendering state and the accused. For instance, certain U.S. treaties flatly prohibit the trial of an extraditee for any offense not included in the extradition request. These treaties are of little or no assistance to a court attempting to determine whether specialty is a right of the accused or of the surrendering state. Treaties that allow either the extraditee, the surrendering state, or both to consent to trial for offenses not listed in the extradition request may be of more help in determining for whose

---

42 *Terlinden v Ames,* 184 U.S. 270, (1902)
43 *Terlinden v Ames,* 184 U.S. 270, (1902)

benefit the principle of specialty exists. Some U.S. treaties allow the extraditee to waive application of the principle. The principles of international law recognize no right to extradition apart from treaty. While a government may, if agreeable to its own constitution and laws, voluntarily exercise the power to surrender a fugitive from justice to the country from which he has fled, and it has been said that it is under a moral duty to do so, the legal right to demand his extradition and the correlative duty to surrender him to the demanding country exist only when created by treaty.

Extradition from one state to another takes place on the order of the governor of the asylum state, that is, the state where the accused is located. The courts in the asylum state have a somewhat limited function in extraditing the accused to the state where she or he is charged with a crime. They determine only whether the extradition documents are in order. For example, they examine whether the papers allege that the accused has committed a crime and that she or he is a fugitive. They do not consider the merits of the charge, since the trial of the accused will take place in the state demanding extradition.

In some cases, courts considering extradition from one state to another may go beyond the procedural formalities and look at the merits of the criminal charge or at allegations by the accused that extradition will lead to harmful consequences beyond a prison term. These cases are rare because under the U.S. Constitution, states are not given the power to review the underlying charge. For example, this problem occurred when the state of New Mexico refused to return a fugitive to the state of Ohio.[44]

The Supreme Court has identified that a court considering an extradition case can only decide four issues: (1) whether the extradition documents on their face are in order, (2) whether the petitioner has been charged with a crime in the demanding state, (3) whether the petitioner is the person named in the request for the extradition, and (4) whether the petitioner is a fugitive.[45]

International extradition is more difficult and is governed in many cases by treaty. While most countries will extradite persons charged with serious crimes, others refuse to extradite if the accused

---

44 *New Mexico ex rel. Ortiz v. Reed*, 524 U.S. 151 (1998),

45 "Extradition and Rendition," *Encyclopedia of Federalism,* Center for the Study of Federalism, October 2018.

may get the death penalty.[46] One very serious matter as regards the United States is whether, should the national government assure a foreign nation that the person will not be tried from capital crime, the federal government can actually prevent one of its states from seeking the death penalty.

Extradition from one nation to another is handled in a similar manner, with the head of one country demanding the return of a fugitive who is alleged to have committed a crime in that country. Extradition between nations is usually based on a treaty between the country where the accused is currently located and the country seeking to place him or her on trial for an alleged crime. The United States has entered into extradition treaties with most countries in Europe and Latin America, and with a few countries in Africa and Asia.

To determine whether an individual can be extradited pursuant to a treaty, the language of the particular treaty must be examined. Some trer certain crimes, set up legal roadblocks, or, as in Canada's case, waties list all the offenses for which a person can be extradited; others provide a minimum standard of punishment that will render an offesed completely if an offense is added to the list.

Even if they do not specifically say so, most treaties contemplate that for an offense to be subject to extradition, it must be a crime under the law in both jurisdictions. The extradition treaties of most countries fall into the second category, since treaties in the first category must be reviity. The name by which the crime is described in the two countries need not be the same, nor must the punishment be the same; simply, the requirement of double criminality is met if the particular act charged is criminal in both jurisdictions.[47]

The applicable extradition statutes of the United States make few references to any aspect of the principle of the principle of specialty. The Secretary of State has discretionary power under to deliver fugitives to foreign governments so that they may "be tried for the offense of which charged."[48] The executive department must protect a fugitive returned to the United States "until the final conclusion of his trial for the offenses specified in the warrant of extradition.[49] As it is, judicial interpretation of these provisions varies according to what

46 Copyright © 1981-2005 by Gerald N. Hill and Kathleen T. Hill. All Right reserved. https://legal-dictionary.thefreedictionary.com/extradition

47 *Collins v. Loisel*, 259 U.S. 309, 42 S. Ct. 469, 66 (1922).

48 18 U.S.C. § 3186

49 18 U.S.C. § 3192

federal circuit rules.

Point of Dissimilarity

There is nothing in the Constitution or laws of the United States that exempts an offender, brought before the courts of a state for an offense against its laws, from trial and punishment, even though he was brought from another state by what may be considered unlawful violence.[50] Specifically, the U. S. Constitution, and laws made pursuant to it, offer no mode by which a person, unlawfully abducted from one state to another and held in the latter state upon process of law for an offense against the state, can be restored to the state from which he was abducted. There exists no comity between the states by which a person held upon an indictment for a criminal offense in one state can be turned over to the authorities of another state, although abducted from the latter. In the *Mahon* case, a person indicted in Kentucky for felony, escaped to West Virginia. While the Governor of West Virginia was considering an application from the Governor of Kentucky for his surrender as a fugitive from justice, he was forcibly abducted to Kentucky, and when there was seized by the Kentucky authorities under legal process, and put in jail and held to answer the indictment. The court held that he was not entitled to be discharged from custody under a writ of *habeas corpus* from the circuit court of the United States.

Neither would the U. S. Supreme Court interfere in cases of abuses of the legal processes.[51] In the Cook case the Supreme Court Court ruled that it would not interfere to relieve persons who have been arrested and taken by violence from the territory of one state to that of another where they are held under process legally issued from the courts of the latter state. A fugitive lawfully extradited from another state may be tried for an offense other than that for which he was surrendered.[52]

The *Lascelles* case involved a single federal question: whether a fugitive from justice who has been surrendered by one state of the union to another state thereof upon requisition charging him with the commission of a specific crime has, under the Constitution and laws of the United States, a right, privilege, or immunity to be exempt from

---

50 *Ker v. Illinois*, 119 U.S. 436, 444 (1886); *Mahon v. Justice*, 127 U.S. 700, 707, 712, 714 (1888).

51 *Cook v. Hart*, 146 U.S. 183, 193 (1892); *Pettibone v. Nichols*, 203 U.S. 192, 215 (1906).

52 *Lascelles v. Georgia*, 148 U.S. 537, 543 (1893).

indictment and trial in the state to which he is returned for any other or different offense than that designated and described in the requisition proceedings under which he was demanded by and restored to such state without first having an opportunity to return to the state from which he was extradited.

Briefly, the facts of the case on which this question was raised were these: in July, 1891, two indictments by a grand jury of Floyd County, Georgia, against the plaintiff, Walter S. Beresford, charged him with the offenses "of being a common cheat and swindler" and with the crime of "larceny after trust delegated," both being criminal acts by the laws of Georgia, and alleged to have been committed in the County of Floyd. The high court ruled that a fugitive from justice who has been surrendered by one state of the union to another State upon requisition charging him with the commission of a specific crime has, under the Constitution and laws of the United States, no right, privilege or immunity to be exempt from indictment and trial in the state to which he is returned for any other or different offense from that designated in the requisition, without first having an opportunity to return to the state from which he was extradited.

This rule is different, however, with respect to fugitives surrendered by a foreign government, pursuant to treaty. In that case the offender may be tried only "for the offense with which he is charged in the proceedings for his extradition, until a reasonable time and opportunity have been given him, after his release or trial upon such charge, to return to the country from whose asylum he had been forcibly taken under those proceedings."[53]

---

53 *United States v. Rauscher,* 119 U.S. 407, 430 (1886).

Interstate Rendition

Soon after the ratification of the U. S. Constitution, Congress adopted legislation in effect enacting the non-self-executing provision of interstate rendition of fugitives from justice. Congress ordered that governors of all states be willing to render up fugitives, but that duty is not absolute. To understand the executive duty we must first understand what legally a fugitive from justice is.[54]

To be a fugitive from justice within the meaning of the interstate rendition clause of the U. S. Constitution, it is necessary that, in the regular course of judicial proceedings, one have been charged with a crime, but it is not necessary that one have left the state after having been charged. It is sufficient that, having been charged with a crime in one state, one is found in another state.[55] During the era (1864-1873) when Chief Justice Salmon P. Chase (1808-1873) led the Supreme Court, Congress had stripped the Court of the authority to hear appeals from *habeas* petitions in the circuit courts, but Congress subsequently restored that power. In *Roberts v. Reilly* (1885), the Supreme Court under Chief Justice Morrison Waite (1816-1888) affirmed a denial of *habeas corpus* on the merits, but held that it had jurisdiction to consider such appeals under the Extradition Act.

It is immaterial what the motive was which had induced the subject to flee.[56] Because the Constitution requires that, upon proper demand, the person charged with crime shall be delivered up to be removed to the state having jurisdiction of the crime, there is no discretion allowed, nor any inquiry permitted, into motives. Nothing is to be said in regard to *habeas corpus*, and the technical sufficiency of the indictment is not open. Questions as to the sufficiency of an indictment charging an admittedly insane person, as was the case here, with having committed a crime are for the courts of the state having jurisdiction of the crime to determine according to the law of that state. They cannot be determined by the courts of another state on *habeas corpus* proceedings in interstate rendition. The constitutionally required surrender of an identified fugitive from justice on a demand

---

54 "Scope of Inquiry on *Habeas Corpus* by Fugitive from Justice in Interstate Rendition" *Columbia Law Review*, 21: 7 (1921), pp. 709-11.

55 *Roberts v. Reilly*, 116 U.S. 80, 95 (1885). See also *Strassheim v. Daily*, 221 U.S. 280 (1911); *Appleyard v. Massachusetts*, 203 U.S. 222 (1906); *Ex parte Reggel*, 114 U.S. 642, 650 (1885).

56 *Drew v. Thaw*, 235 U.S. 432, 439 (1914).

made in due form is not to be interfered with by the summary process of *habeas corpus* upon speculation as to what ought to be the result of a trial in the place where the Constitution provides for its taking place. The case of *Drew v. Thaw* held that "A party to a crime who afterwards leaves the State is a fugitive from justice; and, for the purposes of interstate rendition, it does not matter what motive induced the departure." going." The Supreme Court ruled that "A party to a crime who afterwards leaves the State is a fugitive from justice; and, for the purposes of interstate rendition, it does not matter what motive induced the departure."[57]

Even if a fugitive were brought involuntarily into the state where found by requisition from another state, he may be surrendered to a third state upon an extradition warrant.[58] The *Innes* case involved three states. The governor of Oregon had honored a requisition made by the governor of Texas for the delivery of the plaintiff in error for removal to Texas as a fugitive from the justice of that state. The accused was taken to Texas, tried for murder and a conspiracy to commit murder, as stated in the Texas extradition request, but she was acquitted. She was not released from custody because the governor of Georgia had requested extradition to that state, to be held as a fugitive from justice. The doctrine of asylum applicable under international law by which a person extradited from a foreign country cannot be tried for an offense other than the one for which the extradition was asked does not apply to interstate rendition.[59] The Supreme Court held:

An Act of Congress which leaves a subject with which Congress has power to deal under the Constitution unprovided for does not necessarily take the matters within the unprovided area out of any possible state action, and so held that the exclusive character of § 5278 Revised Statutes. does not relate to the rendition between criminals found in, but who had not fled to, the surrendering state but had been involuntarily brought therein. In construing an Act of Congress, this Court will not presume that, because its provisions were not coterminous with the power granted by Congress, it was so framed for the purpose of leaving the subject, so

---

57 "Interstate Rendition," U.S. Constitution Annotated, US Law, LII Legal Information Institute at cornell.edu. Hereinafter cited as *Cornell law,*

58 *Innes v. Tobin*, 240 U.S. 127 (1916).

59 "Interstate Rendition Clause," The Heritage Guide to the Constitution, The Heritage Guide to the Constitution .

far as unprovided for, beyond the operation of any legal authority what-ever, state or national.[60]

In July 1907 the governor of Rhode Island issued a warrant of arrest based upon information that had been communicated to him by the governor of New York that Jacob Bassing had been charged with the crime of grand larceny in New York, and was a fugitive from the justice of the latter state, and was supposed to be then in Rhode Is-land. Bassing claimed that he had previously been extradited from Rhode Island in March 1907 on the same change, tried, and released in New York. The Supreme Court, however, ruled that Bassing was a fugitive from justice insofar as the governor of Rhode Island was con-cerned and thus had been lawfully taken into custody. Therefore, a person indicted a second time for the same offense is nonetheless a fugitive from justice by reason of the fact that after dismissal of the first indictment, on which he was originally indicted, he left the state with the knowledge of, or without objection by, state authorities: The court held:[61]

> The mere arraignment and pleading to an indictment does not put the ac-cused in judicial jeopardy, nor does the second surrender of the same per-son by one state to another amount to putting that person in second jeopardy because the requisition of the demanding state is based on an indictment for the same offense for which the accused had been formerly indicted and surrendered, but for which he had never been tried. . . . One charged with crime and who was in the place where, and at the time when, the crime was committed, and who thereafter leaves the state, no matter for what reason, is a fugitive from justice within the meaning of the interstate rendition provisions of the Constitution and of § 5278, Re-vised Statutes, and this nonetheless if he leaves the state with the knowl-edge and without the objection of it authorities.[62]

However, person for whose delivery a demand has been made by executive authority of one state upon the executive authority of an-

---

60 *Innes v. Tobin,* 240 U.S. 127 (1916) .See "Ida May Innes, Plff. in Err., v. John W. Tobin, Sheriff of Bexar County, Texas," Supreme Court | US Law | LII / Le-gal Information Institute at cornell.edu. See also "The Uniform Criminal Extra-dition Act," *Columbia Law Review,* 32: 8 (1932), pp. 1411-1424.

61 https://en.wikisource.org/wiki/Bassing_v._Cady/Opinion_of_the_Court. *Bass-ing v. Cady,* 208 U.S. 386 (1908).

62 *Bassing v. Cady,,* 208 US 486 at 388. See "Federal Jurisdiction. "Habeas Cor-pus". Lack of Due Process in Indictment as Bar to Interstate Rendition," *Colum-bia Law Review,* 44: 7 (1933), pp. 1259-61,

other state, and who can show conclusively, based upon conceded facts, that he was not within the demanding state at the time stated in the indictment, nor at any time when the acts were, if ever, committed, is not a fugitive from justice according to the federal statute upon the subject of interstate extradition and rendition.

Hyatt stated that he was arrested and detained on a warrant from the governor of New York, granted on a requisition from the governor of Tennessee, alleging that he had been indicted in that state for grand larceny, and that he was a fugitive from the justice of that state; and that the warrant under which he was held showed that the crimes with which he was charged were committed in Tennessee. He stated that nowhere did it appear in the papers that he was personally present within the state of Tennessee at the time the alleged crimes were committed; that the governor had no jurisdiction to issue his warrant, in that it did not appear before him that he was a fugitive from the justice of the state of Tennessee, or had fled therefrom; that it did not appear that there was any evidence that he was present in Tennessee when the crimes were alleged to have been committed; that it appeared on the face of the indictments accompanying the requisition that no crime under the laws of Tennessee was charged or had been committed.[63]

Denominating a person as a "fugitive" as defined by the statute" implementing the Constitution is the touchstone for rendition. Return cannot be accomplished if the subject was not actually present in the demanding state when the crime was committed, because the courts in construing the statute have held "presence" essential to the definition of "fugitive.'" A defendant cannot be extradited if he was only constructively present in the demanding state at the time of the commission of the crime charged.[64] The cases have split on whether one who leaves the demanding state involuntarily is a "fugitive" within the meaning of the federal rendition statute. An earlier case decided in the opposite way.[65]

For the purpose of determining who is a fugitive from justice, the words "treason, felony or other crime" embrace every act forbid-

---

63 James L. Hyatt, as Chief of Police of the City of Albany, N. Y., Plff. in Err., v. New York on the relation of Charles E. Corkran, 188 U.S. 691 (1903).

64 *Hyatt v. People ex rel. Corkran,* 188 U.S. 691 (1903).

65 *State v. Hall,* 115 N.C. 811, 20 S.E. 729 (1894). See also *Innes v. Tobin,* 240 U.S. 127 (1916).

den and made punishable by a law of a state,[66] including misdemeanors.[67] To be a fugitive from justice within the meaning of this
clause, it is not necessary that the party charged should have left the
State after an indictment found or for the purpose of avoiding a prosecution anticipated or begun. It is sufficient that the accused, having
committed a crime within one State and having left the jurisdiction
before being subjected to criminal process, is found within another
State.[68] The motive which induced the departure is immaterial.[69] Even
if he were brought involuntarily into the State where found by requisition from another State, he may be surrendered to a third State upon
an extradition warrant.[70]

A person indicted a second time for the same offense is nonetheless a fugitive from justice by reason of the fact that after dismissal
of the first indictment, on which he was originally indicted, he left the
State with the knowledge of, or without objection by, state authorities.[71] But a defendant cannot be extradited if he was only constructively present in the demanding State at the time of the commission of
the crime charged.[72] For the purpose of determining who is a fugitive
from justice, the words "treason, felony or other crime" embrace every act forbidden and made punishable by a law of a State, including
misdemeanors.[73]

A governor is not allowed to request rendition until a person
has been charged with a crime in the regular course of judicial proceedings.[74] The person whose rendition has been demanded has no
constitutional right to be heard before the governor of the state in
which he is found on the question whether he has been substantially

---

66 *Kentucky v. Dennison*, 65 U.S. (24 How.) 66, 103 (1861).

67 *Taylor v. Taintor*, 83 U.S. (16 Wall.) 366, 375 (1873).

68 *Roberts v. Reilly*, 116 U.S. 80 (1885). See also *Strassheim v. Daily*, 221 U.S. 280 (1911); *Appleyard v. Massachusetts*, 203 U.S. 222 (1906); and *Ex parte Reggel*, 114 U.S. 642, 650 (1885).

69 *Drew v. Thaw*, 235 U.S. 432, 439 (1914)

70 *Innes v. Tobin*, 240 U.S. 127 (1916).

71 *Bassing v. Cady*, 208 U.S. 386 (1908).

72 *Hyatt v. People ex rel. Corkran*, 188 U.S. 691 (1903).

73 *Kentucky v. Dennison*, 65 U.S. (24 How.) 66, 103 (1861); *Taylor v. Taintor*, 83 U.S. (16 Wall.) 366, 375 (1873).

74 *Kentucky v. Dennison*, 65 U.S. (24 How.) 66, 104 (1861); *Pierce v. Creecy*, 210 U.S. 387 (1908). See also *Marbles v. Creecy*, 215 U.S. 63 (1909); and *Strassheim v. Daily*, 221 U.S. 280 (1911).

charged with crime and is a fugitive from justice.[75] It is improper thereby to inquire into the motives of the governors of the demanding and surrendering States.[76] The role played by writ of habeas corpus is very limited in rendition proceedings. [77]

As we have seen interstate rendition of fugitives is a matter of constitutional concern and is addressed in the U. S. Constitution, Article IV, section 2, clause 2. It is not surprising that the interpretation of the full meaning of this article would require the attention of the U. S. Supreme Court. What is surprising is that it took some sixty years for the matter to appear in the court, but the subject matter, slavery, was most predictable.

Fugitive Slave Rendition

On 7 August 1830, Mary Martin of New Orleans, Louisiana, applied to the City of New York to bring Jack, a man that she claimed was her slave under the laws of Louisiana. Following a hearing, New York granted a certificate authorizing Martin to take Jack back to Louisiana, and Jack was the delivered to be returned as ordered.

Jack applied to the Court of Common Pleas for a writ *de homine replegiando*[78], an ancient common law writ that had been revived in parts of the United States, principally in relation to the fugitive slave law.Jack's principle claim was that because both he and Mary Martin were currently resident in New York, he had become a free man by operation of law. The court rejected this argument, and gave judgment in favor of Mary Martin.

Attorneys J. I. Roosevelt, Jr. and R. Sedgwick. Brought Jack's case to the New York State Supreme Court of Judicature. The Court's

---

75 *Munsey v. Clough*, 196 U.S. 364 (1905); *Pettibone v. Nichols*, 203 U.S. 192 (1906).

76 *Pettibone v. Nichols*, 203 U.S. 192 (1906).

77 *Biddinger v. Commissioner of Police*, 245 U.S. 128 (1917). See also *Rodman v. Pothier*, 264 U.S. 399 (1924); *Sweeney v. Woodall*, 344 U.S. 86 (1952); *Hyatt v. People ex rel. Corkran*, 188 U.S. 691 (1903); *South Carolina v. Bailey*, 289 U.S. 412 (1933); *Munsey v. Clough*, 196 U.S. 364, 375 (1905); and *Michigan v. Doran*, 439 U.S. 282, 289 (1978). Indeed, in California v. Superior Court, 482 U.S. 400 (1987), the Court reiterated that extradition is a "summary procedure."

78 *De homine replegiando* ("personal replevin") is a legal remedy used to liberate a person from unlawful detention on bail, "with a view to try the question of the validity of the law under which he is held in confinement." It is the oldest common law freedom writ. It is similar to the writ of habeas corpus but carried with it the right to a jury trial. *Black's Law Dictionary*.

opinion was written by Judge Samuel Nelson, who examined the constitutionality of the fugitive slave law and concluded that the right to legislate on this subject belonged exclusively to the National Government. Justice Nelson also concluded that, contrary to decades of New York jurisprudence, where a magistrate grants a certificate under the fugitive slave law, a writ of *de homine replegiando* cannot be taken under State law to prevent the owner from removing the slave from New York.

The case came before the Court for the Correction of Errors in December 1935. Jack was represented by G. Wood and R. Sedgwick. In this opinion, Chancellor Walworth ruled that he could find no grant of power in the U.S. Constitution that gave Congress the power to pass a law under which "any free citizen of this State may be seized as a slave or apprentice who has escaped from servitude, and transported to a distant part of the union without any trial except a summary examination before a magistrate." Walworth concluded that the federal Fugitive Slave Law of 1793 was invalid. However, the Court held that New York State was obliged to return Jack to Louisiana under Article 4, Section 2, Clause 3 of the Federal Constitution.[79]

The Prigg Case

The Prigg decision is the first of several important cases the U. S. Supreme Court heard relative to interstate rendition of prisoners and the issue of slavery. The nation had long since divided on the issue of chattel slavery, with the South defending that "peculiar institution" which was very profitable. The North, conversely, had not found slavery to be at all useful and economically useless and so decided that it was also immoral and must be terminated throughout the nation. One major issue that was increasingly divisive was the return of fugitive slaves to their legal owners.

The defendant. Edward Prigg, along with Nathan S. Bemis, Jacob Forward, and Stephen Lewis, Jr., were indicted by the grand jury of York County, Pennsylvania, for that, on the first day of April 1837, upon a certain Negro woman, named Margaret Morgan, with force and violence, they made an assault, and with force and violence, felo-

---

79 *Jack v. Martin*, 12 Wend. 311 (New York Supreme Court of Judicature, 1834); 14 Wend. 507 (Court for the Correction of Errors, 1835). Chancellor Walworth's decision in Jack v. Martin is included as Document 15 of the materials underlying Article 4, Section 2, Clause 3 (Full Faith and Credit–Fugitive Slave Rendition, The Founders Constitution. Liberty Fund, 2008, document 15.

niously did take and carry her away from the County of York, within the Commonwealth of Pennsylvania, to the State of Maryland, with a design and intention there to sell and dispose of the said Margaret Morgan, as and for a slave and servant for life. Edward Prigg pleaded not guilty.

Edward Prigg, a citizen of the State of Maryland, was indicted in York County, Pennsylvania. His crime was that he had forcibly carried away from Pennsylvania, a free state, to the State of Maryland a Negro woman named Margaret Morgan. It was clearly Prigg's intention to sell her as a slave for life, which was contrary to a statute of Pennsylvania passed on the twenty-sixth day of March, 1826. Edward Prigg pleaded not guilty, and the jury found a special verdict on which judgment was rendered for the Commonwealth of Pennsylvania. The case was removed to the Supreme Court of the State, and the judgment of the Court of Oyer and Terminer was *pro forma* affirmed.[80]

The jurors in York County found that the Negro woman, Margaret Morgan came into Pennsylvania from the State of Maryland, some time in the year 1832; that, at that time she was a slave for life, to a certain Margaret Ashmore, a citizen of the State of Maryland, residing in Harford County; and that the said Negro woman, Margaret Morgan, escaped and fled from Maryland, without the knowledge and consent of the said Margaret Ashmore; that, in the month of February, 1837, the defendant, Edward Prigg, was appointed by the said Margaret Ashmore her agent or attorney to seize and arrest the said Negro woman, Margaret Morgan, as a fugitive from labor, and to remove, take, and carry her from Pennsylvania into Maryland, and there deliver her to the said Margaret Ashmore; that, as such agent or attorney, the said Edward Prigg, afterwards and in the same month of February, 1837, before a certain Thomas Henderson, Esquire, then being a justice of the peace in and for the County of York, made oath that the said Negro woman Margaret Morgan had fled and escaped from Maryland, owing service or labor for life, under the laws thereof to the said Margaret Ashmore; that the said Thomas Henderson, so being such justice of the peace as aforesaid, thereupon issued his warrant, directed to one William McCleary, then and there being a regularly appointed constable in and for York county, commanding him to take the said Negro woman, Margaret Morgan, and her children, and bring them before the said Thomas Henderson, or some other justice of the

---

80 *"Prigg v Pennsylvania,"* https://www.quimbee.com/cases/prigg-v-pennsylvania

peace for said county; that the said McCleary, in obedience to said warrant, did accordingly take and apprehend the said negro woman, Margaret Morgan, and her children, in York county aforesaid, and did bring her and them before the said Thomas Henderson; that the said Henderson thereupon refused to take further cognizance of said case.[81]

The jury claimed ignorance of the applicable law and demurred to the court. If the court determined that Prigg was indeed guilty the jurors would go along; if it determined that he had not committed a crime in that case the jury was also willing to acquiesce. Thus there was a special verdict which was made as a result of an agreement between Messrs. Meredith and Nelson, counsel for Edward Prigg, and Mr. Johnson, Attorney-General of Pennsylvania, and, by agreement, the court gave judgment against Edward Prigg on the finding of the jury and the indictment.[82]

At this point the case was carried to the Supreme Court of the United States. Prigg challenged the constitutionality of the law under which the indictment was found. Prigg sought and obtained the counsel of the State of Maryland, a slave state. It was for the defense of the institution of slavery that Maryland had undertaken the defense of Edward Prigg The cause was brought to the Supreme Court, with the acquiescence of both the States of Maryland and Pennsylvania. The question to be answered: Was Margaret Morgan to be a slave for life, as was certain under the laws of Maryland. In its view, Morgan was the chattel property of Margaret Ashmore, a citizen of that Maryland.

In 1832, Morgan had escaped and fled from the State of Maryland into Pennsylvania. Edward Prigg was then duly appointed the agent and attorney of Margaret Ashmore. Knowing Morgan to be living in York County, Pennsylvania, Prigg obtained a warrant from a justice of the peace of York County, which caused Margaret Morgan to be taken, as a fugitive from labor. A constable of the State of Pennsylvania brought Morgan before the magistrate, who refused to recognize the charge and rejected the case entirely. Thereupon Edward

---

81 Levinson, Sanford, "Prigg v. Pennsylvania." in Marbach, Joseph R, Ellis Katz, and Troy E Smith, eds. 2 vols. *Federalism in America: An Encyclopedia.* Greenwood Press, 2006.

82 *Prigg v. Pennsylvania*, 41 U.S. 539 (1842), case brief summary at Law School Case Briefs | Legal Outlines | Study Materials: Prigg v. Pennsylvania case brief summary; Goldstein, Leslie Friedman, "A 'Triumph of Freedom' after All? Prigg v. Pennsylvania Re-examined," *Law and History Review*, 29 (2011), pp. 763–96.

Prigg carried her and her children into Maryland and delivered them all to the ownership of Margaret Ashmore. The children reportedly were born in Pennsylvania, one of them more than a year after Margaret Morgan had fled and escaped from Maryland.[83]

The applicable Pennsylvania law came from an Act of Assembly of Pennsylvania of 25th March, 1826, which provided that "if any person shall, by force and violence, take and carry away, or shall by fraud or false pretense attempt to take, carry away, or seduce any negro or mulatto from any part of the Commonwealth, with a design or intention of selling and disposing of, or keeping or detaining, such negro or mulatto as a slave or servant for life, or for any other term whatsoever, such person, and all persons aiding and abetting him, shall, on conviction thereof, be deemed guilty of a felony. . . ." Punishment as a felony required a fine and imprisonment. Other provisions contained in the act were designed to aid in carrying into effect the Constitution and laws of the United States relating to fugitives from labor, and, on the application from the State of Maryland, to meet the supposed wishes of the State of Maryland on the subject of fugitive slaves. However, the law had failed to produce the good effects intended.

When Prigg forcibly removed Morgan and her children to Maryland, a county judge in that state adjudged them to be slaves. Prigg was charged and convicted under a Pennsylvania law designed to prevent self-help in the return of fugitive slaves. Prigg challenged this law as unconstitutional. The U.S. Supreme Court reviewed the intent of the Pennsylvania law:

> It is historically well known that the object of the clause in the Constitution of the United States relating to persons owing service and labor in one state escaping into other states was to secure to the citizens of the slave holding States the complete right and title of ownership in their slaves as property in every State in the Union into which they might escape from the State where they were held in servitude. The full recognition of this right and title was indispensable to the security of this species of property in all the slave-holding States, and indeed was so vital to the preservation of their domestic interests and institutions that it cannot be

---

83 *Prigg v. Pennsylvania*, 41 U.S. 539 (1842), case brief summary at Law School Case Briefs | Legal Outlines | Study Materials: Prigg v. Pennsylvania case brief summary; https://www.quimbee.com/cases/prigg-v-pennsylvania"*Prigg v Pennsylvania*," ; Nogee, Joseph, "The Prigg Case and Fugitive Slavery, 1842–1850," *Journal of Negro History*, 39: 3 (1954), pp. 185–205.

doubted that it constituted a fundamental article without the adoption of which the Union could not have been formed. Its true design was to guard against the doctrines and principles prevailing in the non-slave-holding States by preventing them from inter-meddling with or obstructing or abolishing the rights of the owners of slaves.

By the general law of nations, no nation is bound to recognize the state of slavery as to foreign slaves within its territorial dominions when it is opposed to its own policy and institutions in favor of the subjects of other nations where slavery is recognized. If it does it, it is as a matter of comity, and not as a matter of international right. The state of slavery is deemed to be a mere municipal regulation founded upon and limited to the range of the territorial laws.[84]

The Court recognized the right of slave holders to retain their property without any regard to alleged rights to freedom and independence on the part of the slave.

The clause of the Constitution of the United States relating to fugitives from labor manifestly contemplates the existence of a positive unqualified right on the part of the owner of the slave which no state law or regulation can in any way qualify, regulate, control, or restrain. Any state law or regulation which interrupts, limits, delays, or postpones the rights of the owner to the immediate command of his service or labor operates pro tanto a discharge of the slave therefrom. The question can never be how much he is discharged from, but whether he is discharged from any by the natural or necessary operation of the state laws or state regulations. The question is not one of quantity or degree, but of withholding or controlling the incidents of a positive right.

Thus it may properly be said to execute itself, and to require no aid from legislation, state or national owner of a fugitive slave has the same right to seize and take him in a State to which he has escaped or fled that he had in the State from which he escaped, and it is well known that this right to seizure or recapture is universally acknowledged in all the slave-holding States. The Court have not the slightest hesitation in holding that, under and in virtue of the Constitution, the owner of the slave is clothed with the authority in every State of the Union to seize and recapture his slave wherever he can do it without any breach of the peace or illegal violence. In this sense and to this extent, this clause in the Constitution does not stop at a mere annunciation of the rights of the owner to seize his absconding or fugitive slave in the State to which he may have fled. If it had done so, it would have left the owner of the slave, in many cases,

---

84 *Prigg v. Pennsylvania*, 41 U. S. (16 Pet.) 539 (1842)

utterly without any adequate redress.[85]

The high court held that the Constitution itself declares that the fugitive slave shall be delivered up on claim of the party to whom service or labor may be due. It is exceedingly difficult, if not impracticable, to read this language and not conclude that it contemplated some remedial redress than that which might be administered at the hand of the owner himself. The law held that "A claim" is to be made. The high court then defined what is meant by "A claim," in a juridical sense. It is a demand of some matter as of right, made by one person upon another to do or to forbear to do some act or thing as a matter of duty. Thus, it cannot be denied that the Constitution requires the delivery of the fugitive on the claim of the master. The natural inference is that the federal government is necessarily clothed with the appropriate authority to enforce the law. The fundamental principle applicable to all cases of this nature would seem to be that, where the end is required, the means are given, and where the duty is enjoined, the ability to perform it is contemplated to exist on the part of the functionaries to whom it is entrusted.[86]

The clause was it then related to fugitive slaves is found in the U. S. Constitution, not in that of any state. It might well be deemed an unconstitutional exercise of the power of interpretation to insist that the states are bound to provide means to carry into effect the duties of the national government nowhere delegated or entrusted to them by the Constitution. On the contrary, the natural, if not the necessary, conclusion is that the federal government, in the absence of all positive provisions to the contrary, is bound, through its own proper departments, legislative, executive, or judiciary, as the case may require, to carry into effect all the rights and duties imposed upon it by the Constitution.[87]

A claim to a fugitive slave is a controversy in a case "arising under the Constitution of the United States" under the express delega-

---

85 *Prigg v. Pennsylvania,* 41 U. S. (16 Pet.) 539 (1842); Finkelman, Paul, "Prigg v. Pennsylvania: Understanding Justice Story's Pro-Slavery Nationalism, *Journal of Supreme Court History,* 2 (1997) pp. 51-64.

86 *Prigg v. Pennsylvania ,* 41 U.S. 539 (1842), Justia US Supreme Court Center; Burke, Joseph C., "What Did the Prigg Decision Really Decide?" *Pennsylvania Magazine of History and Biography,* 93: 1 (1969), pp. 73–85.

87 Finkelman, Paul, "Story Telling on the Supreme Court: Prigg v. Pennsylvania and Justice Joseph Story's Judicial Nationalism," *Supreme Court Review* (1995) pp. 247-294.

tion of judicial power given by that instrument. Congress, then, may call that power into activity for the very purpose of giving effect to the right, and, if so, then it may prescribe the mode and extent to which it shall be applied, and how and under what circumstances the proceedings shall afford a complete protection and guaranty of the right.[88]

The Supreme Court reviewed the provisions of the federal act of 12th February, 1793, relative to fugitive slaves, which it held was clearly constitutional in all its leading provisions. Indeed, with the exception of that part which conferred authority on state magistrates, the act was free from reasonable doubt or difficulty. As to the authority so conferred on state magistrates, while a difference of opinion exists, and may exist on this point in different states, whether state magistrates are bound to act under it, none is entertained by the U. S. Supreme Court that state magistrates may, if they choose, exercise the authority unless prohibited by state legislation. The power of legislation in relation to fugitives from labor is exclusive in the federal government.[89] Where Congress have exclusive power over a subject, it is not competent for state legislation to add to the provisions of Congress on that subject.[90]

The right to seize and retake fugitive slaves, and the duty to deliver them up, in whatever state they may be found is, under the Constitution, recognized as an absolute positive right and duty pervading the whole union with an equal and supreme force uncontrolled and uncontrollable by state sovereignty or state legislation. The right and duty are coextensive and uniform in remedy and operation throughout the whole nation. The owner has the same security, and the same remedial justice, and the same exemption from state regulations and control, through however many State he may pass with the fugitive slave in his possession in *transitu* to his domicile.[91]

The Court Court entertained no doubt whatsoever that the states, as a result of their general police power, possess full jurisdiction to arrest and restrain runaway slaves, and to remove them from their borders and otherwise to secure themselves against their depredations and evil example, as they certainly may do in cases of idlers,

---

88 *Prigg v Pennsylvania,* at U. S. 542; Finkelman, Paul, "Sorting Out Prigg v. Pennsylvania," *Rutgers Law Journal,* 24 (1993), pp. 605-665.

89 *Sturgis v. Crowninshield,* 17 U. S. (4 Wheat.) 122 (1819).

90 *Houston v. Moore,* 18 U. S. (5 Wheat.) at 21-22 (1820).

91 Id. at 41.

vagabonds, and paupers. The rights of the owners of fugitive slaves are in no just sense interfered with or regulated by such a course, and, in many cases, they may be promoted by the exercise of the police power. Such regulations can never be permitted to interfere with or obstruct the just rights of the owner to reclaim his slave derived from the Constitution of the United States or with the remedies prescribed by Congress to aid and enforce the same.[92]

The supreme Court found that the act of the Pennsylvania Legislature upon which the indictment against Edward Prigg was founded was unconstitutional and thus null and void. That unconstitutional legislation attempted to punish as a public offense against the commonwealth the very act of seizing and removing a slave by his master which the Constitution of the United States was designed to justify and uphold.[93]

Kentucky v Dennison

Kentucky v Dennison[94] was argued on 20 February 1861, and decided on 14 March 1861 by the unanimous vote of 8 to 0. Chief Justice Roger B. Taney penned the opinion of the Court. This was the last of four major slave cases heard by the U. S. Supreme Court. The facts of the case were relatively simple. In 1859, Willis Lago, a free black man, had helped a slave named Charlotte escape from Woodford County, Kentucky, into Ohio. Charlotte's owner, C. W. Nuckols, filed an indictment against Lago, and the state requested, via Kentucky Governor Beriah Magoffin, that both Charlotte and Lago be returned to Kentucky. Lago was to be extradited to stand trial for seducing and enticing Charlotte to escape.[95]

Kentucky Governor Beriah Magoffin lodged a request with Ohio governor Salmon P. Chase[96] for the extradition of Lago. Howev-

---

92 Id. at 41-42
93 "Prigg v Pennsylvania," in Wikipedia; Finkelman, Paul, ed. *The Supreme Court: Controversies, Cases, and Characters from John Jay to John Roberts.* ABC-CLIO, 2014, p. 241.
94 *Kentucky v Dennison*, 24 How. (65 U.S.) 66 (1861)
95 "Interstate Rendition: Executive Practices and the Effects of Discretion," *Yale Law Journal,* 66: 1 (1956), pp. 97-120; "Interstate Rendition. Uniform Act on Fresh Pursuit," *Columbia Law Review,* 38: 4 (1938), pp. 705-709; "Habeas Corpus in Interstate Rendition," *Columbia Law Review,* 47: 3 (1947), pp. 470-477; Wolfe, Nancy Travis, "Interstate rendition: Discretionary or mandatory," *American Journal of Criminal Justice,* 5 (1980), pp. 25-44.
96 Salmon Portland Chase (1808-1873) later served as the sixth Chief Justice of

er, Chase, an antislavery advocate, refused to comply, arguing that Lago had not committed any crime recognized under prevailing Ohio law. In 1860, Chase left office and Governor Magoffin renewed the request for extradition with the new Ohio governor, William Dennison, who also refused to comply. Magoffin then sought a writ of mandamus to force Dennison to act. Magoffin sued in the United States Supreme Court, under the court's original jurisdiction for cases between two states.

Chief Justice Roger B. Taney supported Kentucky's right to expect Governor Dennison to respect its laws. He agreed with the Southern governors who had argued throughout the 1830s and 1840s that they had the right to extradite slaves, those who helped free slaves, and anyone else who had been indicted for a crime within their states. The high court rejected the position taken by Ohio that the Extradition Clause required only the delivery of fugitives charged with acts which would be criminal by the law of the asylum State.[97] "Under such a vague and indefinite construction," the Court said, "the article would not be a bond of peace and union, but a constant source of controversy and irritating discussion."[98]

The duty of the Governor of Ohio was merely ministerial, and he had no right to exercise any discretionary power as to the nature or character of the crime charged in the indictment. The word "duty," in the act of 1793, means the moral obligation of the State to perform the compact in the Constitution when Congress had, by that act, regulated the mode in which the duty was to be performed. But Congress cannot coerce a State officer, as such, to perform any duty by act of Congress. The State officer may perform it if he thinks proper, and it may be a moral duty to perform it. But if he refuses, no law of Congress can compel him. The Governor of Ohio cannot, through the Judiciary or any other Department of the General Government, be compelled to deliver up Lago, and, upon that ground only, this motion for a mandamus was overruled.[99] As the high court wrote,

---

the United States. He also served as the 23rd Governor of Ohio, represented Ohio in the United States Senate, and served as the 25th United States Secretary of the Treasury during the Lincoln Administration.

97 "Kentucky v. Dennison," in *The Oxford Companion to the Supreme Court of the United States.* Oxford University Press, 2006.

98 24 How. at 102

99 *Kentucky v. Dennison,* 65 U.S. 24 How. 66 66 (1861). "Kentucky v. Dennison," in *The Oxford Companion to the Supreme Court of the United States.* Oxford

The demand being thus made, the act of Congress declares that "it shall be the duty of the Executive authority of the State" to cause the fugitive to be arrested and secured, and delivered to the agent of the demanding State. The words, "it shall be the duty," in ordinary legislation, imply the assertion of the power to command and to coerce obedience. But looking to the subject matter of this law, and the relations which the United States and the several States bear to each other, the court is of opinion the words "it shall be the duty" were not used as mandatory and compulsory, but as declaratory of the moral duty which this compact created when Congress had provided the mode of carrying it into execution. The act does not provide any means to compel the execution of this duty, nor inflict any punishment for neglect or refusal on the part of the Executive of the State; nor is there any clause or provision in the Constitution which arms the Government of the United States with this power. Indeed, such a power would place every State under the control and dominion of the General Government, even in the administration of its internal concerns and reserved rights. . . . .

It is true that Congress may authorize a particular State officer to perform a particular duty, but if he declines to do so, it does not follow that he may be coerced or punished for his refusal. And we are very far from supposing that, in using this word "duty," the statesmen who framed and passed the law, or the President who approved and signed it, intended to exercise a coercive power over State officers not warranted by the Constitution. But the General Government having in that law fulfilled the duty devolved upon it by prescribing the proof and mode of authentication upon which the State authorities were bound to deliver the fugitive, the word "duty" in the law points to the obligation on the State to carry it into execution.[100]

Chief Justice Taney wrote, "But if the Governor of Ohio refuses to discharge this duty, there is no power delegated to the General Government, either through the Judicial Department or any other department, to use any coercive means to compel him. And upon this ground, the motion for the mandamus must be overruled. Chief Justice Taney admonished Dennison, but found that constitutionally the U. S. Supreme Court could issue no orders that Lago and Charlotte be extradited to Kentucky. Taney ruled that interstate extradition was a matter of gubernatorial discretion, to be performed out of comity and

---

University Press, 2006
100 *Kentucky v. Dennison,* 65 U.S. 24 How. 66 66 (1861). See the Notable Kentucky African Americans Database. University of Kentucky.

good citizenship.[101]

This decision remained good law until overturned by Puerto Rico v. Branstad (1987).[102]

As witness his decision in the Dred Scott decision,[103] Chief Justice Roger B. Taney was profoundly pro-slavery, and deeply antagonistic toward the North. Since serious consideration of secession was already affecting decisions in the South, Taney was hesitant to rule that the Supreme Court or the federal government might have the power to force state governors to act. Taney chose a middle course, similar to Chief Justice John Marshall's stand in *Marbury v Madison*,[104] and chastised the two Ohio governors for not following the criminal extradition clause of the U. S. Constitution, but ruled that the Court had no power to coerce a state to comply with any constitutional obligations. Although it has become desirable to chastise Justice Taney, we note that he was joined by seven other associate justices, with no dissenters[105].

Chain Gang Extradition

In the intervening years little was heard concerning the refusal of various governors to honor requests for rendition of fugitive prisoners. Extraditing such persons was generally routine and without controversy. One interesting exception was based on a best-selling book and highly acclaimed motion picture.

I Am a Fugitive from a Chain Gang, was a great American novel made into an equally dramatic motion picture. Released in 1932, that was an exposé on the life of inmates on chain gangs. It

---

101 See "The Uniform Criminal Extradition Act," *Columbia Law Review*, 32: 8 (1932), pp. 1411-1424.

102 Bunch, Kenyon and Hardy, Richard J., "Continuity or Change in Interstate Extradition? Assessing Puerto Rico v. Branstad," *Publius*, 21: 1 (1991), pp. 51-67.

103 *Dred Scott v. Sandford*, 60 U.S. (19 How.) 393 (1857). It may be noted that this was a 7-2 decision; thus six additional justices agreed with the outcome, if not all the reasoning, of the decision.

104 *Marbury v. Madison*, 5 U.S. (1 Cranch) 137 (1803). Chief Justice John Marshall took the opportunity to excoriate James Madison, with whose Jeffersonian politics he disagreed, and who, as Secretary of State, had not delivered Marbury's commission, but then held that the issuance was invalid.

105 See Finkelman, Paul, "Slavery," in *The Oxford Companion to the Supreme Court of the United States*, Kermit L. Hall, ed. Oxford University Press, 2005. See also "Interstate Rendition: Executive Practices and the Effects of Discretion," *Yale Law Journal*, 66: 1 (1956), pp. 97-120.

awakened social interest in and helped bring an end to the widespread use of chain gangs in the American South. *I Am a Fugitive from a Georgia Chain Gang!* is the amazing true story of one man's search for meaning, fall from grace, and eventual victory over injustice.

The book *I Am a Fugitive From a Chain Gang* was based was based on the real-life experiences of Robert E. Burns. In 1921, Burns was a shell-shocked and penniless veteran who found himself at the mercy of Georgia's barbaric penal system. Desperate, he fell in with a gang of petty thieves. Captured immediately Georgia sentenced him to six to ten years' hard labor for his part in a robbery that netted less than $6.00. Unrepresented by legal counsel, Burns was shackled and led away to serve his time on a county chain gang. After four months of backbreaking work, he made a daring escape. He escaped from the Campbell County Prison Camp in June 1922 after serving a few months of a six- to ten-year sentence. As in the film, his shackles were bent by a sledgehammer wielded by a black inmate, and he fled through the woods and down a river toward Atlanta to evade officials. Dodging shotgun blasts, racing through swamps, and eluding bloodhounds Burns made his way north.[106]

For seven years Burns lived as a free man. He married and became a successful and prosperous Chicago businessman and publisher. During seven years of freedom in Chicago, he lived a highly-respected and honorable life. He became a public speaker and a writer. Burns founded and became editor-in-chief of *The Greater Chicago Magazine* and earned an annual income of $20,000. When he fell in love with another woman, however, his jealous wife turned him in to the police, who arrested him as a fugitive from justice.

Georgia promised him lenient treatment and a quick pardon, but in reality he was back on a chain gang within a month. Despite support from many prominent individuals, including the governor of Illinois, he voluntarily returned to Georgia after being assured that he would be given a full pardon in just a short time, perhaps 90 days. The state authorities in Georgia failed to keep their promise - they soon returned him to the chain gang in LaGrange to serve out the remainder of his original prison sentence. Parole board hearings ignored requests

---

106 Burns, Robert Elliott, *I Am a Fugitive from a Georgia Chain Gang!* (1932); reprint by University of Georgia Press, 1997. See also Mancini, Matthew, "I Am a Fugitive from a Georgia Chain Gang!," in *New Georgia Encyclopedia,* 2003. See also Mancini's forward, to the Brown Thrasher Edition of *I am a Fugitive from a Georgia Chain Gang!*

for an appeal. He worked for a year on the chain gang, and then escaped a second time in September 1930, aided by the assistance of a sympathetic local store owner. He again went North after evading numerous manhunts, became a tax consultant in New Jersey, and wrote a series of magazine articles of his harrowing experiences on the chain gang

The Reverend Vincent G. Burns, an Episcopal priest in New Jersey, brother of Robert Burns, ghost-wrote the book. The story was first serialized in *True Detective Mysteries* (from January - June 1931), and then published by Vanguard Press as a sequel in March 1932 as a novel entitled *I Am a Fugitive From a Georgia Chain Gang*. As a movie the state was omitted. In 1938, Reverend Burns, sued his fugitive sibling for claiming all the money received from the original story.

I Am A Fugitive From A Chain Gang became a motion picture in 1932. The Warner Brothers studio made it as a gritty, uncompromising, critical, and combative look at the unjust and barbaric treatment of criminals in the prison system as existed in the South following World War I. The harsh and grim melodramatic film was one of the first of Warner Brothers' films designed to explore social conscience, reform and protest. This powerful, stark film was adapted by Sheridan Gibney, Brown Holmes, and Howard J. Green. The film reflected the dire effects of a man who was unjustly convicted of a petty robbery, and then twice served and twice escaped from a chain gang in an un-named Southern state. *I Am A Fugitive From A Chain Gang* is a gritty, uncompromising, critical, and combative look at the unjust and barbaric treatment of criminals in a southern state's prison system following World War I. Warner Brothers acquired the movie rights to the book for $12,500 in early 1932. Production head Darryl Zanuck hired fugitive Burns as technical adviser and consultant to the screenwriters. Fearing the worst, Warner Brothers hired security guards to protect Burns on the studio lot. Burns used the name Richard M. Crane to disguise himself.[107]

Today the movie is considered an American film masterpiece. Initially, Warner Brothers feared that it would not resonate with audiences because it had such a downbeat ending: the protagonist slips

---

107 "Bars Chain Gang Extradition," *New York Times*, January 14, 1933; "Fights Chain Gang Extradition," *New York Times*, June 12, 1943. The web site IMDB contains much information on this motion picture.

around in the dark fearing that each shadow might hide an agent bent on his return to the chain gang. Asked how he lives, he responds, "I steal." This realistic and haunting ending made it unique among films of its day. As it was, the film became one of the top box-office hits of its time. The book in its movie version was nominated for a Best Picture Oscar in 1933 and its leading actor, Paul Muni, was nominated for best actor. The film received the year's Best Film honor from the National Board of Review. Unlike so many "true" stories the film is remarkably faithful to the incredible true-life, autobiographical misfortunes and experiences of Burns. Not surprisingly, the film was actually banned in Georgia. Two Georgia prison wardens unsuccessfully sued Warner Brothers. Many southern newspapers cried LIES! in bold headlines. Hollywood had already made a few other prison films, all denouncing the horrific conditions of America's prisons and the inhumane treatment of the inmates. *The Big House*, released in 1930 attacked brutish prison conditions, Howard Hawks made *The Criminal Code* in 1931, again exposing the barbaric conditions in some prisons. *Ladies of the Big House* also released in 1931 showed that the conditions in women's prisons were no better. Probably anticipating the release of *I am a Fugitive*, RKO chief David O. Selznick released director Rowland Brown's *Hell's Highway* in 1932. That film was the first of the hard-hitting movies exposing the evils of the chain-gang.[108]

Unlike the hero of the movie, Burns found sanctuary in New Jersey. Only three weeks after the film was released in mid-November 1932, Georgia officials learned of his whereabouts in New Jersey and sought to arrest him as a fugitive. Governor A. Harry Moore was the first of three New Jersey chief executives to officially refused to extradite him. By 1937, Georgia had outlawed chain gangs had been outlawed in Georgia. In the 1940s, Georgia Governor Ellis Arnall proposed that he would act as Burns' lawyer if he would return and settle the matter. Having once been deceived, Burns courageously returned to the state in 1945, and this time the Georgia Pardon and Parole Board commuted his sentence to time served and restored his civil rights. However, he was not officially given a full pardon because he had admitted being guilty for the holdup.[109]

---

108 "I Was a Fugitive from a Chain Gang," in IMDB. See also "I am a Fugitive from a Chain Gang" in Wikipedia.

109 https://www.goodreads.com/book/show/169213.I_am_a_Fugitive_from_a_Georgia_Chain_Gang_. See also Matthew J. Mancini "I Am a Fugitive from a Georgia Chain Gang" New Georgia Encyclopedia. Burns, Vincent Godfrey, *The Man*

As early as 1904 the federal courts had ruled that service on a chain gang constituted cruel and unusual punishment. A black man was sentenced to seven months on a chain gang for being d runk and disorderly. His chain gang was sub-contracted to a local roads contractor. The petitioner sought relief through *habeas corpus* from the U. S. District Court for the Southern District of Georgia which found that this sentence must be considered "infamous punishment". It had been established in both the United States and in Great Britain "for more than a century, imprisonment at hard labor in the state prison or penitentiary her similar institution has been considered an "infamous punishment."[110] This did not stop the continued use of chain gangs, even for petty off enses.

Other governors have refused to extradite fugitives from southern chain gangs. For example, New Jersey Governor Richard J. Hughes blocked the extradition of two escaped prisoners today. He placed the men one from South Carolina and the other from Florida on indefinite parole.[111] Another chain gang member escaped in 1964 to New York where he was not recognized until 1991. James Harris was 17 years old and a high school truant when he ran into trouble with the law in Alabama in 1962. Beaten, he says, into confessing to a burglary, he was sentenced to 21 years in prison and sent to a chain gang to dig ditches and lay asphalt on Alabama's muddy back roads. In 1964, with $20 and a pair of shoes from his fellow prisoners, Harris escaped to Long Island and began to make a life for himself, although he was involved in petty theft in New York. The governor refused to send him back South.[112]

Woodall, a Negro, was convicted of burglary in Alabama and sentenced to hard labor at a state penitentiary. After six years, he es-

Who Broke a Thousand Chains; The Story of Social Reformation of the Prisons of the South. Washington: Acropolis Books, 1968.

110 *Jamison v Wimbish*, 130 Fed. 351 (1904). See "The Georgia Chain Gang for Petty Offenses," *Yale Law Journal*, 14: 1 (1901), pp. 45-47. The court cited *Ex parte Wilson*, 114 U.S. 428 (1885) regarding infamous punishments.

111 Wright, George "Governor Hughes blocks Extradition of 2 fugitives from Chain Gang," *New York Times*, 22 August 1962. See also Childs, Dennis .*Slaves of the State: Black Incarceration from the Chain Gang to the Penitentiary.* University of Minnesota Press, 2015.

112 Lyall, Sarah, "1964 Chain-Gang Escape Follows Man North to L.I.," *New York Times*, 24 June 1991; Burns, Vincent Godfrey. *The Man Who Broke a Thousand Chains; The Story of Social Reformation of the Prisons of the South.* Washington: Acropolis Books, 1968.

caped and was apprehended in Ohio. Alabama sought to extradite him so that he could be returned to Alabama and serve the balance of his sentence. He thereupon filed this petition for *habeas corpus* to be released from custody. Although he had made no attempt to raise questions in the Alabama courts, he claimed in Ohio that his confinement in Alabama amounted, and would amount again, to cruel and unusual punishment contrary to the Eighth and Fourteenth Amendments

He offered to prove that the Alabama jailers have a nine-pound strap with five metal prongs that they use to beat prisoners, that they used this strap against him, that the beatings frequently caused him to lose consciousness, and resulted in deep wounds and permanent scars. He also alleged that he was stripped to his waist and forced to work in the broiling sun all day long without a rest period.[113]

He applied unsuccessfully to Ohio state courts for release on a writ of *habeas corpus*. After exhausting his remedies in the Ohio courts, he applied to a federal district court in Ohio for *habeas corpus* on the same grounds. Alabama was not a party to that proceeding. Alabama was not a party to that proceeding.[114] Although prevailing initially in the lower federal court, he lost in the U.S. Supreme Court which held that the district court should not have entertain his application on its merits.

The high court noted that the scheme of interstate rendition contemplates the prompt return of a fugitive from justice as soon as the state from which he fled demands him; these provisions do not contemplate an appearance by that state in the asylum state to defend against claimed abuses of the former state's prison system. The prisoner must test the constitutionality of his treatment by Alabama in the courts of that State, where all parties may be heard, where all pertinent testimony will be readily available, and where suitable relief, if any is necessary, may be fashioned.[115]

In other similar cases, the Court of Appeals for the Ninth Circuit,[116] and the Court of Appeals for the Eighth Circuit,[117] have reached a like result. In 1950, the Court of Appeals for the Second Circuit held that a fugitive from Georgia was not entitled to a hearing in the federal courts in his asylum on the ground that the merits had

---

113 *In re Woodall*, 88 Ohio App. 202, 89 N.E.2d 493
114 194 F.2d 542.
115 *Sweeney v. Woodall*, 344 U.S. 86 (1952)
116 *Ross v. Middlebrooks*, 188 F.2d 308 (1951)
117 *Davis v. O'Connell*, 185 F.2d 513 (1950).

been fully heard in the state courts of the asylum and the fugitive's claim disproved.[118]

In 1949, the federal Court of Appeals for the third circuit ruled that on the use of chain gangs. It held that Georgia's use of the chain gang constituted cruel and unusual punishment which constituted a denial of due process of law. Leon Johnson had been found guilty of murder and sentenced to life at hard labor. He escaped and took refuge in Pennsylvania. An escaped convict from a chain gang may contest his extradition proceedings, and because of the denial of due process courts will discharge him from custody.[119] The court seemed to be inviting those condemned to servitude on a chain gang to escape.

The *Middlebrooks* case is another "chain gang" conviction. Midlebrooks was convicted and sentenced in Georgia and escaped from a Georgia chain gang. He was found in California and arrested by the California authorities pursuant to a demand for rendition from the Governor of the State of Georgia. The demand appeared on its face to be valid, and was accompanied by certified copies of the indictments concerned and other papers. Middlebrooks appealed to the California courts that he would be punished in ways inconsistent with the Constitutiobal prohibitions of cruel and unusual punishment. The state courts denied the petitions on the ground that the California courts had no jurisdiction to determine the questions presented.

Middlebrooks then petitioned the United States District Court for the Southern District of California for relief. He alleged, and the District Court found, that (1) the Georgia conviction which gave rise to Middlebrooks' incarceration was void, in that it was procured without a trial, without a plea of guilty, and without the assistance of counsel, in violation of the Fourteenth Amendment; and (2) Middlebrooks had been, and if returned to Georgia would again be, subjected to cruel and unusual punishment, in violation of the Fourteenth Amendment. The district court in *Middlebrooks* recognized the need for a different rule from that of the *Sweeney* case where there is danger of future mistreatment or unavailability of state remedies, and where there are more than mere allegations of future cruel and unusual punishment. On these findings the District Court ordered his release.

---

118 *United States ex rel. Jackson v. Ruthazer,* 181 F.2d 588, 589 (1950)

119 *Johnson v Dye,* 175 F 2d 250 (3d cir. 1949). See also, "The Case of the Fugitive from the Chain Gang," *Standford Law Review,* 2: 1 (1949), pp. 174-83.

On appeal to the United States Court of Appeals for the Ninth Circuit, the district court was reversed. While the District Court found that "as a practical matter, it is extremely remote" that Middlebrooks could secure adequate relief in the courts of Georgia, on appeal Middlebrooks' counsel have conceded that the Georgia judicial system is entirely adequate, and would be available, to give Middlebrooks any relief to which he is entitled. The Constitution requires immediate compliance with the request for rendition, and any question of Middlebrooks' constitutional rights would be decided in the requesting, not the asylum, state.[120]

On 15 February 1976, South Dakota requested extradition of Dennis James Banks. South Dakota alleged that Banks had been convicted of specified felonies in South Dakota and had fled to California while out on bail. California did not questioned the sufficiency of the demand nor did he deny the request. Rather, California chose to exercise its prerogative to "investigate" the equities of the case before acting on South Dakota's demand. South Dakota, on the other hand, insisted that the Governor's extradition function is mandatory, once the conditions of the Extradition Act are satisfied, and sought a writ of mandate to compel the state's California's governor to issue a warrant for Banks' arrest.

The Supreme Court heard the case and determined that a state governor does possess discretionary power to refuse an extradition demand. However, it determined that the governor does have an obligation enforceable by mandamus to exercise that discretion, either by granting or denying South Dakota's demand. The demand was presented to the Governor on February 15, 1976, and since that date the matter presumably has been under the Governor's investigation and subject to the present litigation. No principle of law applicable to the case justifies a refusal by the Governor, within a reasonable time, either to grant or deny the demand properly before him.[121]

Puerto Rico v Branstad

---

120 *Ross v Middlebrooks,* 188 F. 2d 308 (1951). See also "Scope of Habeas Corpus Inquiry in Fugitive Extradition Cases," *Journal of Criminal Law and Criminology,* 44: 2 (1953), pp. 208-13.

121 *State of South Dakota v. Brown*, S.F. No. 23579. Supreme Court of California. (March 20, 1978). See also McMunigal, Kevin C., "Constitutional Law. South Dakota v. Brown: Judicial Enforcement of Governor's Duty to Extradite Fugitives," *California Law Review*, 67: 3 (1979), pp. 643-61.

As we have seen, the Supreme Court had held in *Kentucky v. Dennison* (1861), that the federal courts may not issue writs of mandamus to compel state governors to surrender fugitives. This had been good law until 1987. For over 125 years, *Kentucky v. Dennison* stood for two propositions: first, that the Extradition Clause creates a mandatory duty to deliver up fugitives upon proper demand; and second, that the federal courts have no authority under the Constitution to compel performance of this ministerial duty of delivery. As to the first of these conclusions, the passage of time has revealed no occasion for doubt. The language of the Clause is "clear and explicit."[122] Its mandatory language furthers its intended purposes: "to enable each state to bring offenders to trial as swiftly as possible in the state where the alleged offense was committed," and "to preclude any state from becoming a sanctuary for fugitives from justice of another state."[123] The Framers of the Constitution perceived that the frustration of these objectives would create a serious impediment to national unity, and the Extradition Clause responds to that perception. They wrote, "It would have been far better to omit it altogether, and to have left it to the comity of the States, and their own sense of their respective interests, than to have inserted it as conferring a right, and yet defining that right so loosely as to make it a never-failing subject of dispute and ill-will."[124]

On January 25, 1981, Ronald Calder, then a civilian air traffic controller employed by the Federal Aviation Administration in San Juan, Puerto Rico, struck two people with his automobile. One of the victims, Antonio de Jesus Gonzalez, was injured while his wife, Army Villalba, was killed. Villalba was eight months pregnant; her unborn child did not survive. The incident occurred in the parking lot of a grocery store in Aguadilla, Puerto Rico, after what was apparently an altercation between Calder and De Jesus Gonzalez. According to two sworn statements taken by police, one from De Jesus Gonzalez and one from a witness to the incident, after striking the couple, Calder backed his car two or three times over the prostrate body of Villalba.. Authorities arrested Calder and charged him with first-degree vehicular homicide. Puerto Rican authorities then release Calder after he

---

122*Michigan v. Doran,* 439 U.S. 282, 286 (1978)

123 Id. at 287; see also *Biddinger v. Commissioner of Police,* 245 U.S. 128, 132-133 (1917); *Appleyard v. Massachusetts,* 203 U.S. 222, 227 (1906).

124 *Puerto Rico v. Branstad,* 482 U.S. 219 at 227; "Puerto Rico, petitioner, v. Terry E. Branstad et al.," Legal Information Institute, Cornell University Law School.

posted $5,000 bail.[125]

As it was, Calder did not appear at two preliminary hearings that had been scheduled in the Puerto Rico District Courts. Calder failed to appear at a preliminary hearing on March 4, 1981, and bail was increased to $50,000. Despite representations by counsel that Calder would appear at a preliminary hearing on April 13, 1981, he did not do so. At that time, Calder was declared a fugitive from justice, and bail was increased to $300,000. The court then declared Calder to be a fugitive of justice. The Puerto Rican authorities notified the police in Iowa because they guessed that he had fled to his home state. In April 1981, Calder surrendered to the police in Polk County, Iowa, but was released after he had posted the $20,000 bail that had set by an Iowa District Court magistrate.[126]

In May 1981, the governor of Puerto Rico Governor Carlos Romero Barceló submitted to Iowa Governor Robert D. Ray, a request for extradition. The requesting papers included the arrest warrant, the fugitive resolution, the charging documents, and three sworn statements of witnesses, including one in which the affiant identified a photograph of Calder as depicting the driver of the car. Counsel for Calder requested that the Governor of Iowa hold an extradition hearing, which was conducted by the Governor's counsel on June 17, 1981[127]. This hearing was only partially transcribed, but the record does show that one of Calder's counsel was permitted to testify to his belief that "a white American man . . . could not receive a fair trial in the Commonwealth of Puerto Rico," Calder himself testified to his understanding that, "on numerous occasions," witnesses in Puerto Rican courts had been "bought."[128]

Puerto Rico made several fruitless attempts to negotiate a reduction in charges against Calder. Governor Ray then wrote, in December 1981, to Governor Barceló that in the absence of a "change to a more realistic charge," the request for extradition was denied. After the next Iowa election Puerto Rico made another extradition request, this to to Ray's successor, Governor Terry Branstad. The new gover-

---

125 "Puerto Rico v. Branstad, Governor of Iowa, *et al. certiorari* to the United States Court of Appeals for the Eighth Circuit No. 85-2116. Argued March 30, 1987. Decided June 23, 1987.

126 *Puerto Rico v. Branstad,* 483 U.S. 219 (1987)

127 Id. at at 19.

128 "Puerto Rico, petitioner, v. Terry E. Branstad et al.," Legal Information Institute, Cornell University Law School.

nor also denied the request for rendition of Calder.

In February 1984, the Commonwealth of Puerto Rico filed a petition for a writ of mandamus in the United States District Court for the Southern District of Iowa to order Branstad to proceed with the extradition of Calder. Branstad argued that the Extradition Clause did not apply to Puerto Rico because the island was not a U. S. state. Furthermore, he claimed that Puerto Rico could not invoke the Extradition Act because the federal courts, under *Kentucky v. Dennison,* did not have the power to order governors to follow the Extradition Clause or Act. The District Court agreed and dismissed the case. The-United States Court of Appeals for the Eighth Circuit affirmed.[129]

The Extradition Clause exists in Article IV, Section 2, of the United States Constitution and reads: "A Person charged in any State with Treason, Felony, or other Crime, who shall flee from Justice, and be found in another State, shall on demand of the executive Authority of the State from which he fled, be delivered up, to be removed to the State having Jurisdiction of the Crime."

Congress by legislation created the Extradition Act[130] which effectively reads the same as the Extradition Clause except that it included territories and districts, as well as the states.

The Supreme Court of the United States over-ruled the two lower federal courts. Justice Thurgood Marshall wrote the opinion of the Court. In that Marshall concluded that the precedent established by *Kentucky v. Dennison* was "the product of another time. The conception of the relation between the States and the Federal Government there announced is fundamentally incompatible with more than a century of constitutional development." When *Dennison* was decided in 1861, the practical power of the Federal Government was at its lowest ebb since the adoption of the Constitution. Secession of States from the Union was a fact, and civil war was a threatening possibility Thus, the Supreme Court established the power of federal courts to enforce both the Extradition Clause and the Extradition Act by writs of mandamus. Basically, *Dennison*'s holding that the federal courts have no authority under the Constitution to compel performance by an asylum state of the mandatory, ministerial duty to deliver up fugitives upon

129"Puerto Rico v. Branstad," in Wikipedia.

130 Extradition Act, 18 U.S.C. § 3182. Dennison's holding that the federal courts have no authority under the Constitution to compel performance by an asylum State of the mandatory, ministerial duty to deliver up fugitives upon proper demand can stand no longer. pp. 224-229.

proper demand can stand no longer.[131]

The point that Governor Bransted made arose during oral argument: Does the Extradition Clause applied to Puerto Rico since it is a territory and not a U. S. state. Justice Marshall, joined by five other Justices, undertook an analysis of Puerto Rico's political status. They concluded that its territorial existence is such that Puerto Rico is heir to certain rights comparable to those of the U. S. states. Justice Marshall argued that the Extradition Act clearly includes U.S. territories. Justice O'Connor noted that fact in her concurrence. However she did not join the opinion of the Court regarding Puerto Rico's status. Justice Scalia also did not join that section of the opinion and noted that "no party before us has asserted the lack of power of Congress to require extradition from a State to a Territory." [132]

However, the high court reaffirmed the other proposition for which *Dennison* stood: that the Extradition Clause's commands are mandatory and afford no discretion to executive officers of the asylum State. The *Dennison* holding as to the federal courts' authority to enforce the Extradition Clause rested on a fundamental premise, that is, that the States and the Federal Government in all circumstances must be viewed as coequal sovereigns. This, Justice Marshall wrote, is not representative of current law. It has long been a settled principle that federal courts may enjoin unconstitutional action by state officials. There exists no justification for distinguishing the duty to deliver fugitives from the many other species of constitutional duty enforceable in the federal courts. Because the duty is directly imposed upon the States by the Constitution itself, there is no need to weigh the performance of the federal obligation against the powers reserved to the States under the Tenth Amendment. Even assuming, as respondents contend, that there is an "executive common law" of extradition, developed under *Dennison*, which provides a superior alternative to the "ministerial duty" to extradite provided for by the Constitution, no weight can be accorded to it. Long continuation of decisional law or administrative practice incompatible with the Constitution's requirements cannot overcome this Court's responsibility to enforce those requirements.[133]

---

131 *Puerto Rico v. Branstad,* at 224-29
132 Bunch, Kenyon and Richard J. Hardy, "Continuity or Change in Interstate Extradition? Assessing Puerto Rico v. Branstad," *Publius,* 21: 1 (1991), pp. 51-67.
133 Id. At 221-24; "Puerto Rico v. Branstad," in Encyclopedia.com.

Ortiz Extradition

The State of Ohio had arrested and convicted Timothy Reed of armed robbery and theft of drugs, and sentenced him to a term of twenty-five years in the state prison system. Ohio then paroled Reed from the Ohio correctional system in 1992. In the following year Ohio prison officials told respondent they planned to revoke his parole. Before the scheduled date of his meeting with his parole officer, respondent fled from Ohio to New Mexico. Ohio sought extradition and the Governor of New Mexico issued a warrant directing the extradition of respondent. He was arrested in October 1994, and later that year sought a writ of *habeas corpus* from the New Mexico State District Court. He claimed he was not a "fugitive" for purposes of extradition because he fled under duress, believing that Ohio authorities intended to revoke his parole without due process and to cause him physical harm if he were returned to an Ohio prison. In January 1995, the New Mexico trial court ruled in favor of respondent and directed his release from custody. The State appealed this order, and in September 1997 the Supreme Court of New Mexico affirmed the grant of *habeas corpus*. [134]

The Supreme Court of New Mexico agreed that the first three requirements had been met, but decided that respondent was not a "fugitive" from justice; in the words of the Supreme Court of New Mexico, he was a "refugee from injustice." That court held that respondent fled Ohio because of fear that his parole would be revoked without due process, and that he would be thereafter returned to prison where he faced the threat of bodily injury. It held that this "duress" negated his status as a fugitive under the law. [135] The State petitioned for *certiorari* from that decision.

The State of Ohio, although not a party at that hearing, and the State of New Mexico which was defending the Governor's action was at a considerable disadvantage in producing testimony, even in affidavit form, of occurrences in the State of Ohio. Very likely Ohio was aware of the U.S. Supreme Court's statement that the "scheme of interstate rendition, as set forth in both the Constitution and the statutes which Congress has enacted to implement the Constitution . . . do[es] not contemplate an appearance by [the demanding state] in respon-

134 124 N. M. 129, 947 P.2d 86 (1997).
135 124 N. M, at 146, 947 P.2d, at 103.

dent's asylum to defend against the claimed abuses of its prison system."[136]

In a previous case the U.S. Supreme Court discovered criteria by which rendition should occur. Claims relating to what actually happened in the demanding State, the law of that State, and what may be expected to happen in that State when the fugitive returns are issues to be decided by the demanding State, not the asylum State.[137]

In multiple previous cases the U.S. Supreme Court had held that claims relating to what actually happened in the demanding State, the law of the demanding State, and what may be expected to happen in the demanding State when the fugitive returns, are issues that must be tried in the courts of that State, and not in those of the asylum State.[138]

The Supreme Court of New Mexico also held that the New Mexico Constitution's provision guaranteeing the right "of seeking and obtaining safety" prevailed over the State's duty under Article IV of the United States Constitution. This had been rejected previously and simply is not the case. [139] In 1987 the U.S. Supreme Court had affirmed "the conclusion that the commands of the Extradition Clause are mandatory, and afford no discretion to the executive officers or the courts of the asylum State."[140] And in another case the high court had written, "The Federal Constitution places certain limits on the sovereign powers of the States, limits that are an essential part of the Framers' conception of national identity and Union. . . . The obvious objective of the Extradition Clause is that no State should become a safe haven for the fugitives from a sister State's criminal justice system."[141]

The U.S. Supreme Court heard the case and reversed the opinion of the courts of New Mexico. The U.S. high court ruled, "We accept, of course, the determination of the Supreme Court of New Mexi-

136 *New Mexico ex rel. Ortiz v. Reed,* 524 U.S. 151, (1998).

137 See also *Pacileo v. Walker,* 449 U. S. 86 at 88 (1980).

138 *Drew v. Thaw,* 235 U.S. 432 (1914); *Sweeney v. Woodall,* 344 U.S. 86 (1952). See "Fugitives from Justice under the Federal Rendition Clause," *Columbia Law Review,* 18: 1 (1918), pp. 70-73.

139 *New Mexico ex rel. Ortiz v. Reed,* 524 U.S. 151, (1998). See also Ray, Marshall J., "What Does the Natural Rights Clause Mean to New Mexico," *New Mexico Law Review,* 39: 2 (2009), pp. 375-406.

140 *Puerto Rico v. Branstad,* 483 U.S. 219, 227 (1987)

141 *California v. Superior Court of California, San Bernardino County,* 482 U.S. 400

co that respondent's testimony was credible, but this is simply not the kind of issue that may be tried in the asylum State." It reminded New Mexico that "the Extradition Clause [of the U.S. Constitution] imposes a mandatory duty on the asylum state." It then chided New Mexico for procrastinating.[142] "As is apparent from the length of time this proceeding has taken in the courts of New Mexico, it has been anything but the "summary" proceeding contemplated by the decisions cited above. This is because the Supreme Court of New Mexico went beyond the permissible inquiry in an extradition case, and permitted the litigation of issues not open in the asylum State. The State's petition for *certiorari* is granted, the judgment of the New Mexico Supreme Court was reversed." The Supreme Court found that New Mexico courts had overstepped their authority and ordered the New Mexico Supreme Court to return the fugitive.[143]

Other Cases Defining Rendition

The case of Harold William Doran was heard by the U.S. Supreme Court in 1978 on appeal from Michigan. Doran was arrested in Michigan and charged with receiving and concealing a stolen truck driven from Arizona. Michigan had notified Arizona authorities, Arizona charged respondent with theft, and an Arizona Justice of the Peace issued an arrest warrant reciting, in accordance with Arizona law, that there was "reasonable cause" to believe that respondent had committed the offense. The Governor of Arizona issued a requisition for Doran's extradition accompanied by the arrest warrant, supporting affidavits, and the original complaint whereupon the Governor of Michigan ordered extradition.[144] Doran immediately petitioned for a writ of *habeas corpus*, alleging that the extradition warrant was invalid because it did not comply with the Uniform Criminal Extradition Act in effect in Michigan.[145] The courts denied the petition. The U.S. Supreme Court reversed and ordered Doran's release. It held that Arizona had failed to show probable cause to support its charge. Once the Governor of the asylum state has acted on a requisition for extradition based on the demanding state's judicial determination that probable cause existed, no further judicial inquiry may be had on that issue

---

142 *New Mexico v Ortiz,* 524 U.S. 151 (1998)
143 *New Mexico v Ortiz,* 524 U.S. 151 (1998)
144 401 Mich. 235, 258 N.W.2d 406.
145 18 U.S.C. § 3182 and the Uniform Criminal Extradition Act.

in the asylum state.[146]

In the case, U.S. Supreme Court[147] held that the Extradition Clause imposes a mandatory duty on the asylum State, affording no discretion to its executive officers or courts. Once a Governor has granted extradition, a court considering release on *habeas* can decide only whether (a) the documents on their face are in order; (b) the petitioner has been charged with a crime in the demanding State; (c) the petitioner is the person named in the extradition request; and (d) the petitioner is a fugitive.[148]

In 1975, James Dean Walker escaped from the Arkansas Department of Corrections and was apprehended in California in 1979. In December 1979, the Governor of Arkansas requested the rendition of, alleging that Walker was a fugitive from justice. In February 1980, the Governor of California honored the request of the Governor of Arkansas and duly issued a warrant of arrest and rendition. Walter then challenged the issuance of the warrant in both state and federal courts. The California Supreme Court issued a writ of *habeas corpus* directing a California trial court to conduct an inquiry as to whether the Arkansas penitentiary in which respondent would be confined was in conformance with the Eighth Amendment of the Federal Constitution. On appeal, the U.S. Supreme Court ruled that the Extradition Clause, and its implementing statute, do not give the courts of the asylum state the authority to inquire into the prison conditions of the demanding state. Once the Governor of California issued the warrant, the respondent must be rendered up.[149] In *Pacilio,* the court wrote "Once the Governor of California issued the warrant for arrest and rendition in response to the request of the Governor of Arkansas, claims as to constitutional defects in the Arkansas penal system should be heard in the courts of Arkansas, not those of California."[150]

Mental Competency

When a criminal defendant flees from a requesting state to an asylum state, the requesting state can demand that the asylum state return the fugitive irrespective of his mental state. Only a handful of states have considered a fugitive's right to be mentally competent to

146 *Michigan v Doran*, 439 U.S. 282 (1978).
147 *New Mexico ex rel. Ortiz v. Reed,* 524 U.S. 151, (1998).
148 See *Michigan v. Doran,* 439 U. S. 282 at 289
149 *Pacileo v. Walker,* 449 U.S. 86 (1980)
150 *Pacileo v. Walker,* 449 U.S. 86 (1980).

proceed with an extradition hearing. Some states apply the same standard as in criminal trial competency cases. Others apply a more limited competency standard. At least two states have declared that a fugitive has no right to be competent to proceed in an extradition hearing. The particular legal test adopted affects the nature and scope of the competency evaluation conducted by the psychiatrist or psychologist in the extradition hearing. Additionally, no state has considered what happens to the fugitive if he is ultimately found not competent to proceed. Legislation, either state by state or through amendments to the Uniform Criminal Extradition Act, can be fabricated to provide the legal and psychiatric communities with guidance in assessing competency initially and in taking appropriate steps if the fugitive is ultimately found not competent.

In many American states, a criminal defendant is incompetent to stand trial only if some present mental condition renders him unable to understand the nature and workings of the proceedings and to assist in his defense. Some forensic mental health evaluators have treated the mental-condition requirement as synonymous with, or similar to, the psychiatric condition required in the state's insanity criteria, which requires some specific severe mental disease or defect. The term "mental condition" rarely, if ever, appears in statess criminal codes. There is rarely anywhere in legal documents a definition of a mental illness for purposes of civil commitment. Moreover, many states' adjudicative competency statutes do not explain what conditions or symptoms constitute a mental condition sufficient to render a defendant incompetent.[151]

Most recently, a group of psychiatrists and psychologists has come forth, asserting that if a fugitive is showing the effects of an acute and severe mental illness at the time of the extradition hearing, the asylum state must resolve the question of his mental competency before determining the merits of the extradition. Once competency is at issue, a psychiatrist or psychologist may be asked to perform a forensic mental health examination of the defendant. The competency

151 Tartaro, Christine; Joshua Duntley; Stephanie Medvetz; and Nicole Hafner, "Factors that Predict Murder Defendants' Competence to Stand Trial," *International Journal of Law and Psychiatry,* 59 (2-18), pp. 31-37; Kois, Lauren; James M Wellbeloved-Stone; Preeti Chauhan; and Janet I Warren, "Combined Evaluations of Competency to Stand Trial and Mental State at the Time of the Offense: An Overlooked Methodological Consideration?," *Law and Human Behavior,* 41: 3 (2017), pp. 217-29.

process, however, creates both legal and mental health questions. To date, there is no uniform formula, either legal or psychiatric, by which competency is determined in this context[152]

An early case concerning the mental health of a person whose extradition was sought was *Drew v Thaw.* Thaw was being held on a warrant from the Governor of New Hampshire for his extradition to New York. He was alleged to be a fugitive from justice and a copy of an indictment found by a New York grand jury accompanied the demand. The indictment alleged that Thaw had been committed to the Matteawan State Hospital for the insane because he had been acquitted at his trial upon a former indictment on the ground of insanity. Thaw conspired with others to assist him in escaping from the hospital. By the New York Penal Law an agreement to commit any act for the perversion or obstruction of justice or of the due administration of the laws is a misdemeanor, if an overt act beside the agreement is done to effect the object.[153]

Thaw argued that if he was insane when he contrived his escape he could not be guilty of crime, while if he was not insane he was entitled to be discharged. Writing the opinion of the U.S. Supreme Court, Justice Oliver Wendell Holmes, Jr., rejected that assertion, determined that there was no doubt that Thaw was a fugitive from justice, and ordered Thaw to be extradited forthwith.[154]

Uniform Criminal Extradition Act

While the United States Constitution provides the original authority for interstate rendition, the Congress has amplified and interpreted it by enacting a federal statute. The federal statute and the Constitution place an outer limit on extradition procedures, although the states are free to use more relaxed standards. Among other considerations, federal law recommends that at the *habeas corpus* hearing, it is advisable for the petitioning state to introduce all documents and any

---

152 Piel, Jennifer; Michael J. Finkle; Megan Giske; and Gregory B. Leong, "Determining a Criminal Defendant's Competency to Proceed With an Extradition Hearing," *Journal of the American Academy of Psychiatry and the Law Online*, 43: 2 (2015), pp. 201-209. See also Reisner, Andrew D. and Jennifer L Piel, "Mental Condition Requirement in Competency to Stand Trial Assessments," *American Academy of Psychiatry and Law*, 46: 1 (2018), pp. 86-92.

153 New York Penal Law, §§ 580, 583.

154 *Drew v Thaw*, 235 US 432 (1914). See "Scope of a Habeas Corpus Hearing on Interstate Extradition of Criminals," *Yale Law Journal*, 53: 2 (1944), pp. 359-64.

related papers, so as to compel the court to examine their legal sufficiency. A defect in the supporting papers may rebut the *prima facie*
case established by the Governor's rendition warrant..[155]

In addition, forty-eight of the fifty states have adopted the Uniform Criminal Extradition Act (U.C.E.A.). This act permits extradition under circumstances, and through procedures, not covered by the
federal statute. The U.C.E.A. was proposed in an effort to reduce
confusion and uncertainty about what was required by the various
states. UCEA covered such topics as arrest in asylum State, prepara-
tion of papers in demanding, issuance of governor's warrant in asylum
state, bail after issuance of rendition warrant, and habeas corpus hearing in asylum State. Under U.C.E.A., rendition is possible even if the
accused was never personally present in the demanding state. That
person may be extradited if he undertook acts outside that state inten-
tionally resulting in a crime in the demanding state. [156]

The most recent development in the extradition process is the
adoption by the Commissioners on Uniform State Laws of the Uniform Extradition and Rendition Act (U.E.R.A.), designed to replace
the U.C.E.A. The Uniform Extradition and Rendition Act, completed
in 1980, provides two separate procedures to be used for the retrieval
of wanted persons found in another state. The Commissioners on Uniform State Laws recently adopted the UERA, designed to replace the
UCEA. The National Conference of Commissioners on Uniform State
Law (NCCUSL) created U.E.R.A. It is designed to streamline the extradition process and provide additional protections for the person
sought. The UERA purports to streamline extraditions by adoption
and clarification of the de facto features of the current process. This
act is now regarded by the NCCUSL as a model act, instead of a uniform act, and so it may also be known as the Model Extradition and
Rendition Act. [157]

---

155 18 USCS § 3182. Federal Statute of the U.S. Code per Title 18, Part II, Chapter
   209, Section 3182
156 *Uniform Laws Annotated,* Master Edition, vol. 11 (2003), Appendix I, pp. 294-
   660. See "The Uniform Criminal Extradition Act," *Columbia Law Review,* 32: 8
   (1932), pp. 1411-1424.
157 Murphy, John J., "Revising Domestic Extradition Law," *University of Pennsylvania Law Review,* 131: 5, (1983), pp. 1063-1119; Abramson, Leslie W. "Extradition in America: Of Uniform Acts and Governmental Discretion," *Baylor Law
   Review,* 33: 4 (1981), pp. 793-841.

Extradition in U. S. Law

Extradition is an action wherein one jurisdiction delivers a person accused, or convicted, of committing a crime in another jurisdiction, over to the other's law enforcement. As a diplomatic device, it dates back at least to the thirteenth century BC, when Egyptian Pharaoh, Ramesses II, negotiated an extradition treaty with a Hittite king, Hattusili III. It is a cooperative law enforcement procedure between the two jurisdictions and depends on the arrangements made between them. In addition to legal aspects of the process, extradition also involves the physical transfer of custody of the person being extradited to the legal authority of the requesting jurisdiction.

In an extradition process, one sovereign jurisdiction typically makes a formal request to another sovereign jurisdiction ("the requested state"). If the fugitive is found within the territory of the requested state, then the requested state may arrest the fugitive and subject him or her to its extradition process. The extradition procedures to which the fugitive will be subjected are dependent on the law and practice of the requested state. Extradition between two sovereign nations, and among clusters of sovereignties, are regulated by treaties.[158]

U. S. Supreme Court adjudication of extradition really began with the *Ker* case in 1886. Extradition, of course was an anticipated duty of all modern states, with only specific details to be worked out by international negotiations which result in a treaty.

Ker v. Illinois

George Hunt, Attorney General for Illinois, in a recently discovered document, outlined the case against Frederick M. Ker. Illinois had requested Ker's extradition based on Ker's own admission of embezzlement. Hunt outlined the case fully in an attachment to his brief in the case of *Ker v. Illinois.*:

> Having passed upon the law questions raised by this hearing, the court may have interest enough in the man and the crime which these questions are put forward to shield, to read another page concerning them. In the month of January, 1883, Frederick M. Ker, having been for many years the confidential clerk for Preston, Kean & Co., bankers of

---

158 See "Extradition," in Wikipedia; Sadoff, David A. *Bringing International Fugitives to Justice: Extradition and its Alternatives.* Cambridge University Press, 2016, p. 43.

Chicago, asked permission to go to New Orleans for a rest from his labors. When the time for his vacation expired, the bankers instead of receiving their clerk, received a letter from him, postmarked at Chicago, in which he generously informed them that there were deficits in his accounts, and the amount of the embezzlement would be found to be about $21,000 of the moneys of the bank, and $35,000 of United States bonds belonging to its patrons. The letter contained an intimation that if allowed to take his journey unmolested, the bank would be let alone, but if pursued and brought back, a run would be organized and the bank ruined; and concluded with the cool remark that if successful in future life, he would endeavor to refund the money to those entitled to receive it. Preston, Kean & Co. were not alarmed by the threats, and inaugurated such measures that by the next steamer there went to Aspinwall one of Pinkerton's men, who at Panama found a Chicago overcoat which had been shed and given to a porter. Precaution had been taken to cut the tailor's name from the neck of the coat, but the name of Ker in one of the lappels [sic] of the side pocket remained untouched. Learning from the porter that the owner of the overcoat had sailed for Callao, the detective armed with photograph alone, followed by the next steamer. Arriving there, he went to Lima, and in a few days thereafter, while in a public square, recognized Ker sitting under the shade of a tropical tree, regaling himself with a cigar. An acquaintance followed. Ker could speak French and so could the detective. Becoming interested in each other, a friendship arose. Together they did the city, the theatre and the fandango. Investments were discussed; Ker had money, the detective had more, and thus dreaming and scheming, day passed into weeks and time wore happily away. In the meantime, at Chicago, the victimized bankers obtained the proper demand from the federal Secretary of State, which came by the next steamer to the friend in Lima. At this time, a state of things existed in Peru which rendered the treaty between the United States and that government inoperative. There was no Peru. The government had a nominal existence at Ariquipa, back in the mountains, eighty-five miles from Lima, but General Lynch, of the Chilean forces, was in military occupation of the capital. Pinkerton's man had no passport to go through the lines to present our demand at the mountain camp of the Peruvian government, but did what was perhaps the next best thing, applied to General Lynch. This officer, doubtless thinking that security to criminals was no part of his mission in Peru, dispatched an officer to aid the detective in putting Ker on his way back to the United States. On board the man-of-war, Essex, then in the harbor at Callao, on her way to China, he was conducted to a state-room and transported to Honolulu, where it was expected to intercept the departure of a vessel to San Francisco. It happened, however, that this vessel had sailed when the Essex arrived outside the harbor, and Ker enjoyed the sea breezes on board his country's man-of-war for nearly a month, when the next steamer took him aboard for San Francisco. Having been brought to Chicago, Ker, in the course of time, was placed upon his trial. He interposed no denial of the charges of theft and embezzlement, but relied upon his ability to persuade the United States to take him back to Peru. The court below was not susceptible to these persuasions, and gave him ten years tuition in Juliet to improve his notions of business integrity. With what success his appeal will meet here, remains to be seen.[159]

The substance of the plea was a very long one. It alleged that the defendant, Frederick M. Ker, being in the city of Lima, in Peru, after the offenses were charged to have been committed, was in fact kidnapped and brought to the United States against his will. Governor Hamilton, of Illinois, made his requisition for extradition of Ker, in writing, to the Secretary of State of the United States. That person prepared a warrant requesting the extradition of the defendant, by the executive of the Republic of Peru, from that country to Cook County, Illinois. On the first day of March, 1883, the President of the United States issued this warrant, in due form, directed to Henry G. Julian, a Pinkerton Detective Agent, as a messenger, to receive the defendant from the authorities of Peru. The charge in Illinois was larceny.

Extradition was requested in compliance with the treaty between the United States and Peru on that subject. Ker alleged that Julian, although in possession of the necessary papers with him, arrived in Lima, but, without presenting them to any officer of the Peruvian government, or making any demand on that government for the surrender of Ker. Rather, he forcibly and with violence arrested Ker, placed him on board the United States vessel *Essex,* in the harbor of Callao, kept him a close prisoner until the arrival of that vessel at Honolulu. After holding Ker for a while in detention, he transferred Ker, in the same forcible manner, on board another vessel, the *City of Sydney,* in which he was carried a prisoner to San Francisco, California.[160]

Before Ker's arrival in San Francisco, Governor Hamilton had made a requisition on the Governor of California, under the laws and constitution of the United States for the delivery up of the defendant

---

159 Document reproduced in Fairman, Charles, "Ker v. Illinois Revisited" 47 *American Journal of International Law* 4: 678-86 (1953).

160 Fairman, Charles, "Ker v. Illinois Revisited," *American Journal of International Law,* 47: 4 (1953), pp. 678-86.

as a fugitive from justice, who had escaped to that state on account of the same offenses charged in the requisition on Peru and in the indictment in this case. This requisition arrived and was presented to the governor of California, who made his order for the surrender of the defendant to the person appointed by the Governor of Illinois, Frank Warner, on 25 June 1883. The defendant Ker arrived in the city of San Francisco on 9 July and was immediately placed in the custody of Warner, under the order of the Governor of California. Still a prisoner, Ker was transferred by Warner to Cook County, where the process of the criminal count was served upon him, and he was held to answer the indictment already mentioned.[161]

A plea to an indictment in a state court that the defendant was thus brought from a foreign country to this country by proceedings which are a violation of a treaty between that country and the United states, and which are forbidden by that treaty, raises a question, if the right asserted by the plea is denied, on which this Court can review, by writ of error, the judgment of the state court.[162]

But where the prisoner has been kidnapped in the foreign country and brought by force against his will within the jurisdiction of the state whose law he has violated, with no reference to an extradition treaty, though one existed, and no proceeding or attempt to proceed under the treaty, this Court can give no relief, for these facts do not establish any right under the Constitution or laws or treaties of the United States.

The treaties of extradition to which the United States are parties do not guarantee a fugitive from the justice of one of the countries an asylum in the other. They do not give such person any greater or more sacred right of asylum than he had before. They only make provision that for certain crimes, he shall be deprived of that asylum and surrendered to justice, and they prescribe the mode in which this shall be done.

The trespass of a kidnapper, unauthorized by either of the governments and not professing to act under authority of either, is not a case provided for in the treaty, and the remedy is by a proceeding

---

161 Garcia-Mora, Manuel R., "Criminal Jurisdiction of a State Ov Criminal Jurisdiction of a State Over Fugitives Brought F ought From a Foreign Countr eign Country By Force or Fraud: A Comparative Study," *Indiana Law Journal*, 32: 4 (1957), pp. 427-49.

162 *Ker v. Illinois,* 119 U.S. 436 (1886). Argued 27 April and decided 6 December 1886/

against him by the government whose law he violates or by the party injured. How far such forcible transfer of the defendant so as to bring him within the jurisdiction of the state where the offense was committed may be set up against the right to try him is the province of the state court to decide, and presents no question in which this Court can review its decision.

The plaintiff in error, being convicted of embezzlement in a state court of Illinois, sued out this writ of error. The federal question which makes the case is stated in the opinion of the Court.

> This case is brought here by a writ of error to the supreme court of the state of Illinois. The plaintiff in error, Frederick M. Ker, was indicted, tried, and convicted in the criminal court of Cook County, in that state, for larceny. The indictment also included charges of embezzlement. During the proceedings connected with the trial the defendant presented a plea in abatement, which, on demurrer, was overruled; and, the defendant refusing to plead further, a plea of not guilty was entered for him, according to the statute of that state, by order of the court, on which the trial and conviction took place. [163]

The federal government had hired Henry Julian, a Pinkerton Detective Agency agent, to bring back top the United States a larcenist, Frederick Ker, who had fled to Peru. Julian had all the necessary, proper and legal extradition papers, but found that there was no Peruvian official available to meet his request because of the recent Chilean military occupation of the Peruvian capital, Lima, where Ker was being held. For their part, the civilian as well as military agents of Chile had absolutely no interest in the proceedings. Rather than return home empty-handed, Julian kidnapped the fugitive, with some acquiescence, if not assistance, from Chilean forces. Julian placed Ker on a U.S. vessel heading back to the United States.[164]

The plea is very full of bereavements that the defendant protested, and was refused any opportunity whatever, from the time of his arrest in Lima until he was delivered over to the authorities of Cook county, of communicating with any person, or seeking any advice or assistance in regard to procuring his release by legal process

---

163 Schwabach, Aaron and S. A. Patchett, "Doctrine or Dictum: The Ker-Frisbie Doctrine and Official Abductions Which Breach International Law," *University of Miami Inter-American Law Review,* 25: 1 (1993), pp. 19-56.

164Cardozo, Michael H. "When Extradition Fails, Is Abduction the Solution?". *American Journal of International Law.* 55 (1): 127–135 (1961).

or otherwise; and he alleges that this proceeding is a violation of the provisions of the treaty between the United States and Peru, negotiated in 1870, which was finally ratified by the two governments, and proclaimed by the president of the United States.[165]

The judgment of the criminal court of Cook County, Illinois, was carried by writ of error to the supreme court of that state, and there affirmed, to which judgment the present writ of error is directed. The assignments of error made on appeal are as follows: First, that the supreme court of Illinois erred in affirming the judgment of said criminal court of Cook county, sustaining the demurrer to plaintiff in error's plea to the jurisdiction of said criminal court. Second, the supreme court of Illinois erred in its judgment aforesaid, in failing to enforce the full faith and credit of the federal treaty with the Republic of Peru, invoked by plaintiff in error in his said plea to the jurisdiction of said criminal court.

The grounds upon which the jurisdiction of this court was invoked were three in number. Realistically, however, based upon the briefs and arguments of counsel it was deemed doubtful whether more than one was relied upon. Ker contended, in several places in the brief, that the proceedings in the arrest in Peru, and the extradition and delivery to the authorities of Cook County, were not due process of law with reference to that clause of the Fourteenth Amendment to the Constitution of the United States which declares that no state shall deprive any person of life, liberty, or property "without due process of law." The U. S. Supreme Court found that due process of law there guaranteed is complied with when the party is regularly indicted by the proper grand jury in the state court, has a trial according to the forms and modes prescribed for such trials, and when, in that trial and proceedings, he is deprived of no rights to which he is lawfully entitled. The 14th Amendment did not say that there may not be proceedings previous to the trial, in regard to which the prisoner could invoke in some manner the provisions of this clause of the Constitution. For mere irregularities in the manner in which the appellate may be brought into custody of the law, we do not think he is entitled to say that he should not be tried at all for the crime with which he is charged in a regular indictment. He may be arrested for a very heinous offense by persons without any warrant, or without any previous complaint, and brought before a proper officer; and this may be,

---

165 July 27, 1874. 18 U. S. St. at Large, pt. 3, p. 35.

in some sense, said to be 'without due process of law.' But it could hardly be claimed that, after the case had been investigated and the defendant held by the proper authorities to answer for the crime, that he could plead that he was first arrested without due process of law. So here, when found within the jurisdiction of the state of Illinois, and liable to answer for a crime against the laws of that state, unless there was some positive provision of the Constitution or of the laws of this country violated in bringing him into court, it is not easy to see how he can say that he is there without due process of law, within the meaning of the constitutional provision.[166]

So, also, the appellate made the objection that the proceedings between the authorities of the state of Illinois and those of the the state of California, were not conducted according to the act of Congress on that subject. It was alleged that, at the time the papers and warrants were issued from the governors of California and Illinois, the defendant was not situated within the state of California, and was not there a fugitive from justice. This argument is not much pressed by counsel, and was scarcely noticed in the supreme court of Illinois. However in the pleadings before the U. S. Supreme Court the appellate attempted to connect it as a part of the continued trespass and violation of law which accompanied the transfer from Peru to Illinois. The high court in regard to that part of this case, held that, when the governor of one state voluntarily surrenders a fugitive from the justice of another state to answer for his alleged offenses, it is hardly a proper subject of inquiry on the trial of the case to examine into the details of the proceedings by which the demand was made by the one state, and the manner in which it was responded to by the other.[167]

But the main proposition argued by counsel for plaintiff in error in this court was that, by virtue of the treaty of extradition with Peru, the defendant acquired by his residence in that country a right of asylum,and thus a right to be free from molestation for the crime committed in Illinois. As a consequence he should only be forcibly removed from Peru to Illinois in accordance with the provisions of the treaty,-and that this right is one which he can assert in the courts of the United States in all cases, whether the removal took place under proceedings sanctioned by the treaty, or under proceedings which were in total disregard of that treaty, amounting to an unlawful and

---

166 119 U.S. 436, 440.
167 *Ker V. Illinois,* 119 U. S. 436 (1886), chanrobles.com.

unauthorized kidnapping. This view of the subject is presented in various forms, and repeated in various shapes, in the argument of counsel. The fact that this question was raised in the supreme court of Illinois may be said to confer jurisdiction on this court, because, in making this claim, the defendant asserted a right under a treaty of the United States, and, whether the assertion was well founded or not, this court has jurisdiction to decide it; and we proceed to inquire into it.

There is no language in the applicable treaty, or in any other treaty made by the United States on the subject of extradition, of which the Supreme Court was aware, which says in terms that a party fleeing from the United States to escape punishment for crime becomes thereby entitled to an asylum in the country to which he has fled. Indeed, the absurdity of such a proposition would at once prevent the making of a treaty of that kind. It will not be for a moment contended that the government of Peru could not have ordered Ker out of the country on his arrival, or at any period of his residence there. If this could be done, what becomes of his right of asylum? [168]

Nor can it be doubted that the government of Peru could, of its own accord, without any demand from the United States, have surrendered Ker to an agent of the state of Illinois, and that such surrender would have been valid within the dominions of Peru. It is idle, therefore, to claim that, either by express terms or by implication, there is given to a fugitive from justice in one of these countries any right to remain and reside in the other; and, if the right of asylum means anything, it must mean this. The right of the government of Peru voluntarily to give a party in Ker's condition an asylum in that country is quite a different thing from the right in him to demand and insist upon security in such an asylum. The treaty, so far as it regulates the right of asylum at all, is intended to limit this right in the case of one who is proved to be a criminal fleeing from justice; so that, on proper demand and proceedings had therein, the government of the country of the asylum shall deliver him up to the country where the crime was committed. And to this extent, and to this alone, the treaty does regulate or impose a restriction upon the right of the government of the country of the asylum to protect the criminal from removal therefrom.

In this case before the high court, the plea shows that, although Julian went to Peru with the necessary papers to procure the extradi-

---

168 Preuss, Lawrence. "Kidnaping of Fugitives from Justice on Foreign Territory". *American Journal of International Law.* 29: 3 (1935), pp. 502–507.

tion of Ker under the treaty, those papers remained in his pocket, and were never brought to light in Peru; that no step were taken under them; and that Julian, in seizing upon the person of Ker, and carrying him out of the territory of Peru into the United States, did not act, nor profess to act, under the treaty. In fact, that treaty was not called into operation, was not relied upon, was not made the pretext of arrest, and the facts show that it was clear case of kidnapping within the dominions of Peru, without any pretense of authority under the treaty or from the government of the United States.[169]

In the case of *U. S. v. Rauscher*, the effect of extradition proceedings under a treaty was very fully considered; and it was there held that when a party was duly surrendered, by proper proceedings, under the treaty of 1842 with Great Britain, he came to this country clothed with the protection which the nature of such proceedings and the true construction of the treaty gave him. One of the rights with which he was thus clothed, both in regard to himself and in good faith to the county which had sent him here, was that he should be tried for no other offense than the one for which he was delivered under the extradition proceedings.

If Ker had been brought to this country by proceedings under the treaty of 1870-74 with Peru, it seems probable, from the statement of the case in the record, that he might have successfully pleaded that he was extradited for larceny, and convicted by the verdict of a jury of embezzlement; for the statement in the plea is that the demand made by the president of the United States, if it had been put in operation, was for an extradition for larceny, although some forms of embezzlement are mentioned in the treaty as subjects of extradition. But it is quite a different case when the plaintiff in error comes to this country in the manner in which he was brought here, clothed with no rights which a proceeding under the treaty could have given him, and no duty which this country owes to Peru or to him under the treaty. We think it very clear, therefore, that, in invoking the jurisdiction of this court upon the ground that the prisoner was denied a right conferred upon him by a treaty of the United States, he has failed to establish the existence of any such right.[170]

---

169 Fairman, Charles. "Ker v. Illinois Revisited". 47 *American Journal of International Law*. 4: 678–686 (1953); Wedgwood, Ruth, "The Argument against International Abduction of Criminal Defendants," *American University International Law Review*, 6: 4 (2011), pp 537-69;

170 119 U.S. 436, 444

The question of how far his forcible seizure in another country, and transfer by violence, force, or fraud to this country, could be made available to resist trial in the state court for the offense now charged upon him, is one which the U. S. Supreme Court did not feel called upon to decide, for it did not see that the constitution or laws or treaties of the United States guaranty him any protection. There are authorities of the highest respectability which hold that such forcible abduction is not sufficient reason why the party should not answer when brought within the jurisdiction of the court which has the right to try him for such an offense. However this may be, the high court wrote, the decision of that question is as much within the province of the state court as a question of common law, or of the law of nations, of which that court is bound to take notice.[171]

The Supreme Court opined although it might or might not differ with the Illinois court on that subject, it is one in which it has no right to review their decision. It must be remembered that this view of the subject does not leave the prisoner, or the government of Peru, without remedy for his unauthorized seizure within its territory. Even this treaty with that country provides for the extradition of persons charged with kidnaping, and, on demand from Peru, Julian, the party who is guilty of it, could be surrendered, and tried in its courts for this violation of its laws. Ker would probably not be without redress, for he could sue Julian in an action of trespass and false imprisonment, and the facts set out in the plea would without doubt sustain the action. Whether he could recover a sum sufficient to justify the action would probably depend upon moral aspects of the case, which the Supreme Court chose not to consider. It held that, so far as any question in which the Supreme Court could revise the judgment of the Illinois Supreme Court is presented to it, the judgment must be affirmed.

The bottom line, said the Supreme Court of the United States, is that "such forcible abduction is no sufficient reason why the party should not answer when brought within the jurisdiction of the court which has the right to try him for such an offense, and presents no valid objection to his trial in such court."[172]

Some courts have come to regard *Ker* as the major precedent for the broad rule that, given a defendant's later arrest within the juris-

---

171

172 Preuss, Lawrence (1935). "Kidnaping of Fugitives from Justice on Foreign Territory," *American Journal of International Law,* 29: 3 (1935), pp. 502–507.

diction and his presence before the court, the court may exercise jurisdiction over him. Much criticism has been leveled at the *Ker* rule because it may condone violations of international law. An early critic of *Ker* wrote, ""The result in *Ker* . . . is unsatisfactory in both its procedural and its substantive aspects . . . . [*Ker*] should have had, in relation to the United States, a right to be released from detention procured by a violation of the universally accepted principles of international jurisprudence."[173]

The *Ker* rule allows a court to disregard completely the violation of a foreign state's sovereignty committed by U. S. officials in the arrest and removal of a criminal suspect from the foreign state. A better rule, however, would allow a court to give effect to the international legal condemnation of international kidnapping by declining to exercise jurisdiction over the kidnapped defendant.[174]

The Specialty Principle

The Doctrine of Specialty is a principle of International law that is included in most extradition treaties, whereby a person who is extradited to a country to stand trial for certain criminal offenses may be tried only for those offenses and not for any other per-extradition offenses. Once the asylum state extradites an individual to the requesting state under the terms of an extradition treaty, that person can be prosecuted only for crimes specified in the extradition request. This doctrine allows a nation to require the requesting nation to limit prosecution to declared offenses. U.S. courts have been divided on allowing standing to assert the doctrine when the other nation has not explicitly or implicitly protested certain charges. A person who has been brought within the jurisdiction of the court by virtue of proceedings under an extradition treaty, can only be tried for one of the offenses described in that treaty, and for the offense with which he is charged in the proceedings for his extradition, until a reasonable time and opportunity have been given him, after his release or trial upon such charge, to return to the country from whose asylum he had been

---

173 Dickinson, Edwin D. "Jurisdiction Following Seizure or Arrest in Violation of International Law," *American Journal of International Law,* 28: 1 (1934), pp. 231-45.

174 Selleck, Kathryn "Jurisdiction After International Kidnapping: A Comparative Study," *Boston College International and Comparative Law Review,* 8: 1 (1985), pp. 237-65.

forcibly taken under those proceedings.[175]

The United States Supreme court decided *Rauscher*[176] on the same day that it decided *Ker*. The decision in this case has become known as the specialty doctrine. Extradited criminals cannot be tried for offenses not named in the treaty, or for offenses not named in the warrant of extradition.

The United States and Great Britain had entered into a treaty on August 9, 1842, entitled A treaty to settle and define the boundaries between the territories of the United States and the possessions of her Britannic majesty in North America; for the final suppression of the African slave trade; and for the giving up of criminals, fugitive from justice, in certain cases.[177] The tenth article of the treaty contains all that relates to the subject of extradition of criminals. "It is agreed that the United States and her Britannic majesty shall, upon mutual requisitions by them, or their ministers, officers, or authorities, respectively made, deliver up to justice all persons who, being charged with the crime of murder, or assault with intent to commit murder, or piracy or arson or robbery or forgery, or the utterance of forged paper, committed within the jurisdiction of either. . . ." [178]

William Rauscher, was indicted by a grand jury, for that, on the 9th day of October, 1884, on the high seas, out of the jurisdiction of any particular state of the United States, and within the admiralty and maritime jurisdiction thereof, he being the second mate of the ship *J. F. Chapman*, assaulted one Janssen, a member of the crew of the vessel of which he was an officer, and unlawfully inflicted upon said Janssen cruel and unusual punishment.[179]

According to the doctrine of publicists, authorities, commentators, and writers on international law, the country receiving the offender against its laws from another country had no right to proceed against him for any other offense than that for which he had been delivered up. The high could found that this is a principle which com-

---

175 https://definitions.uslegal.com/d/doctrine-of-specialty/. See also http://www.-duhaime.org/LegalDictionary/D/DoctrineofSpecialty.aspx; "Doctrine Doctrine of Specialty Law, U.S. Legal.com.

176 *United States v. Rauscher*, 119 U.S. 407 (1886)

177 U. S. St. at Large, 8: 576.

178 119 U.S. 407, 411

179 Rogers, Henry Wade, "Supreme Court of the United States. United States v. Rauscher," *American Law Register*, 35: 4 (1887) pp. 218-246. We have followed this initial study of *Rauscher* closely.

mends itself, as an appropriate adjunct, to the discretionary exercise of the power of rendition, because it can hardly be supposed that a government which was under no treaty obligation, nor any absolute obligation of public duty, to seize a person who had found an asylum within its bosom, and turn him over to another country for trial, would be willing to do this, unless a case was made of some specific offense, of a character which justified the government in depriving the party of his asylum. It is unreasonable that the country of the asylum should be expected to deliver up such person to be dealt with by the demanding government without any limitation, implied or otherwise, upon its prosecution of the party. In exercising its discretion, it might be very willing to deliver up offenders against such laws as were essential to the protection of life, liberty, and person, while it would not be willing to do this on account of minor misdemeanors, or of a certain class of political offenses in which it would have no interest or sympathy. Accordingly, it has been the policy of all governments to grant an asylum to persons who have fled from their homes on account of political disturbances, and who might be there amenable to laws framed with regard to such subjects, and to the personal allegiance of the party. In many of the treaties of extradition between the civilized nations of the world there is an express exclusion of the right to demand the extradition of offenders against such laws, and in none of them is this class of offenses mentioned as being the foundation of extradition proceedings. Indeed, the enumeration of offenses in most of these treaties, and especially in the treaty now under consideration, is so specific, and marked by such a clear line in regard to the magnitude and importance of those offenses, that it is impossible to give any other interpretation to it than that of the exclusion of the right of extradition for any others.[180]

The principal question, and the only principle remaining long after this decision was rendered, was: May a person extradited be tried only for the crime noted on the extradition papers, or may that person be tried on charges not noted on those legal forms? The high court pursued every possible learned opinion on the subject before ar-

---

180 119 U.S. 407, 420-21. See also "United States: Supreme Court opinion in United States v. Alvarez-Machain. Extradition Treaty; International Abduction" in *International Legal Materials,* 31: 4 (1992), pp. 900-18; "Article 16. Apprehension in Violation of International Law," American Journal of International Law, 29 "Supplement: Research in International Law (1935), pp. 623-42. .

riving at its conclusion.[181]

First, the Supreme Court noted very able article arising out of the same public discussion at that time, to wit, 1876, is found in the *American Law Review*, said to have been written by Judge Lowell, of the United States Court at Boston, in which, after an examination of the authorities upon the general rule, independent of treaties, as found in the continental writers on international law, he says, that rule is, that the person whose extradition has been granted, cannot be prosecuted and tried except for the crime for which his extradition has been obtained; and, entering upon the question of the construction of the treaty of 1842, he gave to it the same effect in regard to that matter.[182]

In the mid-nineteenth century, David Dudley Field, in his draft of an outline for an international code, published about the same time, adopted the same principle. It is understood that the rule which he lays down represents as well what he understands to be existing law, as also what he supposed it should be.[183]

The high court took cognizance of what it called "a very learned and careful work," published in the United States by Mr. Spear, in 1879, with a second edition in 1884. After considering all the correspondence between the United States and Great Britain upon the subject, the debate in the House of Lords, the articles of Mr. Lawrence and Judge Lowell, as well as the treatise of Mr. Clarke, an English writer, with a very exhaustive examination of all the decisions in this country relating to this matter, arrives at the same conclusion, that is, one may be charged after extradition only with the crime stated on the original request for extradition. The high court remarked that this examination by Mr. Spear is so full and careful, that it leaves nothing to be desired in the way of presentation of authorities.

The only English work on the subject of extradition which the Supreme Court was able to find which discusses this subject was a small manual by Edward Clarke of Lincoln's Inn, published in 1867. He adopted the same view of the construction of this treaty and of the general principles of international law upon the subject.[184]

Justice Gray concurred, writing that it is good law "that the ac-

---

181 "Non-Extradition of Nationals," *Yale Law Journal*, 46: 3 (1937), pp. 525-27.

182 *American Law Review 10:* 617 (1875-76); George, Jonathan, "Toward a More Principled Approach to the Principle of Specialty," *Cornell International Law Journal,* 12: 2 (1979), pp. 309-27.

183 Field, David Dudley. *Field's International Code,* (1867) § 237: 122.

184 119 U.S. 417at 18

cused shall be tried only for the crime specified in the warrant of extradition, and shall be allowed a reasonable time to depart out of the United States, before he can be arrested or detained for another offense." However, Justice Gray wrote, "Upon the broader question whether, independently of any act of Congress, and in the absence of any affirmative restriction in the treaty, a man surrendered for one crime should be tried for another, I express no opinion, because not satisfied that that is a question of law, within the cognizance of the judicial tribunals, as contra distinguished from a question of international comity and usage, within the domain of statesmanship and diplomacy."[185]

Chief Justice Waite dissented, writing, "I am unable to concur in the decision of this case. A fugitive from justice has no absolute right of asylum in a country to, which he flees, and if he can be got back within the jurisdiction of the country whose laws he has violated, he may be proceeded with precisely the same as if he had not fled, unless there is something in the laws of the country where he is to be tried, or in the way in which he was got back, to prevent."[186]

Legal scholars over the years have found that the Supreme Court in the *Rauscher* decision did not rely on a single rationale in its analysis of the principle of specialty. Rather, the Court stated that to ignore the doctrine would amount to "an implication of fraud upon the rights of the party extradited, and of bad faith to the country which permitted his extradition." The analysis is further complicated by the Court's final conclusion that the trial court "did not have jurisdiction of the person at [the] time, so as to subject [Rauscher] to trial.[187] It can be argued that the *Rauscher* decision emphasized the rights of the individual under the principle of specialty, although subsequent lower court decisions, however, have diminished the importance of the rights of the extraditee in the application of the doctrine.

The specialty doctrine is frequently incorporated as a part of an original treaty. The following provision was placed in the extradition treaty of 17 April 1900 between the United States and Chile:[188]

---

185 119 U.S. 433at 34

186 119 U.S. 435at 36

187 Id. at 422. See also Levitt, Kenneth, "International Extradition, the Principle of Speciality, and Effective Treaty Enforcement," *Minnesota Law Review,* 76 (1992), pp. 1017-39.

188 Treaty on Extradition, Apr. 17, 1900, United States-Chile, art. VIII, 32 Stat. 1850.

No person surrendered by either of the high contracting parties to the other shall, without his consent, freely granted and publicly declared by him, be triable or tried or be punished for any crime or offense committed prior to his extradition, other than that for which he was delivered up, until he shall have had an opportunity of returning to the country from which he was surrendered.

In a Canadian case, Justice La Forest of the Supreme Court of Canada used these words in defining this idea: "[The] doctrine of specialty . . . prohibits the requesting state from prosecuting for crimes other than that for which the extradition took place[189] In a case in the United States, Justice Cynthia Hall wrote "The doctrine of specialty prevents the requesting nation from prosecuting the extradited person for any offenses other than those upon which the surrendering country agreed to extradite."[190]

The present question of the doctrine of specialty is whether the principle of specialty confers any rights upon the extradite, or rather operates solely to protect the sovereignty and extradition process of the surrendering state. Whether a court of the requesting state will refuse to try a delivered extraditee for offenses not enumerated in the extradition request will often depend on what the court perceives to be the rationale supporting the principle of specialty. In the classical view the principle of specialty involves a right of the surrendering nation only. Under this theory, international law is concerned only with the relationships between nations, and absolutely not between nations and individuals. Hence international law provides and enforces the rules of extradition, and any violation of the principle of specialty is an issue for the contracting nations to the extradition treaty to resolve. Therefore, if the surrendering state fails to file a timely protest, a court of the requesting state may try the accused for offenses not contained in the extradition request.[191]

Less tenable is the alternative view which holds that the specialty rule confers some right on the individual. Such right he may assert as a defense even in the absence of any formal protest by the surrendering state. Such a right may be fundamental, said to exist as an independent human right, legally unassailable as such by both the

189 *U. S. v Lepine*, 1 S.C.R. 286 (1994)

190 *U. S. v Saccoccia*, 18 F. 3d 795 (1994)

191 See George, Jonathan "Toward a More Principled Approach to the Principle of Specialty," 12 *Cornell International Law Journal* 2 (1979).

requested and the requesting state. Or it may be viewed as a derivative right whose origin may be found in treaties, or even in municipal law. Such rights, if they do exist, could be said to limit the court's *in personam* jurisdiction to the offense charged in the extradition request.[192]

Frisbie v. Collins

Acting as his own lawyer, Shirley Collins brought a *habeas corpus* case in a United States District Court seeking release from a Michigan state prison where he was serving a life sentence for murder. His petition alleges that while he was living in Chicago, Michigan officers forcibly seized, handcuffed, blackjacked and took him to Michigan. He claims that trial and conviction under such circumstances is in violation of the Due Process Clause of the Fourteenth Amendment and the Federal Kidnapping Act, and that therefore his conviction is null and void. The District Court denied the writ without a hearing on the ground that the state court had power to try respondent "regardless of how presence was procured." [193]

The Court of Appeals, one judge dissenting, reversed and remanded the cause for hearing.[194] It held that the Federal Kidnapping Act had changed the rule declared in prior holdings of this Court, that a state could constitutionally try and convict a defendant after acquiring jurisdiction by force.

To review this important question the U.S. Supreme court granted *certiorari*.[195] The high court first disposed of the state's contention that the District Court should have denied relief on the ground that respondent had an available state remedy. The Supreme Court found this argument to be "a little cloudy," apparently because of the state attorney general's doubt that any state procedure used could possibly lead to the granting of relief. There is no doubt that as a general rule federal courts should deny the writ to state prisoners if there is "available State corrective process." That general rule is not rigid and inflexible; district courts may deviate from it and grant relief in special circumstances. Whether such circumstances exist calls for a factual appraisal by the court in each special situation. Determination of

---

192 Garcia-Mora, Manuel R. *International Law and Asylum as a Human Right.* Washington: Public Affairs Press, 1956.

193 342 U.S. 519, 520; Reid, Herbert O. "Interstate Rendition and Illegal Return of Fugitives," *Howard Law Journal,* 2: 1 (1956), pp. 76-93.

194 189 F.2d 464

195 342 U.S. 865

this issue, like others, is largely left to the trial courts subject to appropriate review by the courts of appeals.[196]

The trial court, pointing out that the Michigan Supreme Court had previously denied relief, apparently assumed that no further state corrective process was available 5 and decided against respondent on the merits. Failure to discuss the availability of state relief may have been due to the fact that the state did not raise the question; indeed the record shows no appearance of the state.[197] The Court of Appeals did expressly consider the question of exhaustion of state remedies. It found the existence of "special circumstances" which required prompt federal intervention "in this case." It would serve no useful purpose to review those special circumstances in detail. They are peculiar to this case, may never come up again, and a discussion of them could not give precision to the "special circumstances" rule. It is sufficient to say that there are sound arguments to support the Court of Appeals' conclusion that prompt decision of the issues raised was desirable. Thus, the Supreme Court accepted ther findings of the appellate court in this regard.[198]

Justice Black wrote the opinion of the court. Citing *Ker,* the U.S. Supreme Court found that the fact that a person was forcibly abducted and taken from one state to another to be tried for a crime does not invalidate his conviction in a court of the latter state under the Due Process Clause of the Fourteenth Amendment. He argued that the Supreme Court had never departed from the rule announced in the *Ker* decision,[199] which held that the power of a court to try a person for crime is not impaired by the fact that he had been brought within the court's jurisdiction by reason of a "forcible abduction." No persuasive reasons were now presented to justify overruling this line of cases. These cases, indeed, rest on the sound basis that due process of law is satisfied when one present in court is convicted of crime after having been fairly apprised of the charges against him and after a fair trial in accordance with constitutional procedural safeguards. There is nothing in the Constitution that requires a court to permit a guilty per-

196 *Darr v. Burford*, 342 U.S. 519, 521

197 "An applicant shall not be deemed to have exhausted the remedies available in the courts of the State, within the meaning of this section, if he has the right under the law of the State to raise, by any available procedure, the question presented."

198 Reid, *op. cit.; "Frisbie v Collins,"* in Wikipedia.

199 *Ker v. Illinois*, 119 U.S. 436, 444

son rightfully convicted to escape justice because he was brought to trial against his will.

Despite the several precedent decisions, the Court of Appeals, relying on the Federal Kidnapping Act, held that respondent was entitled to the writ if he could prove the facts he alleged. The Court thought that to hold otherwise after the passage of the Kidnapping Act "would in practical effect lend encouragement to the commission of criminal acts by those sworn to enforce the law." In considering whether the law of our prior cases has been changed by the Federal Kidnaping Act, we assume, without intimating that it is so, that the Michigan officers would have violated it if the facts are as alleged. This Act prescribes in some detail the severe sanctions Congress wanted it to have. Persons who have violated it can be imprisoned for a term of years or for life; under some circumstances violators can be given the death sentence. Nonetheless, Justice Black reasoned that the Kidnapping Act cannot fairly be construed so as to add to the list of sanctions detailed a sanction barring a state from prosecuting persons wrongfully brought to it by its officers. It may be that Congress could add such a sanction. The high court refused to do so. Thus, the judgment of the Court of Appeals was reversed and that of the District Court was affirmed.[200]

The rule of international law violated by official international kidnapping was upheld by the United States when, after an attempted abduction by Soviet officials of a Soviet citizen in the United States, the U.S. State Department declared: "the Government of the United States cannot permit the exercise within the United States of the police power of any foreign government." Although courts of the United States traditionally have held that an arrest in violation of customary international law is no bar to their exercise of jurisdiction over the arrestee, a rule to the contrary could find precedential support.

For example, in his concurring opinion in *United States v. Lira,* Judge Oakes commented: "[T]here is a very strong policy which would be operative if the abduction here were from an objecting country . . . or in violation of a treaty. That policy is of course respect for the law of nations, the requirements of world society, and the integrity and independence of other nations, not only under formal char-

---

200 Scott, Austin W. Jr., "Criminal Jurisdiction of a State over a Defendant Based upon Presence Secured by Force or Fraud," *Minnesota Law Review,* 37: 2 (1953), pp. 91-107; "Federal Kidnapping A ct," in Wikipedia.

ters . . . but as unwritten obligations of international law."[201]

Mahon v Justice

Neither the Constitution nor the laws of the United States make provision for relief of a person, unlawfully abducted from one state to another and held in the latter state upon process of law for an offense against the state. That person can not be restored to the state from which he was abducted.

There is no comity between the states by which a person held upon an indictment for a criminal offense in one state can be turned over to the authorities of another state, although abducted from the latter.

In the case at hand, Kentucky had indicted Plyant Mahon for a felony, but he escaped to West Virginia. While the Governor of West Virginia was considering an application from the Governor of Kentucky for his surrender as a fugitive from justice, he was forcibly abducted to Kentucky, and when there was seized by the Kentucky authorities under legal process, and put in jail while awaiting the outcome of the indictment. The court ruled that he was not entitled to be discharged from custody under a writ of *habeas corpus* from the circuit court of the United States.[202]

West Virginia argued that during the month of December, 1887, or January, 1888, Plyant Mahon, while residing in West Virginia, was seized, in violation of her laws, and of the Constitution and laws of the United States, without warrant by a body of armed men from Kentucky. These men forcibly carried Mahon out of West Virginia into the Pike County, Kentucky, and there confined him in the cpunty jail, where he has been ever since.

On the 1st of February, 1888, the Governor of West Virginia made a request to the Governor of Kentucky that Plyant Mahon be released and returned to West Virginia. The Governor of Kentucky refused to honor that demand, refusing on the ground, among others, that the questions involved were judicial, and not executive. The Governor of West Virginia then asked that the writ of *habeas corpus* be granted, directed to the keeper of the jail, commanding him to pro-

---

201 *U. S. v. Lira,* 515 F.2d 68 (1975). Philippe, Julie and Laurent Tristan, "International Law, Extraterritorial Abductions and the Exercise of Criminal Jurisdiction in the United States," *Willamette Journal of International Law and Dispute Resolution,* 1 (2004), pp. 61-80.

202 Fairman, Charles, "Ker v. Illinois Revisited," *American Journal of International Law,* 47: 4 (1953), pp. 678-86.

duce the body of said Plyant Mahon, together with the cause of his detention. He requested that judgment be rendered that would order Plyant Mahon to be discharged from confinement and custody and be safely returned within the jurisdiction of the State of West Virginia. At the same time, another petition was presented to the court by one John A. Sheppard, representing that he was a citizen of West Virginia and setting forth substantially the facts contained in the petition of the governor, and praying for a like writ of *habeas corpus*. Subsequently the name of Plyant Mahon was substituted for that of John A. Sheppard, and the proceedings on the petition were conducted in his name.[203]

The court ordered the writ to be issued, directing the jailer of Pike County to produce the body of Mahon before the District Court of the United States in the City of Louisville on the 20th of the month, and there to abide such order as might be made in the premises. The jailer of Pike County, Abner Justice, made a return to the writ substantially as follows: that he held Plyant Mahon in custody and confined in the jail of Pike County by virtue of and in obedience to three writs issued by the clerk of the criminal court of the county, under its order, each for the arrest of Mahon to answer an indictment pending against him and others for the crime of willful murder, alleged to have been committed in that county, a crime for the trial of which that court had full jurisdiction, and commanding the officer arresting Mahon to deliver him to the jailer of the county, copies of which writs were annexed to the return; that under the writ of *habeas corpus,* he was proceeding to the City of Louisville to produce the body of Mahon before the United States district court there when he was met on his way by the United States marshal of the district of Kentucky, who, by virtue of the order of the district court, took Plyant Mahon into his custody. He further returned that three indictments against Mahon and others for willful murder were found by the grand jury of Pike County, Kentucky, and returned into the circuit court of said county at its September term, 1882, at which time that court had jurisdiction of the crime charged; that by order of the court, made at each subsequent term, writs were issued by the clerk thereof for the arrest of Plyant Mahon to answer the indictments, until the criminal court of the county was established by act of the General Assembly of Kentucky in 1884, by which the jurisdiction previously vested in the circuit court

203 "*Mahon v Justice,*" in Wikisource.

was transferred to and vested in said criminal court; that by orders of this latter court from term to term, writs were issued by the clerk thereof for the arrest of Mahon to answer the indictments; but none of them were executed upon him until January 12, 1888, when he was arrested in Pike County by the sheriff thereof and delivered by him to the respondent, jailer of said county, in obedience to the writs which were issued, and under the command and authority of which he was held by the respondent as jailer in custody in the jail of said county, when the writ of *habeas corpus* was served upon him.[204]

The jailer made a further return in which he stated that a requisition was made by the Governor of Kentucky upon the Governor of West Virginia for the arrest and rendition to Kentucky of said Plyant Mahon; that it was accompanied by a copy of the indictments referred to, certified by the Governor of Kentucky to be authentic; that at the same time the governor appointed on Frank Phillips as the agent of the state to receive and bring to the State of Kentucky the said Mahon, as provided by law in such cases; that on the 30th of September, 1887, the Governor of West Virginia returned said requisition to the Governor of Kentucky, informing him that an affidavit, as required by the statute of West Virginia, should accompany the requisition before the same could be complied with; that thereafter the Governor of Kentucky returned the requisition to the Governor of West Virginia, accompanied by the affidavit required; that afterwards, about the 12th of January, 1888, Frank Phillips and others, seized Mahon in the State of West Virginia and brought him against his will into the County of Pike in the State of Kentucky, where the writs mentioned in the respondent's original return were executed upon him by the Sheriff of Pike County; that at that time, no warrant for the arrest of Mahon had been issued or ordered to be issued by the Governor of West Virginia in compliance with said requisition, and afterwards, on the 30th of January, 1888, he informed the Governor of Kentucky that he declined to issue his warrant for the arrest of Plyant Mahon, in compliance with the requisition made upon him, because he had become satisfied, upon investigation of the facts, that Mahon was not guilty of the crime charged against him in the indictments, and that subsequently, on the 1st of February, 1888, the Governor of West Virginia made

---

204 "Hatfields and McCoys: American family feud," *Encyclopedia Britannica.*
   Plyant Morgan (1849-1925) Family genealogy and brief biography at at Plyant
   Mahon (1849 - 1925) - Genealogy (geni.com).

upon the Governor of Kentucky a demand for the release of Mahon from the jail of the County of Pike and his safe conduct back into West Virginia, with which demand the Governor of Kentucky declined to comply on the ground that Mahon was in the custody of the judicial department of the commonwealth, and that the question of his release upon the grounds alleged in the demand was one which the courts alone could determine, and that the adjudication thereof was not one within the purview of his powers and duties as governor.[205]

The facts thus detailed were established before the court on the hearing upon the writ, and are contained in its findings. On the 3d of March, the court denied the motion for the discharge of Plyant Mahon and ordered the marshal to return him to the jailer of Pike County. From this order an appeal was taken to the circuit court of the United States and there affirmed.[206]

205 Federal Reporter, Volume 34 (resource.org)
206 *Mahon v. Justice,* 127 U.S. 700 (1888); "Interstate Renditions Clause," Interstate Renditions Clause: Doctrine and Practice | Constitution Annotated | Congress.gov | Library of Congress, See also *Pettibone v. Nichols,* 203 U.S. 192 (1906). See also "Effect of Illegal Abduction Into the Jurisdiction on a Subsequent Conviction ," *Indiana Law Journal,* 27: 2 (1952), pp. 292-300.

Interpreting and Perfecting Ker

It was inevitable that the U. S. Supreme Court would find it both necessary and expedient to expand upon the *Ker* decision, if only because it involved such utterly unique circumstances, such as the war going on when the Pinkerton agent arrested Ker.

In 1911, the U.S. Supreme Court held that "One who is never within the State before the commission of a crime producing its results within its jurisdiction is not a fugitive from justice within the rendition provisions of the Constitution, but if he commits some overt and material act within the State and then absents himself, he becomes a fugitive from justice when the crime is complete; if not before. Although absent from the State when the crime was completed in this case, the party charged became a fugitive from justice by reason of his having committed certain material steps toward the crime within the State, and the demanding State is entitled to his surrender under article IV, section 2, of the Constitution of the United States and the statutes providing for the surrender of fugitives from justice."[207]

Church v Hackenberg

In New York Walter Church pleaded guilty to attempted robbery, on which charge he was sentenced by the New York State court to serve a term of two and a half to five years. In August 1933, New York State paroled Church. On October 1, 1933, the Parole Commission revoked the parole of Church on the ground that he failed to report as his parole required. In January 1934, Church was arrested at White Plains, New York, charged with passing and having in his possession counterfeit money and simultaneously identified as a parole violator. New York authorities turned him over to federal authorities. In July 1934, Church was indicted in the United States District Court for the unlawful passing and possessing of counterfeit money. Church, on July 19, 1934, entered a plea of guilty and was sentenced to serve three years on three different counts. He was removed from New York to the United States Northeastern Penitentiary at Lewisburg, Pennsylvania. He was confined until November 8, 1936, at which time he was released. Prior to his release, the Governor of New York instituted extradition proceedings against Church, charging that he was a parole violator and had fled from justice of the State of New York. The Gov-

---

207 *Strassheim v. Daily*, 221 U. S. 280 (1911).

ernor of Pennsylvania had found'that Church was a fugitive from justice of the State of New York. The Governor of Pennsylvania granted extradition."[208]

Church fought extradition, claiming that he was found in Pennsylvania because he was taken there [to jail] forcibly and against his will. New York authorities responded only that he was a parole violator on a criminal charge, and should be sufficient ground to sustain extradition to New York.

The judge of the Court of Common Pleas on Union County, Pennsylvania, Judge Curtis Lesher rejected this contention, holding that Church was not a fugitive from justice of the State of New York. Lesher wrote, "As a matter of fact, Church was not allowed the opportunity to return to his own state when released from the United 8tates Penitentiary at Lewisburg, Pennsylvania. He was met at the gates of the penitentiary-at the time of his release by the Sheriff of Union County, Pennsylvania, and immediately taken into custody and placed in jail. . . . the Governor of Pennsylvania had no authority to issue a warrant for the delivery of the petitioner to the New York authorities for the purpose of returning him to the State of New York, and the prayer of the petition must be granted, and the Sheriff of Union County must be directed to release the petitioner, Church."[209]

Pettibone v Nichols

On 12 February, 1906, a criminal complaint charged Pettibone with having murdered Frank Steunenberg at Caldwell, Idaho, on 13 December, 1905. Thereupon, the Governor of Idaho requested Governor of Colorado, in which state the accused was alleged then to be, to arrest of Pettibone, and to turn him over to an agent of Idaho, to be conveyed to the latter state and there dealt with in accordance with law. The papers on which the Governor of Idaho based his requisition distinctly charged that Pettibone was in that state at the time Steunenberg was murdered and was a fugitive from its justice.

A requisition by the Governor of Idaho was accordingly issued

---

208 Black, Forrest Revere, "Interstate Rendition as Applied to a Person Brought Involuntarily into the Surrendering State," *American Institute of Criminal Law & Criminology* , 29: 309 (1938-1939), pp. 309-28. See also Moore, John Bassett. *Extradition and Interstate Rendition,*(1891). 2 vols. 2: 848-50.

209 *Commonwealth of Pennsylvania ex rel Walter Church v. Hackenburg, Sheriff of Union Co., Pa.,* by Curtis J. Lesher, Common Pleas Judge for Union Co., Pa., No. 100, January Term, 1937.

and was duly honored by the Governor of Colorado, who issued a warrant commanding the arrest of Pettibone and his delivery to the authorized agent of Idaho, to be conveyed to the latter state. Pettibone was arrested under that warrant and carried to Idaho by its agent, and was there delivered by order of the probate judge into the custody of the warden of the state penitentiary

The accused Pettibone claimed that his presence in Idaho had been procured by connivance, conspiracy, and fraud on the part of the executive officers of Idaho, and that his detention was in violation of the provisions of the Constitution of the United States and of the act of Congress relating to fugitives from justice. On 7 March 1906, the Idaho grand jury returned an indictment against Pettibone, William D. Haywood, Charles H. Moyer, and John L. Simpkins, charging them with the murder of Steunenberg on 13 December, 1905, at Caldwell, Idaho. The officer holding Pettibone made an amended return stating the fact of the above indictment.[210]

The officers having Pettibone in custody moved to strike from the answer of the accused all allegations relating to the manner and method of obtaining his presence within the state. That motion was sustained on 12 March 1906, and the prisoner was remanded to await his trial under the above indictment. The Supreme Court of Idaho held the action of the Governor of Colorado to be at least quasi-judicial and, in effect, a determination that Pettibone was charged with the commission of a crime in the former state and was a fugitive from its justice; that, after the prisoner came within the jurisdiction of the demanding state, he could not raise in its courts the question whether he was or had been, as a matter of fact, a fugitive from the justice of that state; that the courts of Idaho had no jurisdiction to inquire into the acts or motives of the executive of the state delivering the prisoner; that "one who commits a crime against the laws of a state, whether committed by him while in person on its soil, or absent in a foreign jurisdiction, and acting through some other agency or medium, has no vested right of asylum in a sister state."

In *Pettibone v. Nichols*,1 the U.S. Supreme Court ruled on this case. It held that even if the arrest and deportation of one alleged to be a fugitive from justice may have been effected by fraud and connivance arranged between the executive authorities of the demanding

---

210 "Interstate Rendition. Uniform Act on Fresh Pursuit," *Columbia Law Review*, 38: 4 (1938), pp. 705-09.

state and the surrendering state so as to deprive him of any opportunity to apply before deportation to a court in the surrendering state for his discharge, and even if on such application to any court, state or federal, he would have been discharged, he cannot, so far as the Constitution and laws of the United.States are concerned, when actually in the demanding State, in the custody of its authorities for trial, and subject to the jurisdiction thereof, be discharged on *habeas corpus* by the federal court. It would be improper and inappropriate in the Circuit Court to inquire as to the motives guiding or controlling the action of the governors of the demanding and surrendering states. "No obligation is imposed by the Constitution and laws of the United -States on the agent of a demanding state to so time the arrest of one alleged to be. a fugitive from justice and so conduct his deportation from the.surrendering.State as to afford him a convenient opportunity, before some judicial tribunal, sitting in the latter State, to test the question whether he was a fugitive from justice and, as such liable, the act of Congress, to be conveyed to the demanding state for trial there. "[211]

Lascelles v Georgia

In July, 1891, the grand jury of Floyd County, Georgia, issued two indictments against the plaintiff, under the name of Walter S. Beresford, which charged him with the offense of being a "common cheat and swindler" and with the crime of "larceny after trust delegated." At the time, the plaintiff was residing in New York. In September, 1891, the governor of Georgia made a requisition on the governor of New York for the arrest and surrender of the plaintiff to designated officials of Georgia. In all legal papers, he was named Walter S. Beresford. On 6 October 1891, a new grand jury issued another indictment against him for the crime of forgery, but naming him as Sidney Lascelles, which, it was discovered, was his true and proper name. Thereafter he was put upon his trial in Floyd County upon this last indictment.

Prior to his arraignment, Lascelles moved the court to quash said indictment on the ground that he was being tried for a separate and different offense from that for which he was extradited from New York to Georgia, without first being allowed a reasonable opportunity

---

211 *Pettibone v Nichols,* 203 U. S. 192 (1906). The same doctrine was announced in the cases of the co-defendants Haywood and Moyer; *Haywood v. Nichols,* 203 U. S. 222 (1906) .and *Moyer-v. -Nichols*, 203 U. S. 222 (1906).

to return to New York. This motion was overruled, and he was put upon trial. Thereupon he averred that he could not be lawfully tried for a separate and different crime from that for which he was extradited. This plea was overruled, and, having been put upon his trial under the indictment, he was found guilty of the offense charged. His motion for a new trial being refused, Lascelles filed a bill of exceptions, and carried the case to the supreme court of Georgia. That court sustained the action of the lower court in all respects. He the n appealed to the United States Supreme Court.

In *Lascelles v. Georgia*,[212] the U.S. Supreme court held that "a fugitive from justice who has been surrendered by one State of the Union to another State, upon requisition charging him with the commission of a specific crime, has, under the Constitution and laws of the United States, no right, privilege or immunity to be exempt -from indictment and trial, in the State to which he is returned, for any other or different offense from that -designated." [213]

Cook v Hart

In May 1889, Cook, and Frank Leake opened a banking office at Juneau, in Dodge county, known as the Bank of Juneau. They engaged in a general banking business, with a pretended capital of $10,000, and continued in such business, soliciting and receiving deposits up to and including 20 June 1890, when the bank closed its doors. During this time Cook had the general supervision of the business, and was the principal owner of the bank. All business was transacted by him personally, or under his direction by a man named Richardson, acting as his agent. Cook frequently visited the bank, and well knew its financial condition. From January 6 to June 20, 1890, Cook received deposits from the citizens of that county to the amount of $25,000. A the time that the bank failed Cook drew out of the bank all of its pretended capital stock, if any were ever put in, and also all the deposits, except the sum of $5,048 in money and securities, which was in the bank at the time it closed; that on June 23, 1890.

Cook and Leake assigned their property for the benefit of their creditors. By 6 January, 1890, Cook knew that the bank was insolvent. On 20 June 1890, at about 4 o'clock in the afternoon, Cook and Leake

---

212 *Lascelles v. Georgia*, 188 U. S. 691 (1903). See also "Fugitive Criminals in International Extradition," *Columbia Law Review*, 23: 2 (1923), pp. 176-179.

213 Larremore, Wilbur, "Inadequacy of the Present Federal Statute Regulating Interstate Rendition," *Columbia Law Review*, 10: 3 (1910), pp. 208-220.

accepted a deposit in the bank from Herman Becker to the amount of $175 in money and that deposit was received by direction and order of the said Cook, he knowing that said bank was unsafe and insolvent. There was also annexed a complaint setting forth substantially the same facts, and a warrant issued by a justice of the peace for Dodge County for the apprehension of Cook. The governor of Illinois issued his warrant for the arrest of Cook to the executive authority of Wisconsin. Cook was arrested by the sheriff of Cook County, Illinois, and on the same day, and while still in the custody of the sheriff, procured a writ of *habeas corpus* from the circuit court of Cook County to test the legality of his arrest.

The Cook County Court, on 6 June1891, decided that the arrest was legal, and remanded Cook to the custody of the sheriff. He was thereupon delivered to the executive agent, and conveyed to Wisconsin, where he was examined before the magistrate issuing the warrant, and held to answer the charge. During the September term of the circuit court of that county, information was filed against him, charging him with the offense set out in the original complaint. Upon his application the trial was continued to the term of said court beginning in February, 1892.

The case of *Cook v. Hart*[214] was heard on appeal by the United States Supreme Court. Cook had acquiesced in the disposition of his case in the courts of Illinois, making no effort whatever to have the supreme court of Illinois review the judgment of the lower court. Upon his arrival in Wisconsin and just as his trial had begun in that state, he sued, requesting another writ of *habeas corpus* in the circuit court of the United States, alleging that he was unlawfully deprived of his liberty. He alleged in that court that he was not a fugitive from Wisconsin when arrested in Illinois and that therefore he was illegally deported from that State. The Federal court in Wisconsin decided against him and he appealed to the Supreme Court of the United States which affirmed the judgment of the lower court.

The court reaffirmed the doctrine in the case of *Mahon v. Justice,* holding that "the supreme court will not interfere to relieve persons who have been arrested and taken by violence from the territory

---

214 *Cook v Hart,* 188 U. S. 691 (1903). See also Black, Forrest Revere, "Interstate Rendition as Applied to a Person Brought Involuntarily into the Surrendering State," *American Institute of Criminal Law & Criminology* , 29: 309 (1938-1939), pp. 309-28.

of one State to that of another, where they are held under process legally issued from the courts of the latter State. That the question of the applicability of this doctrine to a particular case is as much within the province of a State court, as a question of common law or of the law of nations, as it is of the courts of the United States." The court further held that it was too late for the alleged fugitive from justice to object to even jurisdictional defects, after he is brought within the territory of the demanding State and further declared that, the authorities tended to support the theory that the executive warrant has spent its force, when the accused has been delivered to the demanding State. [215]

Mahon v. Justice

Mahon was indicted for murder in Kentucky but before his arrest he fled to West Virginia. The governor of Kentucky then demanded that the executive of West Virginia arrest and surrender of Mahon as a fugitive from justice. For some reason which was never made clear the West Virginia governor refused. An agent of Kentucky, assisted by several others, seized Mahon by force and brought him back to Kentucky. The chief executive of West Virginia demanded that the governor of Kentucky return of Mahon, which was refused. The governor of West Virginia sued, using a writ of *habeas corpus* in the Federal court of Kentucky, demanding the discharge of Mahon, alleging that Mahon's detention in Kentucky was unlawful because he had not been removed from West Virginia in accordance with the Constitution and laws of the United States.

In the initial hearing the writ was quashed and the petition was dismissed, the court holding that Mahon was lawfully held in custody in Kentucky. An appeal was taken to the Supreme Court of the United States, and, after due consideration, the judgment of the lower court was affirmed, using this language: "So in this case, it is contended that, because under the Constitution and laws of the United States a fugitive from justice from one State to another can be surrendered to the State where the crime was committed, upon proper proceedings taken, he has the right of asylum in the State to which he has fled, unless removed in conformity with such proceedings, and that this right can be enforced in the courts of the United States. But the plain answer to this contention is, that the laws of the United States do not

---

215 Larremore, Wilbur, "Inadequacy of the Present Federal Statute Regulating Interstate Rendition," *Columbia Law Review,* 10: 3 (1910), pp. 208-220.

recognize any such right of asylum, as is here claimed on the part of a fugitive from justice in any State to which he has fled; nor have they, as already stated, made any provision for the return of parties, who, by violence and without lawful authority, have been abducted from a State. There is therefore, no authority in the courts of the United States to act upon any such alleged right."[216]

Justice Bradley wrote a strong dissenting opinion in the Mahon decision with which Justice Harland concurred.[217] Justice Bradley argued:

I dissent from the judgment of the court in this case. In my opinion the writ of *habeas corpus* was properly issued, and the prisoner, Mahon, should have been discharged and permitted to return to West Virginia. He was kidnapped and carried into Kentucky in plain violation of the Constitution of the United States, and is detained there in continued violation thereof. It is true, he is charged with having committed a crime in Kentucky. But the Constitution provides a peaceable remedy for procuring the surrender of persons charged with crime and fleeing into another State. This provision of the Constitution has two objects: the procuring possession of the offender, and the prevention of irritation between the States, which might arise from giving asylum to each other's criminals, and from violently invading each other's territory to capture them. It clearly implies that there shall be no resort to force for this purpose. The Constitution has abrogated, and the States have surrendered, all right to obtain redress from each other by force. The Constitution was made to "establish justice" and "insure domestic tranquillity;" and to attain this end as between the States themselves, the judicial power was extended "to controversies between two or more States," and they were enjoined to deliver up to each other fugitives from justice when demanded, and even fugitives from service. This manifest care to provide peaceable means of redress between them is utterly irreconcilable with any right to redress themselves by force and violence; and, of course, what is unconstitutional for the States is unconstitutional for their citizens. It is undoubtedly true that occasional instances of unlawful abduction of a criminal from one State to another for trial, have been winked at; and it has been held to be no defence for the prisoner on his trial. Such precedents are founded on those which have arisen where a criminal has been seized in one country and forcibly taken to another for trial, in the absence of any international treaty of extradition. It is obvious that such cases stand on a

---

216 *Mahon v Justice,* 127 U. S. 714 (1887); *In re Mahon* (1887) 34 Fed. 525

217 Id. 716-17. See also "The Uniform Criminal Extradition Act," *Columbia Law Review,* 32: 8 (1932), pp. 1411-24.

very different ground. It is there a question between independent nations bound by no ties of mutual obligation on the subject, and at liberty to adopt such means of redress and retaliation as they please. But where an extradition treaty does exist, and a criminal has been delivered up under it, he cannot, without violating the treaty, be tried for any other crime but that for which he was delivered up.[218] This shows that, even when rightfully obtained for one offence, he cannot be prosecuted for another. It is true that in the same volume is found the case of *Ker*, in which it was held not to be a good plea to an indictment, that the prisoner was kidnapped from Peru, with which country we had an extradition treaty. But this was because, as before said, the prisoner himself cannot set up the mode of his capture by way of defence, if the State from which he was abducted makes no complaint. Peru made none.[219]

In a similar state case heard in Vermont, the same doctrine was announced by the Supreme Court of that state. There it appeared that the prisoner charged with crime had escaped to Canada, and was brought back against his will, and without the consent of the authorities of that Province, and he sought to plead his illegal capture and forcible return in bar of the indictment; but his application was refused, the court observing that the escape of the prisoner into Canada did not purge the offence, nor oust the jurisdiction of the court, and he being within its jurisdiction it was not for it to inquire by what means or in what manner he was brought within the reach of justice. Said the court: "If there were anything improper in the transaction it was not that the prisoner was entitled to protection on his own account. The illegality, if any, consists in a violation of the sovereignty of an independent nation. If that nation complain it is a matter which concerns the political relations of the two countries, and in that aspect is a subject not within the constitutional powers of this court."[220]

In yet another state case, the Supreme Court of Iowa declared the same doctrine, and stated the distinction between civil and criminal cases where the party is by fraud or violence brought within the jurisdiction of the court. The defendants were charged with larceny, and were arrested in Missouri and brought by force and against their will, by parties acting without authority, either of a requisition from the governor or otherwise, to Iowa, where an indictment against them had been found. In Iowa they were rearrested, and turned over to the

218 *United States v. Rauscher,* 119 U.S. 407
219 *Ker v. Illinois,* 119 U.S. 437
220 *State v. Brewster,* 7 Vt. 118

civil authorities for detention and trial. It was contended that their arrest was in violation of law; that they were brought within the jurisdiction of the State by fraud and violence; that comity to a sister State and a just appreciation of the rights of the citizen, and a due regard to the integrity of the law, demanded that the court should under such circumstances refuse its aid; and that there could be no rightful exercise of jurisdiction over the parties thus arrested. But the court answered that "the liability of the parties arresting the defendants without legal warrant, for false imprisonment or otherwise, and their violation of the penal statutes of Missouri, may be ever so clear, and yet the prisoners not be entitled to their discharge. The offence being committed in Iowa, it was punishable here, and an indictment could have been found without reference to the arrest. There is no fair analogy between civil and criminal cases in this respect. In a civil case, the party invoking the aid of the court is guilty of fraud or violence in bringing the defendant or his property within the jurisdiction of the court. In the criminal case, the people, the State, is guilty of no wrong. The officers of the law take the requisite process, find the prisoners charged within the jurisdiction, and this, too, without force, wrong, fraud, or violence on the part of any agent of the State or officer thereof. And it can make no difference whether the illegal arrest was made in another State or another government."[221]

Constructive Presence: Round One

The legal definition of presence refers to the existence of a person in a particular place. In many judicial proceedings it is necessary that the parties should be present in order to reader them valid; for example, a party to a deed when it is executed by himself, must personally acknowledge it, when such acknowledgment is required by law, to give it its full force and effect, and his presence is indispensable, unless, indeed, another person represent him as his attoruey, having authority from him for that purpose. In the criminal law, presence is actual or constructive. When a larceny is committed in a house by two men, united in the same design, and one of them goes into the house, arid commits the crime, while the other is on the outside watching to prevent a surprise, the former is actually, an the latter

---

221 *State v. Ross,* 21 Iowa, 467. See also "Judicial Decisions on Criminal Law and Procedure," *Journal of the American Institute of Criminal Law and Criminology,* 17: 3 (1926), pp. 458-62.

constructively, present. It is a rule in the civil law, that he who is incapable of giving his consent to an act, is not to be considered present, although he be actually in the place; a lunatic, or a man sleeping, would not therefore be considered present. And so, if insensible or if the act were done secretly so that he knew nothing of it.The English statute of fraud directs that all devises and bequests of any lands or tenements shall be attested or subscribed in the presence of said devisor. Under this statute it has been decided that an actual presence is not indispensable, but that where there was a constructive presence it was sufficient; as, where the testatrix executed the will in her carriage standing in the street before the office of her solicitor, the witness retired into the office to attest it, and it being proved that the carriage was accidentally put back, so that she was in a situation to see the witness sign the will through the window of the office.[222]

The Governor of Tennessee filed extradition documents with the Governor of New York demanding the arrest and delivery of Corkran who was alleged to have committed the crimes of grand larceny and false pretenses in Tennessee. The documents alleged that Corkran was a fugitive from justice and had been present in the state when the crimes were committed. The Governor of New York issued an arrest warrant for Corkran. Hyatt was the chief of police of Albany, New York, who arrested Corkran. Thereafter, Corkran filed a writ of *habeas corpus* in a New York supreme court seeking his release. At a hearing, Corkran testified that he had travelled from New York to Chattanooga, Tennessee, on business and, after completing the business, returned home to New York and was not in Tennessee on the dates the alleged crimes took place. The supreme court rejected Plaintiff's request for release and the decision was affirmed by the appellate division of the supreme court of New York. However, the Court of Appeals of New York reversed those decisions and ordered Plaintiff released. Hyatt appealed and the U.S. Supreme Court granted certiorari to review.

The issue was whether an individual must be extradited from one state to a demanding state if it is shown that the individual was actually present in the demanding state at the time the alleged crimes occurred and that he was a fugitive from justice from the demanding

---

222 "Presence": in Electric Law Library Lexicon. See also *Black's Law Dictionary.* See also "Interstate Renditions Clause," Constitution Annotated, https://constitution.congress.gov/

state.

In this decision the Supreme Court of the United States has repudiated the doctrine of *constructive presence* within the State where the crime was committed. In the *Hyatt* decision the U. S. Supreme Court wrote: "The language of section 5278, Revised Statutes, provides, as we think, that the act shall have been committed by an individual who was at the time of its commission personally present within the State which demands his surrender .... Thus the person who is sought must be one that has fled from the demanding State, and he must have fled (not necessarily directly) to the State where he is found. It is difficult to see how a person can be said to have fled from the State in which he is charged to have committed some act amounting to a crime against that State, when in fact he was not within the State at the time the act is said to have been committed. How can a person flee from a place that he was not in? He could avoid a place that he had not been in; he could omit to go to it; but how can it be said with accuracy that he has fled from a place in which he had not been present? This is neither a narrow, nor, as we think, an incorrect interpretation of the statute, it has been in existence since 1793, and we have found no case decided by this court wherein it has been held that the statute. covered a case where the party was not in the State at the time when the act is alleged to -have been committed."[223]

Constructive Presence: Round Two

Michigan alleged that Daily made false representation that certain machinery, to be sold to the state, was new, whereas in fact it was secondhand and used. Under this false representation Daily obtained from the state of $10,000. A certain Armstrong was warden of the Michigan state prison at Jackson, and, in conjunction with the board of control of the prison, was authorized to buy machinery for a cordage plant in the prison; that he was authorized to accept the machinery and to pay for it from the funds of the state under his control. Armstrong contracted with the Hoover & Gamble Company, acting through Daily, the agent, and one Eminger, the secretary of the company, for the purchase of the required machinery, all of which, according to the terms of the contract, was to be new. Armstrong, Daily, and

---

223 *Hyatt v. People ex rel. Corkran*, 221 U. S, 280 (1911). See also "Duty to Surrender Fugitives From Justice," Legal Information Institute, Cornell Law School.

Eminger had agreed beforehand to substitute old, worn, and second-hand machinery, of less value, for that which was contracted for. Thus, the board being ignorant of their intent, was deceived and defraued by the substitution; that the secondhand machinery. Armstrong, Daily, and Eminger, with intent to cheat the state, falsely pretended that the machinery furnished was the new machinery required by the contract, and rendered bills for the same at the contract prices. Armstrong audited the bills, and the machinery paid for as new machinery. Thus, Armstrong, Daily, and Eminger, by means of the false pretenses set up, obtained from the state of Michigan money, to wit, $ 10,000.

Agents of the governor of Illinois, acting under a request for extradiction, arrested Daily, directing his extradition to Michigan as a fugitive from justice from that state. Daily had been indicted in Michigan for bribery and also for obtaining money from the state by false pretenses. The district judge who issued the *habeas corpus* was of opinion, however, that the facts alleged in the indictment for obtaining money by false pretenses did not constitute a crime against the laws of Michigan, and that the evidence failed to show that Daily was not a fugitive from justice.

In *Strassheim v. Daily* Justice Oliver Wendell Holmes, Jr., wrote the opinion of the court. If a jury should believe the evidence and find that Daily did the acts that led Armstrong to betray his trust, deceived the Board of Control, and induced by fraud the payment by the State, the usage of the civilized world would warrant Michigan in punishing him, although he never had set foot in the State until after the fraud was complete. Acts done outside a jurisdiction, but intended to produce and producing detrimental effects within it, justify a State in punishing the cause of the harm as if he had been present at the effect, if the State should succeed in getting him within its power.[224] We may assume therefore that Daily is a criminal under the laws of Michigan.

One who is never within the State before the commission of a crime producing its results within its jurisdiction is not a fugitive from justice within the rendition provisions of the Constitution, but if he commits some overt and material act within the State and then absents

---

224 Citing *Commonwealth v. Smith,* 11 Allen, 243, 256, 259. *Simpson v. State,* 92 Georgia, 41. *American Banana Co. v. United Fruit Co.,* 213 U.S. 347, 356. *Commonwealth v. Macloon, 101 Massachusetts,* 1, 6, 18. See also Kreimer, Seth F. "Lines in the Sand: The Importance of Borders in American Federalism," *University of Pennsylvania Law Review,* 150: 3 (2002), pp. 973-1019.

himself, he becomes a fugitive from- justice when the crime is complete; if not before. Although absent from the State when the crime was completed in this case, the party charged became a fugitive from justice by reason of his having committed certain material steps toward the crime within the State, and the demanding State is entitled to his surrender under article IV, section 2, of the Constitution of the United States and the statutes providing for the surrender of fugitives from justice.

Of course we must admit that it does not follow that Daily is a fugitive from justice.[225] On the other hand, however, we think it plain that the criminal need not do within the State every act necessary to complete the crime. If he does there an overt act which is and is intended to be a material step toward accomplishing the crime, and then absents himself from the State and does the rest elsewhere, he becomes a fugitive from justice, when the crime is complete, if not before. . . . . when, as here, it appears that the prisoner was in the State in the neighborhood of the time alleged it is enough."[226]

Constructive Presence: Part Three

In *Ex parte Hoffstot* the petitioner was a resident of New York who had been indicted in Pennsylvania for conspiracy to bribe members of the Pittsburgh city council. Following Hyatt, the initial ruling was that he could not be extradited in the absence of some proof that he had been physically present in Pennsylvania when the offense was committed. In the absence of such proof he could not be a fugitive from the justice of that state. In this case the U.S. Suprenme Court held that there was indeed specific evidence that petitioner, a resident of New York, participated in Pennsylvania in a conspiracy to bribe members of the city council of Pittsburgh. The object of the bribe was the selection of certain banks in Pittsburgh, one of which petitioner was president, as city depositories. There was enough evidence from which a jury would be justified in drawing the inference that petitioner was in Pittsburgh on a day when some acts in furtherance of the conspiracy were performed. Thus, there was evidence enough that he was a fugitive from justice to justify his extradition to Pennsylvania.

---

225 Citing *Hyatt v. Corkran,* 188 U.S. 691, 712. See also Reeder, Frank G., "International Law: Criminal Law: Jurisdiction over Aliens for Crimes Committed Abroad," *Michigan Law Review.* 60: 1 (1961), pp. 109-12.

226 *Strassheim v. Daily,* 116 U.S. 80 (1885). See "Reaching the Out-of-State Mail-Order Insurer," *Harvard Law Review,* 64: 3 (1951), pp. 482-90.

Ex parte Hoffstot, said that "Where accused has committed a crime in one State, and afterwards leaves it, the right of extradition exists, without reference to his purpose inith the knowledge and without the objection of its authorities."[227]

Roberts v Reilly

A New York grand jury found that William S. Roberts and Edward H. Walton were to stand trial for the crime of grand larceny in the first degree. Roberts and Walton, with force and arms, stole ten bonds issued by the Georgetown and Lane's Railroad Company, a corporation duly existing under the laws of the State of South Carolina, and called first mortgage bonds. Each bond indebted the railroad company in the sum of one thousand dollars, and which said sum the said railroad company thereby promised to pay, on the first day of January, A.D. 1913, with interest.

In the initial hearing it was alleged that the crime with which the defendant was charged was committed in the state of Georgia; that the papers accompanying the demand of the governor of New York were not authenticated, as required by that act; that it nowhere appears that the relator was personally within the limits of the state of New York at the precise time when said alleged crime is stated to have been committed; that it nowhere appears that any evidence was before the governor of New York, at the time he issued his demand, that relator was personally within the limits of New York state when the crime is alleged to have been committed.

The case came before the United States Supreme Court as *Roberts v Reilly.* Justice Matthews wrote the opinion of the court. He said, "On the question of fact, whether the appellant was a fugitive from the justice of the State of New York, there was direct and positive proof before the governor of Georgia, forming part of the record in this proceeding. There is no other evidence in the record which contradicts it. The appellant in his affidavit does not deny that he was in the State of New York about the date of the day laid in the indictment when the offense is alleged to have been committed, and states, by way of inference only, that he was not in that State on that very day; and the fact that he has not been within the State since the finding of the indictment is irrelevant and immaterial. To be a fugitive from justice, in the sense of the act of Congress regulating the subject under consideration, it is not neces-

---

227 *Ex parte Hoffstot,* 218 U. S. 665 (1910).

sary that the party charged should have left the State in which the crime is alleged to have been committed, after an indictment found, or for the purpose of avoiding a prosecution anticipated or begun, but simply that having within a State committed that which by its laws constitutes a crime, when he is sought to be subjected to its criminal process to answer for his offense, he has left its jurisdiction and is found within the territory of another."[228]

---

228 *Roberts v Reilly.* 116 U.S. 80 (1885). See "Habeas Corpus in Interstate Rendition Proceedings," *Columbia Law Review,* 14: 8 (1914), pp. 665-667; "Scope of Inquiry on Habeas Corpus by Fugitive from Justice in Interstate Rendition," *Columbia Law Review,* 21: 7 (1921), pp. 709-711.

The Nature of Extradition Treaties

At present the United States has extradition treaties with more than 100 countries. Traditionally, the U. S. has maintained extradition treaties with all civilized nations, excepting only a few with which there are political and ideological differences. The United States extradites to other countries only under the authority of bilateral extradition treaties with those nations. U. S. will, however, accept fugitives from countries whether based on an extradition treaty, the provisions of a multilateral treaty, or other means of return. A list of countries with which the United States has extradition treaties may be found in the United States Code.[229]

Extradition treaties are essentially contracts which obligate the contracting parties to comply with the request of another state party to that treaty to arrest and deliver a person when the treaty's requirements are met and no exceptions apply. They have been honed, tested, perfected, and improved especially over the last hundred years.

Because extradition treaties are individually negotiated they vary in their provisions. This is done in order to accommodate the various legal systems, preferences, and priorities of the negotiating countries. These treaties, however, generally share certain common elements. They establish requirements for both the country sending the extradition request (called the requesting country) as well as the country receiving the request (called the requested country). We will now examine some of the elements common to treaties.

All these treaties define which crimes are covered by extradition. Treaties made prior to the 1970s typically include a list of specific extraditable offenses. Commonly, these arrangements cover felonies such as murder, manslaughter, theft and larceny. Only the crimes that are listed in the treaty can be invoked in requesting extradition. However, more recent treaties have largely abandoned these lists, however, and use a concept known as "dual criminality" instead. Double criminality, or dual criminality, is a requirement in the extradition law of many countries. It states that a suspect can be extradited from one country to stand trial for breaking a second country's laws only if a similar law exists in the extraditing country.[230] Thus, if Coun-

---

229 18 U.S.C. § 3181. This list is reproduced as the list of United States extradition treaties.

230 Bassiouni, M. Cherif, *International Extradition and World Public Order: The*

try A has no laws against blasphemy, for example, double criminality could prevent a suspect being extradited from Country A to face blasphemy charges in another country. This more flexible approach examines the conduct that serves as the subject of the request. The doctrine of specialty has long been a standard requirement in extradition treaties. This doctrine requires that the person whose extradition is being requested may be tried in the requesting country only for the crimes for which extradition was sought.[231]

Exceptions Specified in Treaties

If these are to be exceptions to extradition treaties these must be noted specifically. Every extradition treaty contains exceptions to the parties' extradition obligations. Among the most common exceptions are the following:

Nationality. Many countries refuse to extradite their own nationals, and extradition treaties often note exceptions for this policy. The U. S. government has long taken the view that nationality should not be a bar to extradition, since the requesting country in an extradition case should have the right to pursue criminal charges against persons who violate its laws regardless of nationality. Under the nationality principle, also known as the active personality principle, a state is entitled to exercise jurisdiction over its nationals, even when they are found outside the territory. Thus, in private international law, national law often follows the nationals outside the territory as far as his personal status is concerned. The U. S. government accordingly extradites its nationals and seeks to limit nationality-based denials in new U. S. extradition treaties. We shall deal in depth with this later in the *Sheinbein* Case.[232]

Political and Military Offenses. These provisions are aimed at crimes such as treason, sedition, and other offenses that could be used to target political opponents or otherwise cause the requested country to become entangled in the domestic politics of the requesting coun-

---

Law and Practice of the United States. Oceana, 1975. See also Moore, John Bassett. *Extradition and Interstate Rendition* (1891). 2 vols. Dobbs Ferry: Oceana, 1974, p. 322.

231 https://www.loc.gov/law/help/extradition-of-citizens/chart.php

232 *State of Maryland v. Samuel Sheinbein* (Case No. 3D00051782, District Court of Maryland for Montgomery County) and State of Maryland v. Samuel Sheinbein (Case No. 81039C, Circuit Court for Montgomery County), accessible on the Maryland Judiciary Case Search System.

try. To clarify and limit the contours of the political offense exception, most bilateral treaties to which the United States is a party now remove such violent acts such as bombings and kidnappings from that exception, even if the subject alleges that the conduct in question was politically motivated.[233]

Capital Punishment. Many nations, especially members of the European Community, no longer impose the death penalty domestically and therefore will not agree to extradite to the United States in any case where the death penalty is possible. Such nations at least reserve the right to deny extradition if the crime could invoke the death penalty .Although the United States usually attempts to limit the application of this exception, many its treaties have provisions permitting the requested country to demand assurances that the death penalty will not be imposed. [234]

Double Jeopardy. Known legally as non bis in idem these provisions are included in extradition treaties in order to protect subjects from transnational double jeopardy.[235] They preclude extradition in cases in which a person has already been convicted or acquitted for the same conduct.[236]

Family Rights. Article 8 of the European Convention on Human Rights[237] has been invoked to stop extradition from proceeding. This provision holds that everyone has the right to the respect of their

---

233 Blakesley, Christopher L. "The Evisceration of the Political Offense Exception to Extradition". *Denver Journal of International Law and Policy* (1987). See also Cantrell, Charles L. "The Political Offense Exemption in International Extradition: A Comparison of the United States, Great Britain and the Republic of Ireland". *Marquette Law Review*. 60: 3 (Spring 1977).

234 Stefanovska, Vesna, "Right to Life vs. Capital Punishment in Extradition Proceedings: a Legal Aspect" *International Journal of Scientific & Engineering Research*, 7: 1 (January 2016).

235 *Non bis in idem*, which translates literally from Latin as "not twice in the same [thing]", is a legal doctrine to the effect that no legal action can be instituted twice for the same cause of action.

236 Goldstein, Shelley. "Extradition and Double Jeopardy" *North Carolina Journal of International Law,* 6:1 (2016).

237 The European Convention on Human Rights (ECHR) (formally the Convention for the Protection of Human Rights and Fundamental Freedoms) is an international treaty to protect human rights and fundamental freedoms in Europe. Drafted in 1950 by the then newly formed Council of Europe, the convention entered into force on 3 September 1953. All Council of Europe member states are party to the Convention and new members are expected to ratify the convention at the earliest opportunity.

private and family life. This is achieved by way of balancing the potential harm to private life against the public interest in upholding the extradition arrangement. While this article is useful as it provide for a prohibition to extradition, the exact conditions required to meet this prohibition is high. Article 8 does explicitly provide that this right is subject to limits in the interests of national security and public safety, so these limits must be weighed in a balancing of priority against this right. Cases where extradition is sought usually involve serious crimes so while these limits are often justified there have been cases where extradition could not be justified in light of the individual's family life. Cases to date have mostly involved dependent children where the extradition would be counter to the best interests of this child.[238]

Suicide Watch. Cases where there is risk of the individual committing suicide have also invoked article 8 of The European Convention on Human Rights against extradition. European courts have held that the public interest of extraditing must be considered in light of the risk of suicide by the individual if extradited.[239] In the case of Lori Love extradition was refused because of the high risk of suicide which had been assessed to exist for the individual if extradited.

Extraterritoriality. Some extradition treaties limit their scope to crimes committed within the territorial jurisdiction of the requesting country. There is a certain conflict with the universality rule which holds that any nation may punish certain crimes that are universally abhorrent, such as piracy. Although this is not the case for the United States some nations will try their own nationals for acts committed anywhere and not just within the territory of that state. The passive personality principle of international law allows states, in limited cases, to claim jurisdiction to try a foreign national for offenses committed abroad that affect its own citizens.[240] This principle has been used by the United States to prosecute terrorists. The United States has attempted to eliminate this restriction.[241]

Rule of Specialty. The Doctrine of Specialty is a principle of International law that is included in most extradition treaties, whereby

238 McKay-Panos, Linda. "Human Rights and Extradition" *Law Now*, 5 March 2019.

239 *Jasons v Latvia*, EWHC 1845 (2004)

240 *https://www.britannica.com/topic/passive-personality-principle*

241 Lowe, A. V. and Warbrick, Colin. "Extraterritorial Jurisdiction and Extradition" *International and Comparative Law Quarterly*, 36: 2 (1987) 398-410.

a person who is extradited to a country to stand trial for certain criminal offenses may be tried only for those offenses and not for any other pre-extradition offenses.[242] We will be discussing this concept at length later in this work.[243]

Procedural and documentation requirements. The requesting country must typically support requests with information about the identity of the person sought, documentation showing the facts and procedural history of the case, copies of the judgment (or conviction if applicable), and any other information the requested country deems appropriate and useful in evaluating the request. The United States requires that there be evidence sufficient to satisfy the requirement known as probable cause under American law.[244]

Statute of Limitations. Statutes of limitations vary enormously from nation to nation, just as they do in the United States from state to state. Treaties may include provisions specifying which country's statute of limitations apply, often the limitations of the requesting nation being the more important. Treaties entered into by the United States typically specify that the statute of limitations in the requesting state alone is relevant.[245]

Extradition from the United States

The extradition process commences when the requesting state sends an extradition request to the State Department which is ordinarily done through diplomatic channels. The State Department next determines that there is a treaty in force between the United States and the requesting country, and whether the conduct alleged in the request is covered under that treaty as an offense for which extradition may be invoked. The State Department will also review the documents submitted, frequently consulting with the Justice Department, to confirm that the request is motivated by *bona fide* legal concerns. It may also

---

242 Iraola, Roberto. "The Doctrine of Specialty and Federal Criminal Prosecutions," 43 *Valpariso University Law Review.* 43: 89 (2008). Available at: http://scholar.valpo.edu/vulr/vol43/iss1/2

243 See *United States v. Rauscher,* 119 U.S. 407 (U.S. 1886)

244 https://www.oas.org/juridico/mla/en/arg/en_arg_mla_des_extrad_proce.pdf

245 Forde, Michael and Kelly, Kieran. *Extradition Law and Transnational Criminal Procedure.* Roundhall, 4th ed., 2011. See also https://en.wikipedia.org/wiki/Political_offence_exception. See also Jeffress,Amy and Witten, Samuel. "Demystifying International Extradition." Advisory. Published in *Law360,* 10 February 2017.

pose questions to the foreign government, and may ask that the request be supplemented or resubmitted if it has determined that the materials in the request are incomplete or unclear.

Modern extradition treaties frequently allow the requesting state to seek the provisional arrest of the subject of the request while it prepares the formal request, which can reduce the possibility that a fugitive will flee while the request is being finalized and sent.

If it appears that Jasons v Latvia [2004] EWHC 1845. all treaty requirements are in order and none of the treaty exceptions create a limitation, the State Department will officially forward the request to the Office of International Affairs (OIA) of the U. S. Department of Justice. OIA then reviews the request to verify that the request is complete and that the documents establish probable cause to believe that subject committed the crime charged. If the request satisfies the treaty's requirements and the probable cause standard, OIA forwards the request to the U. S. Attorney's Office in the district in which the subject is located with instructions on how to proceed. An Assistant United States Attorney then files a complaint in US district court and seeks a warrant for provisional arrest if the subject has not yet been arrested.

An arrest warrant is then issued. When the subject is located and detained, he or she will be brought before a magistrate or district court judge for a preliminary hearing. The exact issues addressed during the hearing will depend on provisions of the treaty. This is a probable cause hearing, not a trial. The court determines whether a case is made out which will justify the holding of the accused and his surrender to the demanding nation. The subject may offer evidence to refute a finding of probable cause, but the rules of evidence and criminal procedure as found in a criminal trial do not apply.

If the court finds that the probable cause standard and other treaty requirements are met, the court will prepare a certification of extraditability, which it sends to the Department of Justice in Washington and from there to the Department of State for use in connection with the Secretary's decision on whether to approve the extradition. Ultimately, the Secretary of State has the final discretion to determine whether the subject should be released or extradited. At this stage, the Secretary may take into account "any humanitarian or other considerations for or against surrender," as well as "written materials submitted by the fugitive, his or her counsel, or other interested parties."

These court findings regarding extraditability can not be appealed. The sole challenge to a finding of probable cause or extraditability is by application of a writ of *habeas corpus* which may be issued by a federal district court. Such a writ may be sought at any point during the extradition process. A court decision which denies a writ of *habeas corpus* may be appealed. *Habeas corpus* review by a district court is generally available whenever an individual "is in custody in violation of the Constitution or laws or treaties of the United States", and is provided for several different types of detention in addition to extradition, such as detention after a criminal conviction, and for military purposes. As part of its *habeas* review, the court will normally accept the factual findings of the extradition magistrate, while legal issues are considered anew. The scope of review of a writ of *habeas corpus* in extradition is limited, based usually on whether: first, the extradition magistrate acquired jurisdiction over the individual and the matter; second, the crime for which extradition is sought is included within the treaty as an extraditable offense, and, third, whether there is probable cause to commit the relator to trial. Many courts, however, have adopted an "expanded" scope of *habeas* review that additionally considers issues about the violation of constitutional rights.

Petitioners in extradition cases may contest the legality of their detention though a *habeas* proceeding by arguing, for example, that the extradition treaty is not in force, that the alleged crime constitutes political behavior subject to exception, that the determination of extraditability by the magistrate has not been made according to the requirements of the applicable United States statutes and treaty, that the extradition procedure does not comply with the Constitution, and that the relator has not been formally charged.[246]

Once the Secretary of State decides on the extraditability of an individual, the Department of State will promptly notify the diplomatic personnel of the requesting country. If the request is approved, the subject's transportation to the requesting country will be arranged in coordination with that country and the subject will be escorted to that country by officials of the U. S. Marshals Service.[247]

---

246 The procedure is contained in 28 U.S.C. § 2241 et. seq

247 "Extradition To and From the United States: Overview of the Law and Contemporary Treaties" CRS Report, 4 October 2016. See also Webber, Diane, "Extradition to the United States," Centre for the Response to Radicalisation and Terrorism Policy Paper No. 5 (2015).

Extradition to the United States

First, the appropriate federal, state, or local prosecutor forwards extradition request to the Office of International Affairs (OIA) of the U. S. Department of Justice. Such requests, initiated by federal, state, and local prosecutors, must be reviewed and approved by the Department of Justice's Office of International Affairs before they are forwarded to the Department of State. According to standard American practice, the Justice Department's Office of International Affairs is responsible in the first instance for reviewing possible outgoing extradition requests, ensuring that they are legally sufficient, and deciding whether to ask the State Department to make a formal extradition request through diplomatic channels.[248]

After receiving a request, OIA, consulting with State as needed, confirms the following: (1) an extradition treaty is in place between the United States and the requested country; (2) the offense or offenses for which extradition is sought are subject to extradition under terms of the applicable treaty (3) the subject is procedurally extraditable based on various factors, including nationality, facts of the offense, and status of the case; and (4) statutes of limitations have not lapsed. The Department of Justice may also evaluate issues such as where the crime was committed and whether capital punishment may be sought.[249]

All requests for extradition must be sent through diplomatic channels for the Department of State is the sole vehicle for the conduct of foreign relations. While the formal request for extradition is being prepared, the Justice Department may request the provisional arrest of the subject, a procedure that is modern in origin. Depending on the provisions of the relevant extradition treaty, detention under a provisional arrest warrant may be limited to specific time periods. If an individual is arrested under a provisional arrest warrant, the person will ordinarily be released if the American government does not submit a formal extradition request within a time period which is usually specified in the treaty.

After receiving a request from the State Department, the ap-

---

248 Pierson, Brendan and Stempel, Jonathan, "How Does Extradition to the U. S. Work?" Reuters World News, 6 December 2018.

249 U. S. Department of Justice at https://www.justice.gov/jm/jm-9-15000-international-extradition-and-related-matters. See also Jeffress, Amy; Samuel Witten; and Kaitlin Konkel, "International Extradition: A Guide to U.S. and International Practice," Advisory by Arnold and Porter, November 10, 2020.

propriate authorities in the requested country will then undertake their own review of the extradition request. Procedures vary by country, but many advanced nations conduct reviews in ways that are similar to those employed in the United States. These usually include executive approval and judicial review. Extradition determinations may be subject to appeal and, as in the United States, may take months or years to complete.[250]

Once the requested country reaches a decision regarding an American extradition request, it will notify the U. S. Department of State. If the request is denied, the OIA may choose to work with prosecutors and the Department of State to create other methods to obtain custody of the individual, one of which is deportation. Although rejected as an alternative by many nations, kidnapping[251] may work as it did for Israel in the Adolf Eichmann case and the United States in the case of Dr. Alvarez-Machain.

Procedural and legal requirements of extradition provide several possible defenses to extradition requests. Each extradition treaty is individually negotiated and the provisions in each treaty should therefore be considered when developing possible defenses. The most common defenses are the following.

First, the subject may argue that although a crime was committed, the alleged crime is not covered by the treaty. A treaty is based on a specific list of extraditable offenses. Thus, the defense may involve a somewhat straightforward dismissal if the offense is not on the list, the subject prevails. Most treaties have replaced the list of crimes with a "dual criminality" approach as discussed above. While this may simplify the process of making new crimes extraditable, it complicates the analysis of the alleged crime covered. If the subject can establish that the conduct that is the basis of the extradition request is not a crime in both countries, or otherwise does not meet the treaty requirements, he or she can avoid extradition.[252]

Second, there may be a failure to meet legal standard. In this case the subject asserts that the request fails to provide sufficient information to meet the required legal standard, which in American courts is known as probable cause. Such a challenge might argue that

---

250 "Extradition of Fugitives to the United States" at https://fam.state.gov/FAM/07FAM/07FAM1620.html

251 Bassiouni, *op. cit.*, 124-26

252 Pierson, Brendan and Stempel, Jonathan, "How does extradition to the U.S. work?" Reuters, 6 December 2018.

the information supplied is unnecessarily vague or merely speculative.

Nearly all treaties include provisions that political offenses are not extraditable. Using this defense, the subject may choose to argue that the request is politically motivated, that the request is being made simply to seek to extradite a dissident, political opponent,or former official who actually committed no crime. Former state officials who committed genocide, torture, and similar crimes may be extradited.[253]

Subjects may argue that extradition should be denied because of human rights concerns. The most substantial human rights concerns involve the subject's likely treatment if returned to the country seeking extradition. This ties in well with the Convention against Torture and Other Cruel, Inhuman or Degrading Treatment or Punishment.[254] The U. S. State Department has sometimes been willing to place limitations and conditions on the extradition to ensure that the person will have legal protections that they may not otherwise be entitled to in the foreign country.

Doctrine of *aut dedere aut judicare*

Related to extradition is the concept of *aut dedere aut judicare*.[255] This maxim represents the principle that states must either surrender a criminal within their jurisdiction to a state that wishes to prosecute the criminal or prosecute the offender in its own courts. The *aut dedere aut judicare* clause appears in various forms in some 30 multilateral treaties and in 18 regional conventions. The first convention containing an extradite or prosecute clause was the International Convention for the Suppression of Counterfeiting Currency (1929), which provided that where a State's domestic law did not allow the extradition of a state's nationals, those offending nationals returning to their State after committing a crime under the Convention should be punished in the same manner as if the crime had been committed in

---

253 "Understanding American Extradition Laws" at https://www.hg.org/legal-articles/understanding-american-extradition-laws-30994

254 Adopted and opened for signature, ratification and accession by United Nations General Assembly resolution 39/46 of 10 December 1984. entry into force 26 June 1987.

255 The Latin term *aut dedere aut judicare* may be translated as "either extradite or prosecute" and refers to the legal obligation of states under public international law to prosecute persons who commit serious international crimes where no other state has requested extradition.

that State.[256]

Many international agreements contain provisions for *aut dedere aut judicare*. These include all four 1949 Geneva Conventions, the U.N. Convention for the Suppression of Terrorist Bombings, the U.N. Convention Against Corruption, the Convention for the Suppression of Unlawful Seizure of Aircraft, the Convention Against Torture and Other Cruel, Inhuman or Degrading Treatment or Punishment, the Convention for the Protection of Cultural Property in the Event of an Armed Conflict, and the International Convention for the Suppression and Punishment of the Crime of Apartheid.[257]

Many contemporary scholars hold the opinion that *aut dedere aut judicare* is not an obligation under customary international law but rather is a specific conventional clause relating to specific crimes." Some multilateral extradition treaties also include an *aut dedere aut judicare clause*. Some examples include: the Second Montevideo Convention on Extradition of 1933; the Arab League Extradition Agreement of 1952; and the European Convention on Extradition of 1957. These accords oblige a State which chooses not to surrender a national to prosecute the national itself.[258]

One proof that this is apparently not a rule of customary international law, was shown by the failure to follow its provisions in the case of the destruction of an airplane over Lockerbie, Scotland. On 21 December 1988 270 people were killed by the explosion of a bomb bringing down Pan Am flight 103 over the small town Lockerbie in Scotland.[259] Libyan dictator Gaddafi accepted responsibility for the

---

256 Fitz-Maurice, Ernestine, "Convention for the Suppression of Counterfeiting Currency," *American Journal of International Law*, 26: 3 (1932), pp. 533-551.

257 Macedo, Stephen, ed. U*niversal Jurisdiction: National Courts and the Prosecution of Serious Crimes under International Law.* University of Pennsylvania Press, 2003. See also Calatayud, Esperanza Orihuela, "La obligación aut dedere aut iudicare y su cumplimiento en españa," *Revista Española de Derecho Internacional*, 68: 2 (2016), pp. 207-28.

258 Mitchell, Claire, "*aut dedere, aut judicare*: the Extradite or Prosecute Clause in International Law," Open Edition Books. This well-documented paper provides an excellent over-view of this important doctrine.

259 Stigall, Dan E. "Ungoverned Spaces, Transnational Crime, and the Prohibition on Extraterritorial Enforcement Jurisdiction in International Law". *Notre Dame Journal of International & Comparative Law* 3: 1 (February 2013); Weiss, Peter, "Universal Jurisdiction: Past, Present and Future," *Proceedings* of the Annual Meeting of the American Society of International Law, 102 (2008), pp. 406-09.

Lockerbie bombing but no one was extradited or prosecuted.[260] The obligation arises regardless of the extraterritorial nature of the crime and regardless of the fact that the perpetrator and victim may be of alien nationality. Thus, it is an obligation that only exists when a state has voluntarily assumed the obligation.[261]

The Consultative Assembly of the Council of Europe authorized its Council of Ministers to prepare recommendations regarding international terrorists who have escaped from the nation wherein they committed their terroristic acts and have sought political asylum. On 24 January 1974 the Council of Ministers adopted a resolution which asserted that terrorists should not escape punishment even if not extradited. Extradition is the most certain way of insuring that acts of terrorism do not go unpunished. If extradition is refused, then the requested state's government should consider the possibility of prosecuting the matter, making its decision in the same manner as it would an ordinary case in its domestic courts.[262] That recommendation follows the guidelines established in the Hague Convention for the Suppression of Unlawful Seizures of Air Craft (1970), which reads as follows:[263]

A.4(2) Each Contracting State shall likewise take such measures as may be necessary to establish its jurisdiction over the offence in the case where the alleged offender is present in its territory and it does not extradite him pursuant to Article VIII to any of the States mentioned in paragraph 1 of this Article

---

260 The Lockerbie Cases before the International Court of Justice (ICJ) deal with the request made by the United States of America ('US') and the United Kingdom ('UK') to Libya to surrender two Libyan citizens, Abdelbaset Aliu Mohmed Al Megrahi and Al Amin Khalifa Fhimah, who were charged by the British Lord Advocate and a US Grand Jury for their involvement in the case. The two suspects were alleged to be intelligence. The Lockerbie Cases were noted as *Libyan Arab Jamahiriya v United Kingdom and United States of America*.

261 Kelly, Michael J. "Cheating Justice by Cheating Death: The Doctrinal Collision for Prosecuting Foreign Terrorists—Passage of *Aut Dedere Aut Judicare* into Customary Law & Refusal to Extradite Based on the Death Penalty". *Arizona Journal of International and Comparative Law,* 20: 491 (2003).

262 Costello, Declan, "International Terrorism and the Development of the Principle 'aut dedere aut judicare,'" *Irish Jurist,* 9: 2 (1974), pp. 209-22. Reydams, Luc. *Universal Jurisdiction: International and Municipal Legal Perspectives*. Oxford University press, 2003.

263 "Hague Convention for the Suppression of Unlawful Seizures of Air Craft," United Nations Treaties, 12325, 16 December 1970, Article 4: 1.

A.7. The Contracting State in the territory of which the alleged offender is found shall, if it does not extradite him, be obliged, without exception whatsoever and whether or not the offence was committed in its territory, to submit the case to its competent authorities for the purpose of prosecution. Those authorities shall take their decision in the same manner as in the case of any ordinary offence of a serious nature under the law of that State.

Virtually all regional conventions which are purely criminal in nature, made since c.1970, have included an extradite or prosecute clause. The regional conventions which post-date the development of the "Hague formula", with its saving clause allowing for prosecutorial discretion, will therefore contain an obligation to submit the case to prosecutorial authorities, rather than the stricter obligation to prosecute or "to take proceedings against" the alleged offender.

Five Principles of International Law and Extradition

Five principles have emerged in international law as legitimate bases for the exercise of the criminal jurisdiction of States over alleged offenders: territoriality, nationality, passive personality, protective, and universality. As the Permanent Court of International Justice (PCIJ) held almost a hundred years ago in one of its most important ruling, "'[T]he first and foremost restriction imposed by international law upon a State is that – failing a permissive rule to the contrary – it may not exercise its power in any form in the territory of another State." The international court continued, [A]ll that can be required of a State is that it should not overstep the limits which international law places upon its jurisdiction. The territoriality of criminal law, therefore, is not an absolute principle of international law and by no means coincides with territorial sovereignty."[264] That ruling was reiterated by one of the first decisions of the International Court of Justice (ICJ): 'Between independent States, respect for territorial sovereignty is an essential foundation of international relations."[265] This principle ordinarily bars states from exercising jurisdiction beyond its borders, although there are some possible exceptions including the principle of nationality, passive personality principle, the protective principle, and possibly the universal jurisdiction in extreme cases of human rights

---

264 Case of the S.S. 'Lotus (*France v. Turkey*), judgment, 7.9.1927, p. 18
265Corfu Channel Case (*United Kingdom of Great Britain and Northern Ireland v. Albania*), judgment, 25.3.1948, p. 35

violations. In a case where a person accused of committing a crime is not to be found within the territory of that state, the state may not exercise its jurisdiction in the territory of another. Instead, states must act in terms of both international and domestic law, which involves extradition.[266]

Territoriality assumes that the offense was committed within the territory of the state asserting jurisdiction, including on ships and in aircraft registered to them. This is the simplest base of criminal jurisdiction, covering the overwhelming majority of criminal prosecutions. However, the question of whether an offense actually takes place within the territory is not always easily answered. It is even more difficult to determine when an act committed outside a state's territory, yet having effects inside of its territory comes, within the scope of legitimate territorial jurisdiction. The territoriality principle is the most basic principle of jurisdiction in international law. It is the most fundamental and commonly accepted method of exercising jurisdiction to prescribe in criminal matters. The generally accepted view in public international law is that the primary basis of criminal jurisdiction for any state is territorial.[267]

In the widest application of the qualified territoriality principle, a state can exercise its jurisdiction over a crime when at least one of its constituent elements, either the criminal conduct (subjective territorial jurisdiction) or the result (objective territorial jurisdiction), occurred within its territory. Thus, the territorial principle has two aspects: the subjective aspect and the objective aspect. Under the subjective aspect of territorial jurisdiction a sovereign is recognized as having the power to adopt criminal laws that apply to crimes that are physically committed within his territorial borders. The subjective territoriality principle permits the State to exercise jurisdiction over acts performed abroad, but which are originated within its territory. Sub-

---

266 Crawford, James, ed. *Brownlie's Principles of Public International Law.* 8th edition; Oxford University Press, 2012; Lauterpacht Hersch. *The Development of International Law by the International Court.* Stevens & Sons, 1958, p. 164. See also Blakesley, Christopher L., "A Conceptual Framework for Extradition and Jurisdiction Over Extraterritorial Crime," *Utah Law Review,* (1984) in Scholarly Works, https://scholars.law. unlv.edu/facpub/319.

267 Berge, Wendell, "Criminal Jurisdiction and the Territorial Principle,"*Michigan Law Review,* 30: 2 (1931), pp. 238-269; "Territorial Jurisdiction,"*American Journal of International Law,* Vol. 29, Supplement: Research in International Law (1935), pp. 480-508.

jective territorial jurisdiction can be claimed and exercised by the state on the territory of which a criminal conduct occurred. Under the objective aspect of territorial jurisdiction a sovereign is recognized as having the power to adopt a criminal law that applies to crimes that take effect within its borders even if the perpetrator performs the act outside of its borders. The objective principle asserts the jurisdiction of the state in respect of offenses began outside the territory of the state but consummated within the territory.[268]

The subjective and objective applications of the territoriality principle on occasion have been combined, as complementary, based upon the conclusion that, taken alone, neither of them can be made sufficiently comprehensive to serve as a rationalization of contemporary practice. The most important principle is always the place in which the criminal has committed a crime, that is, the principle of territoriality.[269]

The nationality principle, also called the active personality principle, assumes that the person charged with the offense is a national of the state asserting jurisdiction. In most instances in which criminal jurisdiction is exercised by a state, the circumstances would satisfy both the territoriality and the active personality principles, because the criminal act is perpetrated by a national within the geographic confines of the home country.[270] Thus, the real need for invoking the active personality principle principally arises when the offense is committed by a national extra-territorially. The active personality principle usually also covers those persons who serve the State in different capacities, such as members of the diplomatic service. It has also been extended at times to include permanent residents, who may, in effect, have become unofficial nationals, if not citizens.[271]

---

268 *United States v. Ivanov,* 175 F. Supp.2d 367 (D. Conn. 2001); See also Kratochwil, F. "Subjective Territorial Principle," *World Encyclopedia of Law;* also Grant, John P. and J. C. Barker, eds. *Encyclopaedic Dictionary of International Law.* 3 ed.; Oxford University Press, 2009.

269 Ryngaert, C. *Jurisdiction in International Law*, 2nd ed. Oxford University Press, 2015. Preuss, Lawrence, "American Conception of Jurisdiction with Respect to Conflicts of Law on Crime," *Transactions* of the Grotius Society, 30 (1944), pp. 184-208. These principles are also defined in Encyclopedia Britannica and Oxford Reference.

270 Stilz, Anna. "Nations, States, and Territory," *Ethics,* 121: 3 (2011), pp. 572-601.

271 Jacob, G. H. Lloyd, "Nationality and Domicile; With Special Reference to Early Notions on the Subject," *Transactions* of the Grotius Society, 10 (1924), pp., 89-114. See also Miller, David, "The Ethical Significance of Nationality,"

The passive personality arises in regard to the nationality of the victim of the offense. The fact that, irrespective of the location of the offense, or the nationality of the perpetrator, the victim is a national of the State asserting jurisdiction. Many legal authorities have voiced strong opposition against invocation of the passive personality principle. In at least some instances, the passive personality principle is well entrenched in state practice. Passive personality principle as a basis of jurisdiction is found in customary international law which permits a state, in limited cases, to exercise extraterritorial jurisdiction to try a foreign national for offenses committed abroad that affect its own citizens.[272]

The protective principle is concerned with protection of certain vital national interests of various states. It is a rule of international law which allows a sovereign state to assert jurisdiction over a person whose conduct outside its boundaries threatens the states security or interferes with the operation of its governmental functions. It authorizes a state to exercise criminal jurisdiction irrespective of location or nationality, even when the alleged offenders are foreigners who acted extra-territorially. It is supported because it acts against threats to the national security of a state, including such crimes as counterfeiting its currency, national emblems, seals or stamps; forgery, fraud or perjury committed in connection with official documents, especially passports and visa permits; and improper use of or insult to the national flag.[273]

The universality principle allows for the assertion of jurisdiction in cases where the alleged crime may be prosecuted by all states, presently including war crimes, crimes against the peace, crimes against humanity, slavery, and piracy. It is the authority of the state to punish certain crimes wherever and by whomsoever committed. This authority, which is vested in every state regardless of territory and nationality, is limited to the exercise of jurisdiction over *delicta juris*

Ethics, 98: 4 (1988), pp. 647-662. See also "Nationality Principle," in Encyclopedia Britannica; Miller, David. *On Nationality.* Oxford University Press, 1997.

272 Moore, J. B. *Digest Of International Law.* Washington, 1906, 2: 228; *United States vs. Yunis,* 681 F. Supp at 900 (D.D.C. 1998).

273 "Protective Principle of Jurisdiction Applied to Uphold Statute Intended to Have Extra-Territorial Effect," *Columbia Law Review,* 62: 2 (1962), pp. 371-375. See also Ferris, Elizabeth G. *The Politics of Protection: The Limits of Humanitarian Action.* Brookings Institution Press, 2001, pp. 40-61.

gentium [acts defined as crimes by international law].[274] For example, Article 6 of the Convention on the Prevention and Punishment of the Crime of Genocide (1948) makes that crime punishable by any nation.[275]

There are those who posit the need for reshaping all extradition laws in order to counter the unjust refusal of states to pay heed to extradition treaties and harbor criminals. It can be said that the extradition principle is one of the sacrosanct rules existing under the international criminal law. The question for future lawmakers is: is extradition a mandatory or optional duty of states? There are cases involving the principle of double criminality whereby a crime is an offense recognized in the territorial as well as in the requesting state. There is a worthy goal of internationally thereby reducing crimes and prevention of flight of fugitives from one state to another in order to escape punishment for their offenses.[276]

The Yunis Case

Fawaz Yunis and several accomplices hijacked a Jordanian airliner while it was on the ground in Beirut. The plane flew to several locations around the Mediterranean Sea, and eventually flew back to Beirut, where the hijackers blew up the plane and then escaped. The only connection between the whole event and the United States was that several Americans were on board the whole time. Yunis was indicted for violating the Hostage Taking Act.[277]

In September 1987, during the Reagan administration, the United States executed an extraordinary extradition, code-named "Goldenrod," in a joint FBI-CIA operation. American agents lured Fawaz Yunis onto a boat off the coast of Cyprus and taken to international waters, where he was arrested. The Reagan administration had

---

274 Bradley, Curtis A., "Unuversal Jurisdiction and U.S. Law," *Universality of Chicago Legal Forum*, 1 (2001), pp. 323-50; Randall, Kenneth C. "Universal Jurisdiction Under International Law, *Texas Law Review*, 66 (1988), 785-806. But see Kissinger, Henry, "The Pitfalls of Universal Jurisdiction," *Foreign Affairs*, 80: 4 (2001), pp. 86-96.

275 Convention on the Prevention and Punishment of the Crime of Genocide, proposed by U.N. General Assembly Resolution 260 of 9 December 1948 and declared in force on 12 January 1951. By 2019, 152 states had signed it.

276Agrawal, Isha, "Extradition under International law: Aid for the Angst of Fugitives," *International Journal of Law and Legal Jurisprudence Studies*, 3: 3 (1995), pp. 453-66.

277 18 U.S.C. § 1203

not undertaken this kidnapping lightly. FBI Director William H. Webster opposed an earlier bid to snatch Yunis, arguing that the United States should not adopt the extralegal tactics of Israel, which had abducted Adolf Eichmann on a residential street in Buenos Aires, Argentina, in 1960 . In 1984 and 1986, following a wave of terrorist attacks, Congress passed laws making air piracy and attacks on Americans abroad federal crimes. Ronald Reagan added teeth to these laws by signing a secret covert-action directive in 1986 that authorized the CIA to kidnap, anywhere abroad, foreigners wanted for terrorism. A new word entered the dictionary of U.S. foreign relations: rendition.[278]

Yunis was apprehended, and later indicted under the Destruction of Aircraft Act.[279] He moved to dismiss on grounds of lack of proper jurisdiction. The Federal District Court held that indeed the national government may prosecute an airline hijacker irrespective of his connection with the United States. The court ruled that there was jurisdiction under both international and domestic law which allowed for successful prosecution of this case. Under prevailing international law, the U.S. Congress had extraterritorial application of its law. International law recognizes several bases for a nation to give extraterritorial application to its laws. One is the universality principle which asserts that some acts are considered to be so heinous and contrary to civilization that any court may assert jurisdiction.[280]

The acts that fall within this category are mainly defined by international convention. The universality principle applies because numerous conventions condemn hijacking, which is simply a form of piracy, the first crime to be universally condemned and the first which allowed universal jurisdiction and prosecution. Hostage taking has been subsequently added to the list of crimes which may be universally prosecuted, and that was done by treaty.[281]

The *Yunis* case is of particular interest because it illustrates several possible bases of jurisdiction which are acceptable under pre-

---

278 Cobain, Ian; and Ball, James, "New Light Shed on U.S. government's Extraordinary Rendition Programme," *The Guardian*, 22 May 2013; Mayer, Jane, "Outsourcing torture," *The New Yorker*, 14 February 2005.

279 18 U.S.C. Â§ 32

280 *United States v. Yunis*, 681 F. Supp. 896, (1988); United States v. Yunis, 924 F.2d 1086 (1991).

281 International Convention against the Taking of Hostages, General Assembly Res. 146 (XXXIV), 34th Sess., Supp. No. 46, at 245, U.N. Doc. A/34/46 (1979), entered into force 3 June 1983.

vailing international law. These are territorial, nationality, and protective Of the five generally recognized jurisdictional grounds, the passive personal principle has been met with the most resistance by U.S. courts and officials. The passive personality principle is also relevant, because it applies to offenses against a nation's citizens abroad. The United States has been slow to recognize this principle, but it is now generally agreed upon.[282]

---

282 Lowenfeld, Andreas F. "U.S. Law Enforcement Abroad: The Constitution and International Law," *American Journal of International Law,* 83: (1989), pp. 880-94; and 84: 2 (1990), pp. 444-493.

The Non-refoulement Rule

On a regular basis, the United States responds favorably to international inquiries for the extradition of various individuals to foreign countries to face trials for crimes they allegedly committed in those countries. This is the obvious case also with the various nations of the world, barring only a very few closed authoritarian regimes. As in the United States, these courts do not inquire into the procedures or treatment which await these surrendered fugitives in the requesting countries. Instead, the courts apply a rule of non-inquiry, restricting their focus to the issues of whether sufficient evidence exists to extradite the subject and whether the terms of the extradition treaty have been met. The rule of non-inquiry bars the courts from denying extradition even when it is clear that the person will be the victim of torture or cruel and inhumane treatment. Torture and inhumane treatment have always been a widespread problem in most of the international community. Responses of governments to international treaties that seek to mitigate harsh punishments and bizarre court proceedings has not always been favorable. It is obvious to anyone studying comparative governments that standards of justice vary immensely as do the mechanisms that states use to administer justice, both in trials and subsequent punishment.

American courts, when deciding issues of extradition and *habeas corpus*, are faced with two often diametrically opposed concepts: non-inquiry into the justice of a requesting nation; and protection of the basic human rights of the detainee called the principle of non-refoulement. The older, long-established rule of non-inquiry contains a stable core that prohibits inquiring closely into claims about the motives of the requesting government, except to the extent the claim falls within the political offense exception, about that country's ordinary criminal procedures, or about its ordinary penal policies, such as the length of prison sentences. The rule of non-inquiry, like extradition procedures generally, is shaped by concerns about institutional competence and by notions of separation of powers. Outside that basic core, where the subjects faces unusual procedures or possible personal injury, the rule is less unwavering, and courts not only inquire into the merits but also sometimes find ways to refuse extradition or signal the executive branch that caution is warranted. The non-refoulement rule has emerged because an advanced concept of justice has determined that there is something amiss with the forcible return of refugees or asylum seekers to a country where they are liable to be subjected to persecution.[283] The non-inquiry rule emerged in U. S. Supreme Court cases that made little effort to provide a theoretical or policy basis for it, even though the instability of the rule creates a need for some kind of grounding or justification. Recent courts have therefore not surprisingly turned to the amorphous idea of "the conduct of foreign affairs" to justify the rule. The foreign relations argument has the double value of associating the rule with constitutional principles while relieving courts of responsibility for any mistreatment that a person might suffer after extradition. Thus, to the extent the rule has a theory, it draws partly from a substantive policy about allocation of authority that overlaps with an institutional stance of deference. It would seem highly probable that the courts will, through a prolonged series of cases, try to establish a base line between the two rules.[284]

Defining Non-refoulement

Dictionary.com defines refoulement as "the forcible return of refugees or asylum seekers to a country where they are liable to be subjected to persecution, and notes that international and European Union law prohibit refoulement. Wikipedia defines it as follows:

> Non-refoulement is a fundamental principle of international law that forbids a country receiving asylum seekers from returning them to a country in which they would be in likely danger of persecution based on "race, religion, nationality, membership of a particular social group or political opinion". Unlike political asylum, which applies to those who can prove a well-grounded fear of persecution based on certain category of persons, non-refoulement refers to the generic repatriation of people, including refugees into war zones and other disaster locales. It is a principle of customary international law, as it applies even to states that are not parties to the 1951 Convention Relating to the Status of Refugees or its 1967 Protocol. It is also a principle of the trucial law of nations.[285]

The Merrian-Webster dictionary defines refoulement as " the

---

283 Sullivan, David B. "Abandoning the Rule of Non-inquiry in International Extradition," *Hastings International and Comparative Law Review,* 15: 1 (1991).

284 Quigley, John, "The Rule of Non-inquiry and the Impact of Human Rights on Extradition Law," *North Carolina Journal of International Law and Commercial Regulation,* 15: 3 (1990), pp. 401-39.

285 "Refoulement," Wikipedia."; "Refoulement" in Dictionary.com.

act of forcing a refugee or asylum seeker to return to a country or territory where he or she is likely to face persecution Since 1980, United States law has defined refugees as people with a "well-founded fear of persecutions" in their home country and thus entitled to sanctuary or political asylum." Oxford/ Lexico say simply, "The forcible return of refugees or asylum seekers to a country where they are liable to be subjected to persecution." And the Cambridge dictionary wrote the refoulement is " the practice of sending refugees or asylum seekers (= people trying to escape war, danger, threats, etc. in their own country) back to their country or to another country where they are likely to suffer bad treatment:

Under international human rights law, the principle of non-refoulement guarantees that no one should be returned to a country where they would face torture, cruel, inhuman or degrading treatment or punishment and other irreparable harm. This principle applies to all migrants at all times, irrespective of migration status. The Office of the High Commissioner, United Nations Human Right Commission, defines non-refoulement as follows:

The principle of non-refoulement forms an essential protection under international human rights, refugee, humanitarian and customary law. It prohibits States from transferring or removing individuals from their jurisdiction or effective control when there are substantial grounds for believing that the person would be at risk of irreparable harm upon return, including persecution, torture, illtreatment or other serious human rights violations. Under international human rights law the prohibition of refoulement is explicitly included in the Convention against Torture and Other Cruel, Inhuman or Degrading Treatment or Punishment (CAT) and the International Convention for the Protection of All Persons from Enforced Disappearance (ICPPED). In regional instruments the principle is explicitly found in the Inter-American Convention on the Prevention of Torture, the American Convention on Human Rights, and the Charter of Fundamental Rights of the European Union. International human rights bodies, regional human rights courts, as well as national courts have guided that this principle is an implicit guarantee flowing from the obligations to respect, protect and fulfill human rights. Human rights treaty bodies regularly receive individual petitions concerning non-refoulement, including the Committee Against Torture, the Human Rights Committee, the Committee on the Elimination of Discrimination Against Women and the Committee on the Rights of the Child.[286]

The prohibition of refoulement under international human rights law is applicable to all forms of removal or transfer of persons, irrespective of status, where there certainly are, or likely to be, substantial grounds for believing that the individual would be at risk of suffering irreparable harm upon return because of torture, ill-treatment or other serious disregard of human rights obligations. As an inherent element of the prohibition of torture and other forms of ill-treatment, the principle of non-refoulement is characterized by its absolute nature without any exception.[287]

In this respect, the scope of this principle under relevant human rights law treaties is broader than that contained in international refugee law. The prohibition applies to all persons, irrespective of citizenship, nationality, statelessness, or migration status, and it applies wherever a State exercises jurisdiction or effective control, even when outside of that State's territory. Among the many serious human rights violations, including torture, and other cruel, inhuman or degrading treatment; denial of due process and the right to a fair trial; possible risks of violations to the rights to life, integrity and/or freedom of the person; serious forms of sexual and gender-based violence; use of the death penalty; mutilation of female genitalia; and prolonged solitary confinement.[288]

Principle of Non-refoulement

Non-refoulement is a fundamental principle of international law that prohibits a country which has received asylum seekers from returning these people to a country in which they would be in likely danger of persecution based on "race, religion, nationality, membership of a particular social group or political opinion". Under prevailing internatuional law, the principle of non-refoulement is binding for states, that is, there is an unconditional ban on the extradi-

286 ThePrincipleNon-RefoulementUnderInternationalHumanRightsLaw.pdf (ohchr.org)

287 Human Rights Committee, General Comment No. 31, para 12. See also Zimmermann, Kalin et al., eds. *The 1951 Convention Relating to the Status of Refugees and Its 1967 Protocol: a Commentary; Article 33, para. 1.* New York: Oxford University Press, 2011, pp. 1345–46.

288 Human Rights Committee, General Comment No. 20, 1994, para 6. See also Bruin, Rene; and Wouters, Kees, "Terrorism and the Non-derogability of Non re-foulement". *International Journal of Refugee Law*, 15: 1 (2003), pp. 5–29.

tion of persons to countries where they may find themselves at risk of torture and ill-treatment.[289] Merriam-Webster's definition of the principle of non-refoulement, which it dates only to 1960 is as follows: "a principle of international law providing a refugee or asylum seeker with the right to freedom from expulsion from a territory in which he or she seeks refuge or from forcible return to a country or territory where he or she faces threats to life or freedom because of race, religion, nationality, membership in a particular social group, or political opinion."[290]

Of non-refoulement Wikipedia wrote that it "is a fundamental principle of international law that forbids a country receiving asylum seekers from returning them to a country in which they would be in likely danger of persecution based on "race, religion, nationality, membership of a particular social group or political opinion". Unlike political asylum, which applies to those who can prove a well-grounded fear of persecution based on certain category of persons, non-refoulement refers to the generic repatriation of people, including refugees into war zones and other disaster locales. It is a principle of customary international law, as it applies even to states that are not parties to the 1951 Convention Relating to the Status of Refugees or its 1967 Protocol. It is also a principle of the trucial law of nations. It is debatable whether non-refoulement is a *jus cogens* of international law. If so, international law would permit no abridgments for any purpose or under any circumstances.[291]

Article 3 of the 1933 Convention relating to the International Status of Refugees contained the first mention of non-refoulement in

---

289 https://wikimili.com/en/Non-refoulement. Several Wikipedia sites offer the same definition: "A principle of international law which forbids the rendering of a victim of persecution to their persecutor."

290 Office of the High Commissioner, Human Rights, United Nations, "The Principle of Non-refoulement Under International Human Rights Law," https://www. ohchr.org/

291 "Non-refoulement" in Wikipedia See also Trevisanut, Seline (September 1, 2014). "International Law and Practice: The Principle of Non-Refoulement And the De-Territorialization of Border Control at Sea," *Leiden Journal of International Law*, 27: (2014), pp. 661-74; Vang, Jerry (Summer 2014). "Limitations of the Customary International Principle of Non-refoulement on Non-party States: Thailand Repatriates the Remaining Hmong-Lao Regardless of International Norms," *Wisconsin International Law Journal*, 32: 2 (2014), pp. 355–383; Allain, Jean, 2001, "The jus cogens Nature of non-refoulement", International Journal of Refugee Law, 13: 4 (2001), pp. 533-558.

international law and prevented party states from expelling legally-residing refugees or turning away refugees at the borders of their home countries. This treaty was ratified by only a few states and gained little traction in international law.[292]

The principle of "non-refoulement" was given universal recognition in Article 33 of the 1951 Convention Relating to the Status of Refugees. Article 33 contains the following two paragraphs that define the prohibition of the expulsion or return of a refugee: First, "No Contracting State shall expel or return ('refouler') a refugee in any manner whatsoever to the frontiers of territories where his life or freedom would be threatened on account of his race, religion, nationality, membership of a particular social group or political opinion." Second, "The benefit of the present provision may not, however, be claimed by a refugee whom there are reasonable grounds for regarding as a danger to the security of the country in which he is, or who, having been convicted by a final judgment of a particularly serious crime, constitutes a danger to the community of that country."[293] The 1967 Protocol Relating to the Status of Refugees modified Article 33 and created a more inclusive legal standard for defining refugees.[294]

Although the principle of non-refoulement is a non-negotiable aspect of international law, states have interpreted Article 33 of the 1951 Convention in various ways, and they have constructed their legal responses to asylum seeker in corresponding manners. First, the strict interpretation holds that non-refoulement laws only apply to asylum seekers who have physically entered a state's borders. States using this interpretation often enact policies and procedures designed to block asylum seekers from reaching their borders. Second, there is a strict interpretation, with a narrow reading: This position holds that only certain refugees are legally entitled to non-refoulement protection. If the country receiving an asylum seeker does not find that their "life or freedom would be threatened" by refoulement, they can be le-

---

292 Goodwin-Gill, Guy S. "The International Law of Refugee Protection". *The Oxford Handbook of Refugee and Forced Migration Studies*. Oxford University Press, 2014. p. 39. See also League of Nations. "Convention of 28 October, 1933 relating to the International Status of Refugees."

293 Zimmermann, K ed. (2011). *The 1951 Convention Relating to the Status of Refugees and Its 1967 Protocol: a Commentary;* Article 33, para. 1. New York: Oxford University Press, 2011, pp. 1345–1346.

294 United Nations High Commissioner for Refugees. "Convention and Protocol Relating to the Status of Refugees". UNHCR.

gitimately returned to their country of origin.[295]

A third way of viewing refoulement is the collectivist approach which involves international systems designed to process the asylum claim in the country in which a person initially seek asylum and redistribute them among other countries. This approach relies on the assumption that Article 33 does not include language requiring states receiving asylum seekers to permit them to remain permanently, only an obligation not to send them back to a region in which they face likely danger. Refugee relocation agreements between countries must ensure they are not sent back by the new host country. Fourth and last there is a collectivist approach, with laws preventing asylum seekers from reaching sovereign borders: This approach is not an interpretation of Article 33, but a way around it. It combines the strict and collectivist approaches. States using this approach establish non-sovereign areas within their borders, primarily at travel hubs. Asylum seekers presenting themselves at such areas are then sent to another country to have their asylum claims processed.[296] As with traditional collectivism, the asylum seeker cannot be sent to a country in which they face likely danger.

A very fine scholar, in a series of learned articles, has reduced the principle of non-refoulement in the migration context to five key points. First, the principle of non-refoulement is found in different bodies of international law and in treaties with virtual univcersal acceptance among nations. Second, the principle of non-refoulement is applicable whenever a person falls within the jurisdiction of a State. Third, the principle of non-refoulement can protect persons fleeing armed conflicts. In recent years, human rights organizations and various national courts have made it clear that the principle also applies when States operate extraterritorially, including during interception or rescue operations in the high seas.

Fourth, the principle protects against direct and indirect measures that force a person to leave. The principle protects persons from being transferred to a state which may not itself threaten the individual, but which would not effectively protect the person against onward transfer in violation of the principle of non-refoulement. That practice

295 Trevisanut, Seline. "International Law and Practice: The Principle of Non-Re-foulement And the De-Territorialization of Border Control at Sea". *Leiden Journal of International Law.* 27: 3 (2014).

296 D'Angelo, Ellen F. "Non-Refoulement: The Search for a Consistent Interpretation of Article 33" *Vanderbilt Journal of Transnational Law.* 42: 1 (2009).

is known as indirect, chain or secondary refoulement. Fifth and last, he principle of non-refoulement requires procedural safeguards to ensure that a person is not returned to a place where he or she would be in danger of certain fundamental rights violations, essential procedural safeguards are required. Under international and regional human rights law, persons with an arguable claim that they would be returned in violation of the non-refoulement principle have the right to an effective remedy. [297]

Extradition requests issued on the basis of politically motivated prosecutions are also illegal under international law. In cases where individuals are, or may reasonably be expected to be, subjected to prosecution for their political beliefs, criticism of the authorities, or their civic, journalistic or human rights activities extradition is to be denied. In addition to illegal extraditions, cases of forced expulsion or kidnapping of persecuted persons , while commonplace, are also illegal. Such illegal actions have all too frequently been organized in cooperation with the special services of the country of origin and are carried out in secret, without complying with normal judicial procedures, by depriving persons of the opportunity to defend their interests in court. Refugees and asylum-seekers have also frequently faced surveillance and threats from the security services of the state from which they fled. International law also prohibits transfer of asylum-seekers at the stage of consideration of their application for asylum. Another reason for prohibiting extradition is the lack of guarantee of a fair trial, which butts against the traditional non-inquiry rule which presupposes fairness and equity in the judicial systems of all contracting parties.

Generally, in matters of extradition, states rely primarily on bilateral or regional legal assistance agreements rather than upon international human rights law.[298] Illegal extraditions are carried out under the pretense of allegedly protecting the interests of national security or maintaining friendly bilateral relations between states. There are

---

297 Rodenhäuser, Tilman, "Another Brick in the Wall: Carrier Sanctions and the Privatization of Immigration Control," *International Journal of Refugee Law*, 26: 2, (2014), pp. 242-45; Rodenhäuser, Tilman,"The principle of non-refoulement in the migration context," *Humanitarian Law and Policy,* 30 March 2018.See also "Note on migration and the principle of non-refoulement," *International Review of the Red Cross*, IRRC No. 904 (April 2017).

298 Zieck, Marjoleine. *UNHCR and Voluntary Repatriation of Refugees: A Legal Analysis.* The Hague: Martinus Nijhoff Publishers, 1997.

frequently objective and well-founded fears that torture, arbitrary deprivation of liberty and even death are to be the fate of the extradited
person in the country of origin. Governments or courts often do not
choose to analyze the essence of the matter, although there are obvious incidents of fabricating evidence and discriminatory actions by
the investigative body. Instead, the basis for extradition is stated in
diplomatic language expressing full confidence in the guarantees provided by the state requesting extradition.

Simultaneously, the extraditing authority is fully aware of the
worthless nature of such guarantees, as well as previous cases of their
violation, are not taken into account. Technically, those persons who
have fled from the nation seeking extradition are protected under a
wide variety of international accords, including the United Nations
sponsored Convention against Torture, the United Nations Convention
on the Status of Refugees, the European Convention on Human
Rights, the European Convention on Extradition, the European Convention on Mutual Assistance in Criminal Matters, and the International Covenant on Civil and Political Rights.[299]

Boumediene v. Bush

The U. S. Supreme Court, in its decision in *Boumediene v.
Bush*[300], of 2008, seems to be changing traditional conceptions of
sovereignty. Justice Kennedy wrote the opinion for the 5–4 majority
in this heavily divided case, holding that the prisoners held at Guantanamo, Cuba, had a right to the writ of *habeas corpus* under the United States Constitution and that the Military Commissions Act of 2006
was an unconstitutional suspension of that right. The Court applied
the Insular Cases, by the fact that the United States, by virtue of its
complete jurisdiction and control, maintains de facto sovereignty over
this territory, while Cuba retained ultimate sovereignty over the territory, to hold that the aliens detained as enemy combatants on that territory were entitled to the writ of *habeas corpus* protected in Article I,
Section 9 of the U.S. Constitution. The lower court had expressly indicated that no constitutional rights, and not merely the right to

---

299 Vang, Jerry, "Limitations of the Customary International Principle of Non-refoulement on Non-party States: Thailand Repatriates the Remaining Hmong-Lao
Regardless of International Norms". *Wisconsin International Law Journal*. 32:2
(2014), pp. 355–383.

300 *Boumediene v. Bush,* 553 U.S. 723 (2008); Chesney, Robert M. "Boumediene
V. Bush," *American Journal of International Law*, 102: 4 (2008), pp. 848-54.

habeas corpus, were extended to the Guantanamo detainees, rejecting petitioners' arguments. However, the more liberal majority of the U. S Supreme Court saw matters quite differently holding that all fundamental rights afforded by the Constitution extend to the Guantanamo detainees.

Justice Scalia wrote a scathing dissenting opinion which was joined by Chief Justice Roberts and Justices Alito and Thomas. Justice Scalia argued that "the procedures prescribed by Congress in the Detainee Treatment Act provide the essential protections that *habeas corpus* guarantees; there has thus been no suspension of the writ, and no basis exists for judicial intervention beyond what the Act allows." The commission of terrorist acts by some former prisoners at Guantanamo Bay after their release "illustrates the incredible difficulty of assessing who is and who is not an enemy combatant in a foreign theater of operations where the environment does not lend itself to rigorous evidence collection." A consequence of the Court's majority decision will be that "how to handle enemy prisoners in this war will ultimately lie with the branch [the judiciary] that knows least about the national security concerns that the subject entails."[301]

By contrast, the *Munaf* majority repeatedly stressed and relied upon Iraq's "sovereign right" or "prerogative" to punish offenses "committed on its soil." Thus, on the same day in June 2008, the Supreme Court declared both that sovereignty has changed, and that it remains the same. One might ask whether *Munaf's* conception of sovereignty was already outdated or whether it gives the lie to claims that sovereignty has eroded.[302]

Lui and Giant island, Ltd.

Jerry Lui, formerly a senior officer of the British American Tobacco Company [BAT] was charged in Hong Kong, then a British Crown Colony, with conspiring to receive and receiving millions of dollars in bribes from Giant Island Limited [GIL]. The bribes were allegedly given for a virtual monopoly on the export of certain cigarettes to the People's Republic of China and to Taiwan, Nationalist China. The Hong Kong authorities charge that GIL paid bribes in ex-

---

301 Gerald L. Neuman, Gerald L.,"The Habeas Corpus Suspension Clause after Boumediene v. Bush," *Columbia Law Review*, 110: 2 (2010), pp. 537-78.

302 Parry, John T., "International Extradition, the Rule of Non-Inquiry, and the Problem of Sovereignty" *Boston University Law Review*, 90: 1973 [2010].

cess of HK $100 million to a series of BAT executives, including Lui. Other alleged conspirators are also charged with the abduction, torture, and murder of a former GIL shareholder who cooperated with the authorities and, it is said, would have provided evidence of Lui's acceptance of bribes. Lui was away from Hong Kong on a business trip when the Hong Kong authorities sought to question him in April 1994 and he did not return to Hong Kong since, despite representations from his attorney to the authorities that he would return and consent to be interviewed within several weeks. At the request of the United Kingdom, acting on behalf of its Crown Colony, Hong Kong, the United States arrested Lui as he disembarked from a plane at Boston's Logan Airport on December 20, 1995. The arrest was for the purpose of extraditing Lui to Hong Kong to face several charges of bribery. At a December 21, 1995 hearing, the government asked that Lui be detained pending completion of the extradition proceedings. The magistrate judge ordered Lui held temporarily pending a full hearing on the motion. Lui filed a cross-motion to be released on conditions. After a hearing, the magistrate judge denied Lui's request to be released on bail. The magistrate judge found both that there were no special circumstances and there was a risk of flight.[303]

The rule of non-inquiry, like extradition procedures generally, is shaped by concerns about institutional competence and by notions of separation of powers.[304] It is not that questions about what awaits the relator in the requesting country are irrelevant to extradition; it is that there is another branch of government, which has both final say and greater discretion in these proceedings, to whom these questions are more properly addressed.[305]

In an extradition request which the U.S. made on Canada it relied on unsworn statements from law enforcement agents. The accused argued that he should not be extradited because he could be prosecuted on inherently unreliable evidence and that this would violate the Canadian Charter of Rights, section 7, the right to life, liberty, and security of the person.[306] All levels of court rejected this constitu-

---

303 *United States v Lui Kin-Hong,* also known as Jerry Lui, 83 F. 3rd 523 (1996), First Circuit. See also John Dugard, John; and Christine Van den Wyngaert, "Reconciling Extradition with Human Rights," *American Journal of International Law,* 92: 2 (1998), pp. 187-212.

304 *United States v. Smyth,* 61 F.3d 711, (9th Cir. 1995).

305 *Arnbjornsdottir-Mendler v. United States,* 721 F.2d 679, 683 (9th Cir. 1983)

306 The Canadian Charter of Rights and Freedoms (French: *La Charte canadienne*

tional objection and the accused was committed for extradition. The Supreme Court of Canada noted that the principle of comity, which includes deference, mutuality and respect, provided for a presumption that the evidence was reliable, and, as such, a fair hearing would occur.[307]

Non-foulement and Deportation

The principle of non-refoulement applies to expulsion as well as extradition. This concept figured prominently in the *Chahal* case. The Sikh activist, was to be deported from the United Kingdom. Chahal was subject of an investigation of a plot to assassinate an Indian leader during his visit to Great Britain. He was held and to be deported under the Prevention of Terrorism Act of 1984. A heavily divided English judiciary ruled that, despite assurances the Indian government offered, Chahal was very likely to be subjected to torture if expelled, and so disallowed the deportation.[308]

The European Court of Human Rights (ECHR) heard the case of *Chahal v. United Kingdom*, heard in 1996 by Chahal was an Indian national who was involved with the Sikh separatist movement. He had lived in the U. K. since the mid-1970s, before India requested extradition. He had been detained for approximately six years pending deportation to India where he claimed he was be subjected to torture or other degrading treatment. All the time he had been without adequate legal representation or judicial scrutiny, possibly because the government viewed him as an undesirable. He appealed to the ECHR which ordered that Chahal not be extradited because Article 3 of the European Convention on Human Rights afforded him protection which the Convention guaranteed irrespective of the subject's personal conduct or character. The Court also found "a violation of article 5 § 4 of the Convention (which guarantees a right of judicial

---

des droits et libertés), in Canada often simply the Charter, is a bill of rights entrenched in the Constitution of Canada. It forms the first part of the Constitution Act, 1982. The Charter guarantees certain political rights to Canadian citizens and civil rights of everyone in Canada from the policies and actions of all areas and levels of the government. It is designed to unify Canadians around a set of principles that embody those rights. The Charter was signed into law by Queen Elizabeth II of Canada on April 17, 1982, along with the rest of the Act.

307 *United States of America v Latty*, 2006 SCC 33

308 *Chahal v U.K.*, 23 EHRR 413 (1996). See also Michaelsen, Christopher, "The Renaissance of Non-Refoulement," *International and Comparative Law Quarterly*, 61: 3 (2012), pp. 750-765

review of the lawfulness of detention), so far as the domestic courts were not provided with information relating to national security and were thus unable to review whether the decision to detain the applicant was justified; the "procedural short-comings" of the United Kingdom's special advisory panel in security cases meant that it could not be considered to be a "court" for the purposes of the Convention.[309]

In the Suresh case, a native of Sri Lanka moved to Canada and sought status as a refugee. Canadaina uthorities deteremined that it was very likely that Suresh was a member of the Tamil Tigers which had fought a bitter contest against the Sri Lankan government and so sought to deport him. The Supreme Court of Canada ruled that the non-refoulement principle had not been incorportaed into the basic law of Canada. Although the nation was dedicated to protection of human rights, it also had a more basic obligation to protect itself and could deny entry to revolutionaries, even if the person expelled might be subject to torture upon return to the native nation.[310]

Non-refoulement and Repatriation

Unlike political asylum, which applies to those who can prove a well-grounded fear of persecution based on certain category of persons, non-refoulement refers to the generic repatriation of people, including refugees in war zones and other disaster locales. It is a principle of customary international law, because it applies to all nations, even to states that are not parties to the 1951 Convention Relating to the Status of Refugees as amended and amplified. It is also a principle of the law of nations. It is also probable that the non-refoulement principle is properly included as a *jus cogens*[311] of international law. If that be so, international law would not permit chnages, violations, or abridgments for any purpose and under any circumstances. In the 1960s, the European Commission on Human

---

309 *Chahal v United Kingdom,* 23 EHRR 413 (1996). See also "European Court of Human Rights Chahal v. The United Kingdom", *International Journal of Refugee Law,* 9: 1 (1997), pp. 86-121

310 *Suresh v Minister of Citizenship and Immigration of Canada,* SCR 1: 3 (2002). Bourgon, Stephane, "The Impact of Terrorism on the Principle of Non-refoulement of Refugees: The Suresh Case before the Supreme Court of Canada," *Journal of International Criminal Justice,* 1: 1, (2003), pp. 169–185.

311 *Jus Cogens:* the principles which form the norms of international law that cannot be set aside.

Rights recognized non-refoulement as a subsidiary of prohibitions on torture. As the ban on torture is *jus cogens,* this linkage rendered the prohibition on refoulement absolute and challenged the legality of refoulement for the purposes of state security.[312]

Although we may think of the non-refoulement principle would most likely apply to third world nations governed by authoritarian regimes and operating politically charged courts, the principle was tested in a case against the United States. Article 3 of the European Convention on Human Rights (ECHR) guaranteeing the right against inhuman and degrading treatment excludes the use of capital punishment whereas it is allowed within the United States.[313] Jens Soering was a German national, born in 1966, who was brought by his parents to the United States at age 11. In 1984, he was a student at the University of Virginia, where he became a friend of Elizabeth Haysom, a Canadian national. Soering and Haysom decided to kill Haysom's parents. Both were found with their throats slit and with stab and slash wounds to the neck and body.

Soering and Haysom fled to Europe; and were arrested in England, United Kingdom on other charges. The Circuit Court of Bedford County, Virginia, having indicted Soering with the capital murder of the Haysoms, the United States requested extradition for the pair, based on the 1972 extradition treaty. A warrant was issued under section 8 of the Extradition Act 1870 for the arrest of Soering, and he was committed to await the Home Secretary's order to extradite him to the United States. Authorities in Virginia communicated to the British government that they intended to seek the death penalty against Soering. Soering, having received no satisfaction from the British government or lower courts, appealed to the Judicial Committee of the House of Lords, which rejected his claim on 30 June 1988. He then appealed to the EctHR which refused to allow the extradition as long as Soering faced the possibility of execution if convicted.[314] The United States relented, promising to not try Soering for capital murder and he was extradited.[315]

---

312 Allain, Jean. 2001, "The jus cogens Nature of Non-refoulement", *International Journal of Refugee Law,* 13: 4 (2001), pp. 533-558.

313 See "Note on migration and the principle of non-refoulement," *International Review of the Red Cross,* IRRC No. 904 (April 2017).

314 *Soering v United Kingdom,* 161 Eur. Ct. H.R. (ser. A) (1989)

315 Sizemore, Bill. "No Hope for Jens Soering". *The Virginian-Pilot,* 18 February 2007. See also "Soering v United Kingdom" in Wikipedia.

By the 1980s, the European Commission on Human Rights, among others, had shifted preference away from preserving state sovereignty and towards protecting persons who might be refouled. This interpretation permitted no abridgments of non-refoulement protections, even if the state was concerned a refugee may be a terrorist or pose other immediate threats to the state. [316]

The principle of non-refoulement arose from the collective memory of the failure of nations during World War II to provide a safe haven to refugees fleeing certain genocide at the hands of the Nazi regime. Following World War II, the need for international checks on state sovereignty over refugees became apparent to the international community. During the war, several states had forcibly returned or denied admission to German and French Jews.[317] In the past U.S. courts have occasionally refused to consider the threat of persecution, extreme forms of punishment, or other humanitarian concerns as a bar to extradition. A glaring example of non-inquiry into the threat of persecution is the case of one Normano. In his case, the District Court of Massachusetts refused to take judicial cognizance of the potential abuse that Normano, a Jew, might suffer at the hands of Nazi Germany during the 1930s.[318]

The Allies had also returned to communist Russia a considerable number of Soviet citizens who had opposed Stalinist practices and sought protection in the West. The non-refoulement doctrine presents an inherent conflict with state sovereignty, as it infringes on a state's right to exercise control over its own borders and those who reside within them. In legal proceedings immediately following World War II, non-refoulement was viewed as a distinct right which could be abridged under certain circumstances, such as those spelled out in Article 3, Section 2 of the 1951 Convention.[319]

---

316 Padmanabhan, Vijay. "To Transfer or not to Transfer: Identifying and Protecting Relevant Human Rights Interests in Non-Refoulement". *Fordham Law Review,* 80 (2011), pp. 73–123.

317 See, for example, Gross, Daniel A. "The U.S. Government Turned Away Thousands of Jewish Refugees," *Smithsonian Magazine*, 18 November 2015; Between the Nazi rise to power in 1933 and Nazi Germany's surrender in 1945, more than 340,000 Jews emigrated from Germany and Austria. Tragically, nearly 100,000 of them found refuge in countries subsequently conquered by Germany. German authorities would deport and kill the vast majority of them. "Refugees: in *Holocaust Encyclopedia.*

318 *In re Normano,* 7 F. Supp. 329 (D. Mass. 1934)

319 Cossacks, ethnic Russians and Ukrainians who took up arms against the Soviet

As a result of various terrorist attacks in the United States and Europe, many modern states have renewed calls for rejecting modern interpretations of refoulement in the interest of national security. They see repatriation as one of the most effective methods of removing refugees who are seen as presenting a credible threat to national security. Additionally, newer treaties typically include specific obligations that prevent refoulement under essentially any circumstances. These factors have led individual states and the European Union to seek ways around non-refoulement protections that balance security and human rights.[320]

Union, were handed over by British and American forces to the Soviet Union after the Second World War. "Repatriation of Cossacks after World War II" in Wikipedia. See also Naumenko, General V. G. *Great Betrayal.* William Dritschilo, trans. 2 vols. All Slavic Publishing House, (2011-18).

320 Bruin, Rene and Wouters, Kees (2003). "Terrorism and the Non-derogability of Non-refoulement". *International Journal of Refugee Law.* 15.1 (2003), pp. 5–29. See also von Sternberg, Mark R., "The Evolving Law of Non-Refoulement," *In Defense of the Alien,* 24 (2001), pp. 205-23; Michaelsen, Christopher, "The Renaissance of Non-refoulement?" *International and Comparative Law Quarterly,* 61: 3 (2012), pp. ,750-65.

The Non-inquiry Rule

The "rule of non-inquiry," is a judicial construct under which courts hearing extradition cases may not inquire into the procedures or treatment, including possible physical torture, that may await the extraditee in the requesting state. The "rule of non-inquiry," is a judicial concept under which courts hearing extradition cases may not inquire into the procedures or treatment, including possible physical abuse, that await the extraditee in the requesting state.[321] More than just a principle of treaty construction, the rule of non-inquiry tightly limits the appropriate scope of judicial analysis in an extradition proceeding.[322] The rule of non-inquiry, like extradition procedures generally, is shaped by concerns about institutional competence and by notions of separation of powers.[323] The rule has become more flexible with the passage of time and the introduction of the principle of non-refoulement. The rule of non-inquiry seems to need to incorporate some of the many changes in international law that have taken place since the non-refoulement rule was first enunciated.[324]

A major principle which guides courts in matters concerning extradition is the rule of non-inquiry. More than just a principle of treaty construction, the rule of non-inquiry tightly limits the appropriate scope of judicial analysis in an extradition proceeding. Under the rule of non-inquiry, courts refrain from "investigating the fairness of a requesting nation's justice system,"[325] and from inquiring "into the procedures or treatment which await a surrendered fugitive in the requesting country."[326] Various international extradition treaties oblige the United States to surrender to a foreign country such persons as have been charged with, or convicted of, an offense in the requesting nation. Many foreign criminal justice systems lack the substantive rights and procedural safeguards embodied in American law, there ex-

---

321 Parry, John T. "International Extradition, the Rule of Non-Inquiry, and the Problem of Sovereignty," *Boston University Law Review*, 90 (2010),pp. 1073-2073, Lewis & Clark Law School Legal Studies Research 2010-4.

322 *Arnbjornsdottir-Mendler v. United States*, 721 F.2d 679, 683 (9th Cir. 1983).

323 See *United States v. Smyth,* [*111] 61 F.3d 711, 714 (9th Cir. 1995)

324 Parry, John T. "International Extradition, the Rule of Non-Inquiry, and the Problem of Sovereignty," *Boston University Law Review,* 90 (1973-74), pp. 1973-2073.

325*United States vs. Kin-Hong,* 520 U.S. 1206 (1997).

326*Arnbjornsdottir-Mendler v. United States,* 721 F.2d 679, 683 (9th Cir. 1983)

ists a natural tension in which the treaty obligation are in conflict with the rights of the individual whose extradition has been requested. Under the established "rule of non-inquiry," the court determining whether a defendant is extraditable may not examine the requesting country's criminal justice system or take into account the possibility that the defendant will be mistreated, tortured, or denied a fair trial in that country.

The rule of non-inquiry, like extradition procedures generally, is shaped by concerns about institutional competence and by notions of separation of powers.[327] Traditionally, the non-inquiry rule bars the courts from denying extradition even when it is clear that the relator will be the victim of torture or cruel and inhumane treatment. Torture and inhumane treatment have always been a widespread problem in many countries. Modern interpretation of such international rules as prevention of torture treaties have called into question the application of the non-inquiry rule.[328] A defendant who anticipates unfair or abusive treatment following extradition may seek relief on that ground only from the Secretary of State, who has discretion to deny the extradition request.' In the United States and several other nations this power enables the Secretary of State or his foreign equivalent to condition extradition upon assurances from the requesting country that the defendant will receive a fair trial and will not be mistreated.[329]

It has generally been held that the rule of non-inquiry arose by implication, originating in the fact that the U. S. Supreme Court did enumerate all procedures which will occur in the demanding country subsequent to extradition. The Supreme Court stressed the narrowness of *habeas corpus* in general and of extradition *habeas* in particular, and this narrow approach would be consistent with the subsequent non-inquiry doctrine. The earliest federal court cases made no mention of possible conditions awaiting subjects who may be extradited once they arrived at the custody of the requesting party.[330]

Although the concept of *habeas corpus* has evolved consider-

---

327 See *United States v. Smyth,* 61 F.3d 711, 714 (9th Cir. 1995). n11

328 Quigley, John, "The Rule of Non-Inquiry and the Impact of Human Rights on Extradition Law," *North Carolina Journal of International Law,* 15 (1990), pp. 401-39.

329 Semmelman, Jacques, "Federal Courts the Constitution and the Rule of Non-Inquiry in International Extradition Proceedings," *Cornell Law Review,* 76: 6 (1991), pp. 1198-1241.

330 *falina Gallina v. Fraser,* 278 F.2d 77, 79 (2d Cir. 1960).

ably since first noted in Supreme Court decisions, there has been little change in application of the non-inquiry doctrine. In reporting decisions, some courts cite the rule in cases that do not raise non-inquiry issues at all. The courts simply mention the rule as part of a general discussion of extradition or while discussing other issues. Such discussions of non-inquiry in these cases could easily be dispensed with, yet courts sometimes cite them as authority for a broad rule. There is little doubt that in some non-inquiry cases the courts do justice by examining the motives of the requesting country. Not uncommonly, the reality behind the claim of a crime is that the requesting country is seeking to punish the relator for political activities and that the specific crimes for which extradition is sought are mere subterfuges.[331]

There are several common, but important, reasons subjects seek court intervention to prevent extradition. A significant number of non-inquiry cases involve complaints about the ordinary criminal process in the requesting country, such as the use of *in absentia* proceedings or the lack of a jury trial. Courts hear many complaints about conditions of confinement. Such claims usually turn on the length of the potential sentence in the requesting country, not on assertions that the treatment meted out in the foreign prison will be harsh or coercive. There is no question that many foreign courts mete out much harsher sentences for some crimes than do, say, American courts. The largest, category of non-inquiry cases involves claims that the extraditee's physical safety is at risk on return to the requesting country. These cases put the greatest pressure on the non-inquiry doctrine, for it is obviously one thing to return a person to a country with different procedures from the United States, and quite another thing to send him back to certain mistreatment or death. Yet courts rather consistently reject claims in these cases as consistently as they do for those in the other categories.

Ordinarily, American courts do not examine a foreign government's motives for seeking extradition or the fairness of a foreign judicial system. A clear example of the application of the non-inquiry rule was *In re Sindona* , a case in which Italy had applied for the extradition from the United States to Italy of Michele Sindona, William J. Arico, a/k/a "Robert McGovern" and Robert Venetucci. Arico died

---

331 Semmelman, Jacques, "Federal Courts, the Constitution, and the Rule of Non-inquiry in International Extradition Proceedings," *Cornell Law Review*, 76: 6 (1991), pp. 199-1241.

on February 19, 1984, while attempting to escape from the Metropolitan Correction Center where he was detained.

Sindona argued that his extradition should be denied because he would not receive a fair trial in Italy. He submitted affidavits swearing that he would likely be assassinated if extradited to Italy and that he could not obtain a fair trial. He also offered press excerpts which, he argued, indicated he would not be provided with a fair trial. The District Court for the Southern District of New York observed that only the Secretary of State could deny extradition for those reasons:

> The general rule is that an argument of this kind is not properly addressed to the court in the extradition hearing, but must be made to the Department of State, which has the primary responsibility for determining whether the treaties with foreign countries are being properly respected and carried out. The Department of State has the discretion to deny extradition on humanitarian grounds, if it should appear that it would be unsafe to surrender Sindona to the Italian authorities."[332]

The rule of non-inquiry bars the courts from denying extradition even when it seems to be clear that the relator will be the victim of torture or cruel and inhumane treatment. Torture and inhumane treatment have been used quite frequently in many of the nations of the world. There is universal condemnation of the use of torture as witness the existence of treaty law. credible claims of torture exist against more than one-third of the world's governments. Torture has been used, and is still employed, to extract information, suppress ideas, or simply torment persons perceived as enemies.[333]

Neely Case
Charles F. W. Neely was a public employee, specifically the finance agent of the department of posts in the city of Havana, Island of Cuba. On 6 May 1900 he had charge of the collection and deposit of moneys of the department of posts of the said city of Havana, and did unlawfully and feloniously take and embezzle from the public funds of the said island of Cuba the sum of $10,000 and more, being then

332 *In re Sindona,* 450 F. Supp. 672 (S.D.N.Y. 1978).

333 The United Nations Convention against Torture and Other Cruel, Inhuman or Degrading Treatment or Punishment (UNCAT, 1984). See Nowak, Manfred; Birk, Moritz; and Monina, Giuliana. *United Nations Convention against Torture and its Optional Protocol: A Commentary.* Oxford University Press, 2019.

and there moneys and funds which had come into his charge and under his control in his capacity as such public employee and finance agent, as aforesaid, and by reason of his said office and employment, thereby violating the Penal Code of the said island of Cuba, by committing embezzlement of the public funds committed by public officers. In *Neely v. Henkel*, the Supreme Court refused to consider the procedures awaiting an extraditee that might violate the extraditee's basic rights. In *Neely,* the person being extradited to Cuba argued that if surrendered he would be tried under Cuban procedure, which provided for no jury trial, no *habeas corpus* protection, and no protection against bills of attainder or *ex post facto* laws. Rejecting this argument, the Supreme Court said that although the enumerated protections were not available in Cuban courts, the person could, nonetheless, be found extraditable. The Court stated that an extraditee is not entitled to "a trial in any other mode than that allowed to its own people by the country whose laws he has violated and from whose justice he has fled.'" Federal courts follow the approach taken in Neely even if the extraditee refers not to the general mode of trial in the requesting state, but to facts suggesting that he, in particular, may be treated unfairly.

Traditionally, extradition has been an executive function, rather than a judicial one. This claim, in turn, suggests an additional rule, known as the "rule of non-inquiry," under which courts hearing extradition cases may not inquire into the procedures or treatment, including possible physical abuse, that may await the person being extradited in the requesting state. Historically, the rule of non-inquiry has relied on a traditional notion of national, territorial sovereignty.[334]

The U. S. Supreme Court first applied the rule of non-inquiry in the 1901 decision in *Neely v. Henkel*.[335] Writing the opinion of the court, Justice Harlan ordered the extradition of Neely to Cuba pursuant to statutory law, declaring, "When an American citizen commits a crime in a foreign country he cannot complain if required to submit to such modes of trial and to such punishment as the laws of that

---

334 Maaskamp, Vanessa, "Extradition and Life Imprisonment," *Loyola of Los Angeles International and Comparative Law Review,* 25: 3 (2003), pp. 741-66.

335 *Neely v. Henkel* (No. 1), 180 U.S. 109 (1901). On the same day, the Court decided a companion case "[f]or the reasons stated in the opinion just delivered." *Neely v. Henkel* (No. 2), 180 U.S. 126 (1901). See "Habeas Corpus. Jurisdiction. District Court Has Jurisdiction to Issue Writ Although Petitioners Are Confined in Foreign Country," *Harvard Law Review,* 63: 3 (1950), pp. 531-34.

country may prescribe for its own people, unless a different mode be provided by treaty stipulation between that country and the United States." In his appeal, Neely had claimed that the statute authorizing his extradition was unconstitutional because it would allow his surrender to another country for trial without "all of the rights, privileges and immunities that are guaranteed by the Constitution," including *habeas corpus* and trial by jury. The Court rejected that assertion, writing that "those provisions have no relation to crimes committed without the jurisdiction of the United States against the laws of a foreign country."[336] No doubt the U. S. military occupation of Cuba was an important factor in the court's decision.

In its opinion, the high court wrote that constitutional due process guarantees are inapplicable to trials in foreign states for crimes committed outside the United States:

> [These] provisions have no relation to the crimes committed without the jurisdiction of the United States against the laws of a foreign country. In connection with the above proposition, we are reminded of the fact that the appellant is a citizen of the United States. But such citizenship does not . . . entitle him to demand, of right, a trial in any other mode than that allowed to its own people by the country whose laws he has violated and from whose justice he has fled.[337]

The Supreme Court decided another extradition case involving the rule of non-inquiry, *Glucksman v. Henkel*. Russia had requested extradition of Glucksman for fraud and theft. A merchant named Birenzweig, a merchant, alleged that Leiba Glucksman, a merchant in Lodz, in June 1906, endorsed over to him in payment for goods a note for 100 rubles, purporting to have been drawn by a merchant named Tugendreich, who resides in Ozorkov. Soon after, he learned that Glikeman had departed, and that the note was spurious. Fraidenreich, another merchant, made a similar claim, both giving the name of Mosche-Leiba Tugendreich as the one who created the note. For his part, Moschek Leib Jakubov Maerov Tugendreich, a merchant in Ozorkov, claimed that he never drew any notes in Glucksman's favor, and that the signatures on the notes were fraudulent, although he had had dealings with Glucksman.[338]

---

336 *Neely v. Henkel* (No. 2), 180 U.S. 126 at 126.

337 *Neely v. Henkel* (No. 1), 180 U.S. 109 at 122-23.

338 "Habeas Corpus. Jurisdiction. District Court Has Jurisdiction to Issue Writ Although Petitioners Are Confined in Foreign Country," *Harvard Law Review*, 63:

The attorney for Glucksman, the alleged fugitive, argued: "This is an extraordinary proceeding and before a person within the jurisdiction of the United States is to be deprived of his liberty and sent four thousand miles away as a prisoner to stand trial upon a criminal charge the greatest caution should be exercised." He also contended "[t]he papers in this case show that the real purpose of this proceeding is not the forgery charge, but that it had been instituted by creditors as a matter of personal spite, malice and vengeance." [339]

Glucksman did not directly challenge the nature of the criminal proceeding in Russia or the prospective treatment he might receive. However, Justice Oliver Wendell Holmes, writing on behalf of the unanimous Court, did raise the issue, writing, "We are bound by the existence of an extradition treaty to assume that the trial will be fair."[340]

In October and November, 1918, the British consul general at New Orleans filed with the District Judge of the United States for the Eastern District of Louisiana, three separate affidavits, each charging that Charles Glen Collins, who was then within the jurisdiction of that court, had committed at Bombay, India, the crime of obtaining property under false pretenses. Collins stood charged in the Magistrate's Court at Bombay, then under British control. The consul asked that Collins be committed as a fugitive from justice for the purpose of having him returned to India for trial. Warrants of arrest issued, and Collins moved, as to each affidavit, to dismiss for want of jurisdiction, contending that the transactions in question were commercial dealings in which he had merely failed to pay debts incurred. After the hearings were concluded, Judge Foster made two orders or judgment in which he found that the evidence sufficient to sustain the charge under the law and the treaty, and as to each he ordered Collins recommitted to the House of Detention in the custody of the United States marshal for that district. Collins appealed, alleging that his detention was illegal and in violation of rights secured to him by the treaty, because, among other reasons, he he had been refused permission to introduce evidence at the hearings. The U.S. Supreme Court dismissed

3 (1950), pp. 531-53.

339 *Glucksman v Henkel*, 221 U. S. 508 (1911). See Levitan, David M., "Constitutional Developments in the Control of Foreign Affairs: A Quest for Democratic Control," *Journal of Politics*, 7: 1 (1945), pp. 58-92.

340 *Glucksman v Henkel*, 221 U. S. 508 at 511.

Collins' suit and allowed his deportation.[341]

On 29 January 1901 the United States and Peru had signed a treaty allowing mutual extradition. Garcia-Guillern, once Minister of Education in Peru, had been charged with embezzlement and Peru asked that he be extradited. In *Garcia-Guillern v. United States*, the Fifth Circuit observed that it was not "permitted to inquire into the procedure which awaits the appellant upon his return" to Peru.[342] On December 8, 1977, the Government of Mexico, pursuant to the United States-Mexico Extradition Treaty of 1899, requested extradition of two United States citizens, Gaspar Eugenio Jimenez Escobedo and Gustavo Castillo, for prosecution on charges of murder, attempted murder, and attempted kidnapping. In the case of *Escobedo v. United States,* Mexico sought the accused's extradition specifically on the charges of attempted kidnapping of the Cuban consul and a related murder. The Fifth Circuit refused to entertain the accused's objections to the Mexican criminal proceedings despite the fact that his confession may have been obtained by means of torture.[343]

In the case of *Peroff v. Hylton*, the Fourth Circuit was asked to consider the accused's claim that he would be an assassinated should he be returned to a Swedish prison. Peroff was charged with participation in a fraudulent scheme whereby relatively worthless shares of stock in a company called "American International Distributors, Inc.," represented to be stock of the "American International Development Corporation," were furnished as collateral for loans made to Peroff by Swedish citizens which loans were not repaid. In *Peroff,* the court offered the opinion that "[a] denial of extradition by the Executive may be appropriate when strong humanitarian grounds are present, but such grounds exist only when it appears that, if extradited, the individual will be persecuted, not prosecuted, or subjected to grave injustice."[344]

341*Collins v. Miller,* 252 U.S. 364 (1920). See "Appeal and Error: Finality of Segmentary Judgment Where Several Distinct Claims for Relief Are Joined in a Single Suit," *California Law Review,* 31: 1 (1942), pp. 90-95. Case discussed in "International Law. Power of American Courts to Question Validity of Confiscatory Acts of Nazi Officials in Germany," *Virginia Law Review,* 34: 3 (1948), pp. 356-58.

342 *Garcia-Guillern v. United States*, 450 F.2d 1189, 1192 (5th Cir. 1971), cert. denied, 405 U.S. 989 (1972).

343 *Escobedo v. United States,* 623 F.2d 1098, (5th Cir.), cert. denied, 449 U.S. 1036 (1980)

344 *Peroff v. Hylton*, 542 F.2d 1247, 1249 (4th Cir. 1976), cert. denied, 429 U.S.

Samuel Shapiro and a partner had run an investment scheme in Israel for which his partner was arrested, tried and convicted. Israel now sought the extradition of Shapiro to stand trial for the same offenses. Judge Motley of the District Court for the Southern District of New York, signed the warrant pursuant to which Shapiro was arrested at his home in Brooklyn and was brought before Judge Pollack of the Southern District. Shapiro contended that the complaint and warrant for his arrest issued by Judge Motley failed to explicitly state that he was "found" within the Southern District of New York.[345] The Court dismissed that contention as being without merit since the law calls only for a complaint under oath stating that the person sought has committed within the jurisdiction of the requesting country a crime covered by a treaty. His attack upon the validity of his arrest based upon a complaint and a warrant he insisted were defective was rejected. In "seeking a warrant in the Southern District . . ." said the court, "the government was acting on a good faith."[346]

In 1989 in the District Court for the eastern district of New York, Mahmoud El-Abed Ahmad sought a writ of *habeas corpus*[347] to prevent his extradition to Israel to stand trial. Israel alleged that on April 12, 1986, Ahmad attacked a passenger bus with firebombs and automatic weapons fire, causing the death of the bus driver and serious injury to a passenger. Ahmad had become a naturalized United States citizen, although he was formerly a resident of the West Bank. He allegedly fled before he could be apprehended, although his two alleged accomplices were convicted in Israel and sentenced to life imprisonment for their admitted participation in the planning and execution of the attack. In sworn statements, the co-conspirators implicated petitioner and described their mutual membership in the Abu Nidal Organization, an international terrorist group. That group had publicly announced its responsibility immediately following the attack. A year later petitioner was located in Venezuela where officials detained him

---

1062 (1977). See also Evans, Alona E.; M. Cheríf Bassiouni; William S. Kenney; and Sharon A. Williams, "International Procedures for the Apprehension and Rendition of Fugitive Offenders," *Proceedings* of the Annual Meeting of the American Society of International Law, 74 (1980), pp. 274-89.

345 *Samuel Shapiro v Thomas E. Ferrandina*, United States Marshal for the Southern District of New York, 478 F.2d 894 (2d Cir. 1973).

346 *Shapiro v. Ferrandina*, 478 F.2d at 899. See also Evans, Alona E., "Shapiro v. Ferrandina," *American Journal of International Law*, 68: 1 (1974), pp. 127-29.

347 28 U.S.C. § 2241

because of suspected activities there on behalf of the Abu Nidal Organization. Venezuela had no extradition treaty with Israel. The Venezuelan authorities advised the United States that they were going to expel Ahmad. Venezuela placed him on a commercial airline flight from Caracas to the United States, during which flight FBI agents executed a warrant for the provisional arrest of petitioner.[348]

Claiming that torture and inhuman and degrading treatment awaited him if he was deported to Israel, Ahmad sought to avoid extradition on humanitarian grounds. In denying Ahmad's request, the Second Circuit declared: "A consideration of the procedures that will or may occur in the requesting country is not within the purview of a *habeas corpus* judge. . . . It is the function of the Secretary of State to determine whether extradition should be denied on humanitarian grounds."[349]

For its part, the U. S. government relied heavily upon *Hirota v. MacArthur* (1948),[350] a case in which the Supreme Court found it lacked original jurisdiction over citizens of Japan being held by the Allied Powers for the Tokyo War Crimes Tribunal because "the tribunal sentencing [the petitioners] [was] not a tribunal of the United States." In *Munaf* and its companion case of *Omar v. Harvey*[351] the Supreme Court wrote, "it is for the political branches, not the judiciary, to assess practices in foreign countries and to determine national policy in light of those assessments."

The U. S. Supreme Court ruled in *Munaf* that the Constitution does not grant extradition for military transferees such as the Iraquis a *habeas corpus* or due process right to judicial review of conditions in the receiving country before they are transferred. It also refused to consider the likelihood of Iraq employing torture or other forbidden degrading instruments. Persons facing extradition traditionally have not been able to maintain *habeas* claims to block transfer based on conditions in the receiving country. Rather, applying the rule of noninquiry, courts historically have refused to inquire into conditions an extradited individual might face in the receiving country. In *Munaf,* the Supreme Court reaffirmed this precise point, stating "we have rec-

---

348 *Ahmad v. Wigen*, 726 F. Supp. 389 (E.D.N.Y. 1989). See also "Can Israel Try a Palestinian Fairly? Case to Be Argued in Federal Court," *Jewish Telegraphic Agency,* 28 July 1989.

349 *Ahmad v. Wigen,* 726 F. Supp. 389 (1989)

350 *Hirota v. MacArthur,* 338 U.S. 197 (1948)

351 *Omar v. Harvey,* 416 F. Supp. 2d 19, 23-28 (D.D.C.2006)

ognized that it is for the political branches, not the Judiciary, to assess practices in foreign countries."

Throughout history, the Supreme Court wrote, military transferees traditionally have not been able to raise *habeas* claims to prevent transfer based on conditions in the receiving country. Since the Founding, the United States has routinely transferred wartime detainees at the end of hostilities or as part of an exchange, without judicial review of conditions the transferees would face in the other nation. In another case[352] the Supreme Court explained that negotiated exchange of prisoners was "a wartime practice well known to the Framers," and "[j]udicial intervention might have complicated" those negotiations.

The Gallina Rule

An Italian named Gallina had been tried and convicted *in absentia* for robbery. In his extradition hearing he claimed that this was not an ordinary crime, but a political act since he was attempting to raise money for a separatist movement in Sicily. Both the district court and the appellate court ruled that the fact that a person tried and convicted *in absentia* would be imprisoned immediately upon return had no bearing on the extradition. The treaty in force allowed extradition of one already tried   and found guilty. The courts also dismissed the claim of political exemption to extradition was without judicial merit.[353]

In the *Gallina* case, the Second Circuit court suggested the possibility of the recognition of exceptions to the rule of non-inquiry. As we saw, Vincenzo Gallina was denied *habeas corpus* relief despite the fact that he would be imprisoned in Italy without an opportunity to defend himself. The court followed the rule of non-inquiry, but in dicta the court noted that "we can imagine situations where the relator, upon extradition, would be subject to procedures or punishment so antipathetic to a federal court's sense of decency as to require re-examination of the rule of non-inquiry The was suggesting that, in at least some situations, a court could inquire into the potential treatment a relator would receive in the requesting country and deny extradition

---

352 *Boumediene .3d 509, 519–20 & n.6 (D. C. Cir.2009) (Kavanaugh, J., concurring).v. Bush,*553 U.S. 723, 747–48 (2008); see also *Kiyemba v. Obama* ("Kiyemba II"), 561 F

353 *Gallina v. Fraser,* 278 F.2d 77, 79 (2d Cir. 1960). See also "Foreign Trials in Absentia," *Stanford Law Review,* 13: 2 (1961), pp. 370-378.

where the relator would be subjected to inhumane treatment or punishment.[354]

Jan Starks was a member of the United States Air Force (USAF) stationed in China who was arrested at a Chinese residence in Taiwan. The charge made against him stemmed from the discovery of a quantity of marijuana and opium on the premises. Starks was to be transferred to Chinese authorities under an executive agreement. It is clear that Starks' alleged misconduct did not arise in the performance of his official duties. Under the status of forces agreement between the United States and the Republic of China, China retained its right to exercise criminal jurisdiction in this type of case. Upon Starks' conviction, the United States was obliged to surrender custody of him to Chinese authorities.[355]

The Eastern District Court of Wisconsin found that Stark's trial was a mockery of justice and that the executive agreement had therefore been breached. The court granted the temporary restraining order. Although the court based its decision on the breach of the executive agreement, the court quoted the *Gallina* precedent, stating, "failure to grant a temporary restraining order in this matter would result in a 'punishment . . . antipathetic to a federal court's sense of decency." Although the temporary restraining order was issued, Stark's motion for dismissal was denied.[356]

The *Gallina* dicta recognized a significant humanitarian concern for the fate of the subject. It also provided the judiciary with a possible, although limited, exception to the non-inquiry rule. While courts have repeatedly held that such inquiry is the exclusive province of the political branches of government, especially the Secretary of State, nonetheless several courts have at the same time referred to the *Gallina* precedent.[357]

---

354 Sullivan, David B., "Abandoning the Rule of Non-Inquiry in International Extradition," *Hastings International and Comparative Law Review*, 15: 1 (1991), pp. 111-33.

355 *Jan Starks, Plaintiff, v. Robert C. Seamans,* Secretary of the Air Force of the United States, Defendant, 339 F.Supp. 1200 (1972).

356 *Starks v. Seamans,* 334 F. Supp. 1255 (E.D. Wisc. 1971).

357 For example: *Demjanjuk v. Petrovsky,* 776 F.2d 571, 583 (6th Cir. 1985); *Prushinowski v. Samples,* 734 F.2d 1016, 1019 (4th Cir. 1984); *Sindona v. Grant,* 619 F.2d 167, 174 (2d Cir. 1980); *Peroff v. Hylton,* 542 F.2d 1247, 1249 (4th Cir., 1976) cert. denied, 429 U.S. 1062 (1977); *United States ex. rel. Bloomfield v. Gengler,* 507 F.2d 925, 928 (2d Cir. 1974), cert. denied, 421 U.S. 1001; and *Ambjornstdottir-Mendler v. United States,* 721 F.2d 679, 683 (9th Cir. 1983). See

Acts of Terrorism

Cases involving the commission of acts of terrorism appear to constitute an exception to the non-inquiry rule. Dannie W. McMullen had used a false Republic of Ireland passport to enter the United States in early 1978. He was arrested by the Immigration and Naturalization Service (INS) on May 19, 1978, charged with unlawful entry. While in the custody of the INS, McMullen made certain statements to INS investigators regarding his membership in the Provisional Irish Republican Army (PIRA), and his participation in a bombing attack at a British Army barracks in Belfast, Northern Ireland.[358] McMullen provided additional information when he was interviewed by agents of the Federal Bureau of Investigation and officials of the British New Scotland Yard. He again admitted to his participation in the bombing attack at Belfast and also admitted planning and participating in a PIRA sponsored attack at Claro Army Barracks at Ripon, England in 1974.[359]

On June 20, 1978, a Justice of the Peace in Ripon, County of North Yorkshire, England, issued a warrant for McMullen's arrest on two counts of attempted murder and other crimes arising out of the bombing of the Claro Barracks. The United Kingdom thereafter filed a request for the extradition of McMullen. In July of 1978 the United States filed a formal request for McMullen's extradition. Deportation proceedings, previously commenced by the INS to deport McMullen for illegal entry into the United States, were held in abeyance pending the extradition proceeding.[360]

The United States District Court for the Northern District of California held a hearing on the extradition request. He found that McMullen was a member of the PIRA at the time of the Ripon bombing and that the PIRA was then engaged in a political uprising against the British. Because McMullen's crimes were committed at the behest

also Sullivan, David B., "Abandoning the Rule of Non-Inquiry in International Extradition," *Hastings International and Comparative Law Review,* 15: 1 (1991), pp. 111-33.

358 Matter of McMullen In Deportation Proceedings A-23054818 Decided by Board October 1, 1980. Matter of McMullen (justice.gov)

359 "Political Legitimacy in the Law of Political Asylum," *Harvard Law Review,* 99: 2 (1985), pp. 450-71. Se also Hannay, William M., "An Analysis of the U. S.-U. K. Supplementary Extradition Treaty," *International Lawyer,* 21: 3 (1987), pp. 925-37.

360 *In re McMullen,* 989 F.2d 603, 610 (2d Cir. 1993).

of the PIRA and in furtherance of its political objectives, the Magistrate Judge concluded that the crimes in question were encompassed by the political offense exception of the 1977 Treaty, and therefore denied the extradition request.

Deportation hearings then resumed, and McMullen conceded that he had illegally entered the U. S., but requested asylum in the United States, thus preventing deportation to the Republic of Ireland. The immigration judge granted both forms of relief, but that decision was reversed by the Board of Immigration Appeals. The Ninth Circuit held that the Board's decision was not supported by substantial evidence.[361] On remand, the Board again denied the application for asylum, planning still to deport McMullen. On McMullen's second petition to the Ninth Circuit for review, the court agreed with the Board that McMullen was statutorily ineligible for withholding of deportation because there was substantial reason to believe that he had committed serious nonpolitical offenses. The court further held that the Board properly had denied McMullen's application for asylum.[362]

Sweden was confronted with a problem in regard to Ahmed Agiza, an Egyptian citizen who had been charged with being a member of the Islamic Jihad and with being minimally involved through an uncle in the plot to assassinate President Anwar Sadat. Sente nced in abs entia to twenty-five years at hard labor, he had sought asylum in Sweden. The Swedish Migration Board recommended granting asylum, but the government, concerned with acts of terrorism, refused to accept that recommendadion and ordered him to be expelled even though his sentence was almost certainly in violation of human rights standards.[363]

Flexibility in Non-inquiry Rule

As we have seen, extradition is primarily an executive function, rather than a judicial one. This assertion suggests additional rules, notably the "rule of non-inquiry," under which courts hearing extradition cases may not inquire into the procedures or treatment, in-

361 *McMullen v. INS*, 658 F.2d 1312 (9th Cir.1981).

362 *McMullen v. INS*, 788 F.2d 591, 598 (9th Cir.1986). See also Lubet, Steven; and Morris Czackes, "The Role of the American Judiciary in the Extradition of Political Terrorists," *Journal of Criminal Law and Criminology*, 71: 3 (1980), pp. 193-210.

363 Agiza v Sweden, Committee against Torture, communication 1416 of 2005, cited in Michaelsen, *op. cit.* at 755.

cluding possible physical abuse, that await the extraditee in the requesting state. This major principle that guides courts in matters concerning extradition is the rule of non-inquiry. More than just a principle of treaty construction, the rule of non-inquiry tightly limits the appropriate scope of judicial analysis in an extradition proceeding.[364] Under the rule of non-inquiry, courts refrain from investigating the fairness of a requesting nation's justice system, and from inquiring "into the procedures or treatment which await a surrendered fugitivein the requesting country. [365]

The non-inquiry rule is more flexible than courts often purport to believe. Courts can choose to take a more explicitly functional approach which would better serve the issues than the non-inquiry doctrine encompasses and implicates. Traditionally, the rule of non-inquiry's relies upon a static and historical notion of national territorial sovereignty.

When a foreign state approaches U.S. officials and asks for the extradition to its territory of a person it suspects of violating its laws, the Secretary of State makes the final decision whether to surrender the person. Initially, however, a federal magistrate rules on whether the person is extraditable. Only if the magistrate so rules does the matter proceed to the Secretary of State for review.

Occasionally, the person whose surrender is sought asserts that the authorities of the requesting state will torture him, or subject him to some other violation of basic human rights. The response of the magistrate is likely to be that the potential ill-treatment is irrelevant to a finding of extraditability. The federal courts follow the "rule of non-inquiry," which provides that the magistrate does not inquire into the claim of anticipated ill-treatment. Rather, this issue of inquiry is left to the Secretary of State, who may consider potential ill-treatment in deciding whether to surrender the person.[366]

---

364 Parry, John T. "International Extradition: The Rule of Non-Inquiry and the Problem of Sovereignty" *Boston University Law Review*, 90: 1973, (2010).

365 *United States v Lui Kin-Hong*, also known as Lerry lui, 83 F. 3rd 523 (1996), First Circuit.

366 See *Neely v. Henkel*, 180 U.S. 109 (1901) (declaring an act constitutional) although it does not secure rights to an accused in a foreign land); *Koskotas v. Roche*, 931 F.2d 169 (1st Cir. 1991) (reasoning that the rule of non-inquiry precluded the court from inquiring into the motives of foreign government); *Ahmad v. Wigen*, 910 F.2d 1063 (2d Cir. 1990) (holding that the courts will consider only whether the alleged offender's crimes fall within the extradition treaty).

Munaf v Geren

The Multinational Force-Iraq (MNF-I) was an international coalition military unit operating in Iraq which was composed of soldiers from 26 different nations, including the United States. The force operated under the unified command of United States military officers, and served at the request of the Iraqi government, and in accordance with United Nations (U. N.) Security Council Resolutions. Pursuant to the U. N. mandate, MNF-I forces detained individuals who were alleged to have committed hostile or warlike acts in Iraq, pending investigation and prosecution in Iraqi courts under Iraqi law. These consolidated cases concern the availability of *habeas corpus* relief arising from the MNF-I's detention of American citizens who voluntarily traveled to Iraq and are alleged to have committed crimes there.

The U. S. Supreme Court was confronted with two questions. First, do United States courts have jurisdiction over *habeas corpus* petitions filed on behalf of American citizens challenging their detention in Iraq by the MNF-I? Second, if such jurisdiction exists, may district courts exercise that jurisdiction to enjoin the MNF-I from transferring such individuals to Iraqi custody or allowing them to be tried before Iraqi courts? The high court concluded that the *habeas statute* extends to American citizens held overseas by American forces operating subject to an American chain of command, even when those forces are acting as part of a multinational coalition. Under circumstances such as those presented here, however, *habeas corpus* provided petitioners with no relief.

In its 2008 decision in *Munaf v. Geren*[367], for example, the Supreme Court applied this rule to the transfer of two U.S. citizens from U.S. military custody to Iraqi custody for trial in Iraqi courts. In response to their claim that they were likely to be tortured in Iraqi custody, the Court stated that "it is for the political branches, not the judiciary, to assess practices in foreign countries and to determine national policy in light of those assessments."[368]

The United States Supreme Court invoked this rule its 2008 decision in *Munaf v. Geren*,[369] regarding the transfer of two U.S. citi-

---

367 *Munaf v. Geren,* 553 U.S. 674 (2008)

368 Sherman, Mark,"Americans Held in Iraq Get Day in Court," *Washington Post,*
    25 March 2008.

369 *Munaf v. Geren, 553 U.S. 674 (2008)*

zens from U.S. military custody to Iraqi custody for trial in Iraqi courts. In response to their claim that they were likely to be tortured in Iraqi custody, the Court stated that "it is for the political branches, not the judiciary, to assess practices in foreign countries and to determine national policy in light of those assessments." The high court unanimously concluded that the *habeas corpus* statute[370] extends to U.S. citizens held overseas by American forces subject to an American chain of command, even if acting as part of a multinational coalition. But, it found that *habeas corpus* provided the petitioners with no relief, holding that "*Habeas corpus* does not require the United States to shelter such fugitives from the criminal justice system of the sovereign with authority to prosecute them." The case dealt specifically with the appeals from Mohammad Munaf and Shawqi Ahmad Omar, both naturalized citizens of the United States held by American, forces in Iraq. In its arguments, the United States government relied heavily upon *Hirota v. MacArthur,*[371] a case in which the Supreme Court found it lacked original jurisdiction over citizens of Japan being held by the Allied Powers for the Tokyo War Crimes Tribunal because "the tribunal sentencing [the petitioners] [was] not a tribunal of the United States."

One recent author has argued for great inclusion of *habeas corpus* review of extradition decisions. He has sought the unfreezing extradition law and putting it back into the overall structure of federal law and the current of legal change. The rule of non-inquiry would work within, and seek to incorporate, some of the many changes in international law that have taken place since the rule was first announced. Ultimately he argued that there are more than sufficient grounds to contest the notion that foreign affairs concerns require courts to refuse to inquire into constitutional or human rights claims.[372]

Perspectives

One of the major judicial tasks of the future will be to develop a way to balance two opposing concepts. Under the one, a defendant is absolutely entitled to fair and humane treatment is the domestic

---

370 28 U.S.C. § 2241(c)(1)

371 *Hirota v MacArthur,* 338 U.S. 1997 (1948)

372 White, Josh, "U.S. Citizen Sentenced To Death In Iraq," *Washington Post,* 14 October 2006; White, Josh, "U.S. Citizen Sentenced to Death in Iraq Loses Appeal," *Washington Post,* 7 April 2007.

courts of the nation which has requested his extradition. On the other hand, nations are bound to honor various national treaty obligations in the course of foreign relations concerns. How to balance one against the other is a most delicate matter. These competing interests have been effectively reconciled by conferring exclusive responsibility for safeguarding the defendant's rights to the the political branches, not the courts. Allowing a defendant to challenge the fairness of the requesting country's investigative, legal, and penal systems in a United States court requires a doctrinally problematic expansion of the scope of constitutional protection which could undermine important foreign policy concerns, and would entail undesirable, if not impermissible, judicial interference in foreign affairs. For its part, efforts made by the Congress to enact legislation eliminating the rule of non-inquiry have been unsuccessful. Unless and until such legislation is enacted, the rule of non-inquiry seems to have retained the greater judicial attention.[373]

Several recent law review articles, symposia, and forums have suggested that the rule of non-inquiry should be discarded and replaced by a rule more sensitive to humanitarian concerns.[374] Under new rules, courts would allow inquiry when the alleged offender presents evidence of treatment in the requesting state which is "antipathetic to a federal court's sense of decency."[375] This standard would return to that which was first suggested in 1960, in dicta by the Second Circuit in *Gallina v. Fraser,* and has occasionally been recognized by many other courts.[376]

The non-inquiry rule has had its staunch defenders, none more so than Steven Lubet, Professor of Law at Northwestern University. He stated that inquiries forbidden by the rule are inextricably tied to the formulation and conduct of foreign policy and any erosion of the rule by the judiciary would be an encroachment upon the executive's prerogative in foreign affairs. Moreover, he suggested that a foreign nation may only request extradition pursuant to a valid treaty which has been negotiated and executed by the President and ratified by a two-thirds majority of the

---

373 Semmelman, *op. cit.* at 1241.

374 See, for example, Sullivan, David B., "Abandoning the Rule of Non-Inquiry in International Extradition," *Hastings International and Comparative Law Review,* 15: 1 (1991), pp. 111-33.

375 *Gallina v. Fraser,* 278 F.2d 77, 79 (2d Cir. 1960)

376 For example, the *Gallina* dicta was excised by the Second Circuit in *Ahmad v. Wigen,* 910 F.2d 1063 (2d Cir. 1990).

Senate, which translates to a political decision which had been made previously concerning the appropriateness of extradition.[377] Too, despite offering its opinion on human rights considerations, the Second Circuit did explicitly reject any inquiry, acknowledging that it has always been improper for courts to inquire into the conditions a relator may face upon extradition.[378]

---

377 Reform of the Extradition Laws of the United States: Hearings on H.R. 2643 Before Subcomm. on Crime of the House Comm. on the Judiciary, 98th Cong., 1st Sess. 93-97 (1983), pp. 84- 96.

378 *Ahmad v. Wiger*, 910 F.2d 1063 (2d Cir. 1990). See also Sullivan, David B., "Abandoning the Rule of Non-Inquiry in International Extradition," *Hastings International and Comparative Law Review*, 15: 1 (1991), pp. 111-33 at 120-22.

Illegal Seizure

Ordinarily, return of fugitives is a matter of law covered by the terms of extradition treaties.[379] Most such treaties view illegal seizure as essentially kidnapping and prohibit this action. There have been exceptions, especially in earlier international court cases. In the real world of politics, states frequently have successfully attempted to bypass the process either by abducting a fugitive in foreign territory or by bringing the fugitive into the their jurisdiction by deceit or fraud. The abduction is sometimes carried out by official operatives of the states, or by those who are otherwise unaffiliated but who are paid in some way. The most interesting and significant aspect of state-sponsored abduction lies in the fact that the abduction or fraud is consummated by the offending State's own authorities in the territory of the state of refuge. Such action not only violates the sovereignty of the state of refuge, but also breeches various international engagements which may exist between the offending and the asylum states, and also flaunts the international order as expressed in the law of nations.[380]

As a result of clearly established international law, added to the specific language of treaties, we may draw two conclusions which largely operate as a restriction upon the freedom of action of the sov-

---

379 See *Third Restatement of the Foreign Relations Law of the United States,* ch. 7, sub ch. B, Extradition, Introductory Note, at 557 (1987) ("it is accepted that states are not required to extradite except as obligated to do so by treaty"); Wharton, Francis, *A Treatise on the Conflict of Laws, or Private International Law,* § 941, at 597-98 (Philadelphia 1872) ("it has been maintained by high authority, both in Europe and the United States, that the duty of one sovereign to surrender to another fugitives from justice has no basis in international law, and only exists when created by treaty between the two sovereigns concerned. . . . This view['s] . . . chief support has been found in the United States."); Wheaton, Henry, Elements of International Law, 111, (Philadelphia 1836) ("No sovereign state is bound, unless by special compact, to deliver up persons, whether its own subjects or foreigners, charged with or convicted of crimes committed in another country, upon the demand of a foreign state or its officers of justice."). McNair, Lord, *The Law of Treaties,* 333 (1961, reissued 1986) (British Government also "has, at any rate for a very long time, maintained that the surrender of an alleged criminal or an escaped convict cannot, as a matter of international law, be claimed in the absence of a treaty creating an obligation to do so.").

380 O'Higgins, Paul, "Unlawful Seizure and Irregular Extradition," *Brigham Young International Law Review,* 36: 280 (1960).

ereign states involved.[381] First, the determination of the asylum State as to the extradition of the fugitive is by no means dependent upon the exercise of arbitrary discretion on its part. The discretion of the State of refuge must be exercised in conformity with conventional and general international law.[382] Second, regarding the state making the extradition request, it should also be perfectly clear that its jurisdiction over the fugitive is conditioned upon the manner in which such jurisdiction was acquired. This is purely a matter of State competence and the latter is unmistakably regulated by the law of nations, at least in respect to matters in which the interests of other Sates are vitally involved. The result of these two propositions is that neither the asylum nor the requesting state is legally authorized to depart in any way from the forms upon which an agreement has been reached.[383]

Courts in various sovereign states have arrived at very different conclusions about their power to try defendants who were kidnapped from other states, especially if effected by officials of the prosecuting state. In English-speaking nations, especially in the United Kingdom and the United States, the general rule established, beginning with common law, has confirmed the court's power to exercise jurisdiction over the kidnapped individual. There has been substantial challenge mounted in more recent years against this traditional rule in both judicial rulings and academic publications. Concern for the rights of the kidnapped individual, desire to maintain the integrity of the sovereignty of the asylum state, and respect for the rule of law in international affairs, have all had a great bearing on some judicial systems, prompting some to refrain from exercising jurisdiction over a kidnapped defendant.[384]

An early case of extralegal securing of a prisoner occurred in 1889. The governor of California had requested the extradition of a subject from Japan. The U. S. State Department refused to assist be-

---

381 Preuss, Lawrence, "Kidnapping of Fugitives from Justice on Foreign Territory," *American Journal of International Law*, 29: 502 (1935).

382 Scott, Austin W., Jr. "Criminal Jurisdiction of a State over a Defendant Based upon Presence Secured by Force or Fraud". *Minnesota Law Review*. 37: 91. (1953).

383 Garcia-Mora, Manuel R. (1957) "Criminal Jurisdiction of a State Over Fugitives Brought From a Foreign Country By Force or Fraud: A Comparative Study," *Indiana Law Journal*, 32 : 4 (1957), Article 1.

384 Selleck, Kathryn, "Jurisdiction after International Kidnapping" A Comparative Study," *Boston College International and Comparative Law Review*, 8: 1 (1985), article 9.

cause there was, at that time, no treaty of extradition between the United States and Japan. The governor chose to obtain the subject in another way. Following the abduction, Pratt appealed his capture and subsequent trial. The California state Supreme Court ruled that, although the governor's action w as "probably illegal" the courts retained jurisdiction and the conviction stood.[385]

In 1957 the ninth federal circuit court heard a case that held that illegal actions by foreign authorities did not void return of a fugitive. Wentz and Jensen were indicted and convicted as a consequence of a fraudulent scheme wherein Frank X. and Selma Pommer were the victims, losing at least $24,000. It became a federal case because the defendants had arranged the scam using interstate wire services, a Western Union telegraph. Having fled to Mexico, the pair eluded Mexican authorities seeking to extradite them, but they were eventually arrested by local Mexican police and returned to the United States. Defendants Wentz and Jensen sought to void the arrest, principally on the ground that Mexico had violated their civil rights.

He alleged that he was seized and detained by Mexican authorities and he was at all times denied an attorney. No legal proceedings were ever held for him in Mexico. He was transported by automobile by unknown persons from Mexico City through Nuevo Laredo, Mexico, to Laredo, Texas, where he was turned over to "certain agents of the United States government." He requested the indictment be dismissed because of lack of personal jurisdiction, which lack purportedly arose out of the events related above. The court ruled that Jensen's counsel misstated the record facts when in his brief he says, "Personal jurisdiction of appellant was acquired by the federal court through the illegal acts of federal officers." No illegal act of a United States officer were related by Jensen. In the affidavit no action of officers of the United States begins before the defendant is brought to them in the United States. Therefore, the charge, if true, must be that the defendant was denied "due process" in Mexico by Mexicans. If true, that it was of no legal concern of an American court. [386]

In 1974, in *United States v. Toscanino*, the defendant Toscanino was accused of intent to smuggle narcotics into the United States. He was forcibly abducted from Italy and taken back to America. He

---

385 *Pratt v. California*, 78 Cal. 345 (1889).
386 *Wentz v United States*, 244 F 2d 172 (9th circuit, 1957). certiorari denied 355 U.S. 806 (1957).

was abducted from his home in Montevideo, Uruguay on January 6, 1973, by members of the Uruguayan police, who were disguised as guerrilla fighters. This group then crossed the border into Brazil where the defendant was lodged in a prison cell in the City of Porto Alegre, having been turned over to the Brazilian police. Next, he was then taken to a prison in Brazilia where he was alternately interrogated and tortured and was then taken to an office where "high police or army officials" were present, and he was then told that they had made a mistake. These unknown officials advised him that he could not return to Uruguay, but that he could return to Italy, but he was sedated and flown to the United States in the company of two Brazilian policemen.

When he arrived in the United States, he was placed in the custody of special agents of the Drug Enforcement Administration.[387] Once in American custody, authorities tortured him, through electrocution, starvation, and flushing his eyes and nose with alcohol. The court found that this case was something that provides "shocks of conscience." Moreover, the actions of U.S. "seems grossly unjust to the observer." When abduction in and by foreign authorities is accompanied by major aggressive and torturous action, as it did for Toscanino, then it does in fact go against due process of law, and the person must be released irrespective of the horrid nature of his crimes.[388] The Toscanino case focused on the violation of the individual defendant's due process rights when that person is kidnapped by U. S. officials or agents on the territory of a foreign state.[389]

A companion case to *Toscanino* involved an organized under-

---

387 *U. S. v Toscanino*, 398 F. Supp. 916 (1975, E.D.N,Y,). "Constitutional Law. Criminal Law. A Federal Court Lacks Jurisdiction over a Criminal Defendant Brought into the District by Forcible Abduction; The Fourth Amendment Protects an Alien Residing Abroad against Unreasonable Searches and Seizures Conducted by American Agents. United States v. Toscanino, 500 F. 2d 267 (2d Cir. 1974)," *Harvard Law Review,* 88: 4 (1975), pp. 813-82.

388 *U. S. v Toscanino,* 500 F. 2d 267; Evans, Alona E., "United States v. Toscanino. 500 F.2d 267," *American Journal of International Law,* 69: 2 (1975), pp. 406-41; Hunter, Roszell Dulany, IV, "The Extraterritorial Application of the Constitution. Unalienable Rights?" *Virginia Law Review,* 72: 3 (1986), pp. 649-76.

389 Reid, Herbert O., "Interstate Rendition and Illegal Return of Fugitives". *Howard Law Journal* 2: 76 (1956). See also Ross, Barry, "The Forcible Abduction of a Criminal Defendant from a Foreign State Precludes a Federal Court's Acceptance of Jurisdiction," *Brooklyn Journal of International Law,* 1: 1 (1975), pp. 86-100.

world conspiracy to import massive quantities of heroin into the United States, and American agents kidnapping the leading perpetrators from South America to bring them to trial.[390] A grand jury in the Eastern District of New York indicted Lujan and eight others in 1973, charging them with conspiracy to import and distribute a large quantity of heroin. The conspiracy was wide-ranging, involving acts in many nations including France, Brazil, Uruguay, Peru, Mexico, and the United States, and the quantities of heroin involved were enormous. Arrest warrants were issued for all defendants. In the Second Circuit in *United States ex reI. Gengler v. Lujan*[391] found that a simple abduction by U.S. officials does not in itself oblige the court to return the defendant to his *status quo ante* .

The court noted that it required little argument to show that the government conduct of which Lujan complained pales by comparison with what he did and planned to do in the future. Lacking from Lujan's petition is any allegation of that complex of shocking governmental conduct sufficient to convert an abduction which is simply illegal into one which sinks to a violation of due process. Lujan did not allege that a gun blow knocked him unconscious when he was first taken into captivity, nor did he claim that drugs were administered to subdue him for the flight to the United States. Neither is there any assertion that the United States Attorney was aware of his abduction, or of any interrogation following the abduction. Indeed, Lujan disclaimed any acts of torture, terror, or custodial interrogation of any kind.[392]

Jaffe Land Fraud Case

In August 1980 the State of Florida charged Sidney Jaffe with twenty-eight violations of its state law regarding the sale of land. Accredited Surety and Casualty Company posted $137,500 bond for Jaffe. For his part, Jaffe fled to Canada and did not appear for trial in May 1981. In November 1981 the trial jury convicted Jaffe *in absentia* of all twenty-eight charges and added the additional charge of fail-

390 Note "Pirates and Smugglers: Analysis of the Use of Abductions to Bring Drug Traffickers to Trial," *Virginia Journal of International Law*, 32: 233 (1991).

391 *U. S. ex rel Gengler v Lujan*, 510 F.2d 62 (2d Cir.), cert. denied, 421 U.S. 1001 (1975).

392 Evans, Alona E., "United States ex rel. Lujan v. Gengler. 510 F.2d 62. U.S. Court of Appeals, 2d Cir., Jan. 8, 1975," online by Cambridge University Press, 28 March 2017.

ing to appear. Florida State Attorney denied two applications for extradition, based in part on the improper form of the requests, and in part because violations of Florida's Land Sales Act were not among charges for which extradition could be effected under the 1971 U.S.-Canada Extradition Treaty. The bonding company faced the loss of the $137,500 by forfeiture. An agreement was reached which placed the money in an escrow account while allowing the bonding firm an additional ninety days to produce Jaffe.

The bonding company assigned one of its employees to work with a professional bounty hunter to abduct Jaffe and bring him to Florida. They were successful, arresting Jaffe in his apartment in Toronto. They sequestered him in the back of an automobile, drove him to Niagara Falls, New York, and all three flew to Florida.[393] Canada lodged immediate complaints for this illegal abduction. A Florida jury convicted Jaffe, and the judge sentenced him to thirty-five years of imprisonment. He remained free on bail while appealing his sentence. The appeal was successful and the verdict overturned. Although the State Attorney refiled charges of organized fraud, Jaffe again fled to Canada, but retained lawyers to sue the bonding company, its employees, the State of Florida, and the bounty hunter.[394]

Canada now sought the extradition of the two men who had kidnapped Jaffe based on Canada's anti-kidnapping statute. Applicable U.S. Law held that a bail surety cannot exercise the power to seize a fugitive outside the United States.[395] The defendants argued that American anti-kidnapping law would not apply to a Canadian bounty hunter abducting a fugitive in the United States, and the extradition treaty required that, to be extraditable, an offense must be recognized by both nations. The court rejected that argument and extradited both men who were then tried in Canada and convicted and sentenced to twenty-one months in prison.[396] The Canadian trial judged sternly warned American bounty hunters to stay out of Canada. The Americans lost their appeal when the Ontario appeals court ruled that "they were without authority when they seized Jaffe and took him out of Canada." In an act of kindness, however, the appeals court reduced their sentences to time served, noting that Canadian justice had been

---

393 *Jaffe v Boyles*, 616 F. Supp 1371 (W.D.N.Y., 1985).

394 "Canadian Refuses to Face Florida Trial" *Los Angeles Times*, 16 April 1985.

395 Determined in *Reese v United States*, 76 U. S. (9 Wall.) 13 (1869).

396 "Canada Sentences Two for Seizing Businessman" *New York Times*, 10 June 1986; *Los Angeles Times*, 11 June 1986.

well served by establishing that the sovereign nation would not allow random acts of abduction, even for apparent good cause. The appellate court also noted that the two convicted men were otherwise of high moral character while Jaffe was viewed in the opposite way.[397]

The Jaffe case showed that should private citizens, including bondsmen and professional bounty hunters, commit kidnapping in a foreign land, courts of the offended nation may exercise personal jurisdiction over the abductee and those committing kidnapping may be extradited to stand trial for what is undoubtedly a major offense under that nation's municipal law. Bail bondsmen and bounty hunters are legally viewed as private persons when operating abroad and enjoy absolutely no special protection or legal protection outside the United States. Should a subject flee abroad, bondsmen and bounty hunters are restricted to using moral suasion and extradition to recover the fleeing person.[398]

Alvarez-Machain

In February 1985 Mexican drug lords ordered the kidnapping of Enrique Camarena-Salazar, an agent of the U. S. Drug Enforcement Agency (DEA) who had been assigned to do undercover work. Camarena was brutally tortured and finally executed. DEA agent Hector Berrellez and others investigated and eventually obtained an indictment against some twenty-two drug lords, including Verdugo Urquidez and Alvarez Machain, a gynecologist from Guadalajara. Having little trouble arresting Verdugo with the assistance of Mexican police, DEA prosecuted him on charges relating to the sale and distribution of illegal drugs as well as Camarena's murder. Verdugo was sentenced to life imprisonment and four consecutive forty year terms. Eventually, there was some considerable question as to whether DEA had actively participated in the abduction of Verdugo, which had allegedly been carried out freely by Mexican authorities. The other suspect in the murder, Javier Vasquez Velasco, was arrested for his alleged involvement in the murder, convicted, and sentenced to three life sentences.[399]

397 *Queen v Near*, number 498/66, 1989; Ontario Appeals Court, 18 October 1989.
398 *Taylor v Taintor*, 83 U. S. (16 Wall.) 366 (1873). "When bail is given, the principal is regarded as delivered to the custody of his sureties" who have the power to seize defendants anywhere in the United States.
399 See Carlisle, Jeffrey J. "Extradition of Government Agents as a Municipal Law Remedy for State Sponsored Kidnappers," *California Law Review*, 81 (1993),

Rene Martin Verdugo-Urquidez, was a Mexican citizen who was alleged to be a drug-lord who was involved in the torture and murder of DEA agent Enrique Camarena Salazar. With the assistance of Mexican police, Verdugo was arrested and forcibly brought to the United States. The DEA searched the defendant's home after receiving authorization from the Mexican authorities. The agents found documents it believed to show his shipments of drugs to the United States. When the government sought to introduce these documents as evidence in court, the defendant objected, asserting that they were obtained without a warrant, and therefore could not constitutionally be used at trial. The United States District Court agreed, and invoked the exclusionary rule to suppress the documents. The government appealed this ruling, which was affirmed by the Court of Appeals for the Ninth Circuit. The government then appealed to the Supreme Court.[400]

The Supreme Court held that the Fourth Amendment's prohibition against unreasonable searches and seizures did not apply since DEA agents had searched and seized property located in a foreign country which was owned by a nonresident alien in the United States. Chief Justice Rehnquist authored the opinion for the Court, joined by Justices White, Scalia, Kennedy and O'Connor. They contended that "the people" intended to be protected by the Fourth Amendment were the people of the United States, and that the defendant's "legal but involuntary presence" on U.S. Soil, a direct result of his arrest and transport to the United States, failed to create a sufficient relationship with the U.S. to allow him to call upon the Constitution for protection.[401]

DEA unsuccessfully negotiated for some time with Mexico for the arrest and deportation of Alvarez, so Berrellez obtained the permission of his superiors to abduct Alvarez. A DEA informant, Bustamante, formerly an associate in a drug ring, located Alvarez and on 2 April 1990 several armed Mexicans kidnapped Alvarez from his medical office and, with additional assistance, moved him by airplane to El Paso, Texas, where they turned him over to DEA agents.[402] For

---

1541-86.

400 Shenon, Philip, "U.S. Says It Won't Return Mexican Doctor Linked to Drug Killing," *New York Times*, 21 April 1990.

401 *United States v. Verdugo-Urquidez,* 494 U.S. 259 (1990)

402 According to the post on Wikipedia, it actually was, a man named Trent Tompkins of Claysville, Pennsylvania, a paid private citizen in the employ of DEA, actually abducted Alvarez from Mexico.

their part the Mexicans received $20,000 and seven of the kidnappers and their families were brought to the United States for protection, which cost the DEA another $6000 per week. [403] There was no question that the torture of Camarena had been both prolonged and extensive, such as a trained physician would have been able to augment and assist.

Coddling its drug lords[404], and demanding respect for its territorial sovereignty, Mexico launched a series of diplomatic protests, culminating in a demand for the extradition to Mexico of Berrellez and Bustamante. Mexico specifically charged the United States with several violations, notably the kidnapping of Alvarez Machain, of the extradition treaty in place between Mexico and the United States.[405] In May 1990 the Mexican embassy in Washington sent a formal request to the U.S. State Department demanding to know the extent of American involvement in the Alvarez abduction. Largely ignoring the Mexican protestations, the U. S. Attorney General's office proceeded with the prosecution of Alvarez Machain.[406]

The District Court on hearing Alvarez's case agreed with the Mexican position, that indeed DEA had violated the letter of the U. S.-Mexico extradition treaty. Noting that the court was troubled with the apparent involvement in the abduction, at least its monetary payments to Mexicans, it ordered an evidentiary hearing. It warned that, should the court find that the Mexicans were not acting on their own initiative, but only acting as paid agents of DEA, it would order the release of Alvarez Machain and his return to Mexico.[407] The Ninth Circuit Court affirmed the lower court's reading of the treaty obligations as applied to the rights of the accused. Its opinion may have been in-

403 Lowenfeld, Andreas F. "Kidnapping by Government Order," *American Journal of International Law*, 84: 3 (1990).

404 See Nadelmann, Ethan E. "The DEA in Latin America: Dealing with Institutionalized Corruption," *Journal of Interamerican Studies and World Affairs*, 29: 4 (1987-1988), pp. 1-39.

405 U. S. Treaties 31: 5059.

406 Gonzalez, Guadalupe and Tienda, Marta, eds. *The Drug Connection in U.S.-Mexican Relations*. San Diego: Bilateral Commission on the Future of U.S.-Mexican Relations, 1989. This work contains several articles that bear on the impact of the Alvarez ker case.

407 *U. S. v Caro-Quintero,* 745 F. Supp 604.United States v. Caro-Quintero, et aL, 745 F. Supp. 599, 610 (C.D. Cal. 1990) (Rafeedie, J.). Although captioned by the name of the lead defendant in the pending indictment, this opinion deals solely with defendant Humberto Alvarez-Machain.

fluenced in part by *amici curiae* briefs submitted by both Mexico and Canada.[408]

The government appealed its case to the U. S. Supreme Court. It threw out the judgment of the lower courts, holding that there was nothing in the U.S.-Mexico extradition treaty that prevented or precluded abduction. Likewise, there was nothing in that treaty that indicated that extradition was the sold and exclusive way to obtain a person under indictment in the United States. The high court claimed that *Ker* had granted it the power to exercise jurisdiction in cases of forcible abduction, unless there was a violation of a valid treaty in force. It readily conceded that this abduction may well have constituted a clear violation of the law of nations, but nonetheless allowed the abduction to stand.[409] The Supreme Court returned the case to trial court where in December 1992 the presiding judge dismissed it for lack of evidence.[410]

The matter was not over. The courts had warned that Alvarez might seek civil damages, which he did, suing under the Alien Tort Statute (ATS). Although winning initially in the lower federal courts, in June 2004, the Supreme Court unanimously ruled that ATS did not create a separate ground of suit for violations of the law of nations. Instead, that act was intended only to give courts jurisdiction over violations accepted by the civilized world and defined acts such as piracy, violations of rights of ambassadors, and safe conducts. Because Alvarez-Machain's claim did not fall into one of the traditional categories, it was not permitted.[411] The Court ruled that the arrest had taken place outside the United States and so was exempted from the Act. The Court rejected Alvarez-Machain's argument that the exemption should not apply because the arrest had been planned in the United States.[412]

The Alvarez Machain case demonstrated that, should govern-

---

408 *U. S. v Alvarez Machain,* 946 F. 2d 1466 (9th Circuit, 1991).

409 *U. S. v Alvarez Machain,* 12 S Ct 2193 (1992)

410 For a detailed discussion of the wide variety of opposing judicial opinions see Lowenfeld, Andreas F. "Still More on Kidnapping," *American Journal of International Law,* 85: 4 (1991), pp. 2503-62.

411 Wedgwood, Ruth, "The Argument against International Abduction of Criminal Defendants," *American University International Law Review,* 6: 4 (2011), pp 537-69; Bush, Jonathan A., "How Did We Get Here? Foreign Abduction after Alvarez-Machain," *Stanford Law Review,* 45: 4 (1993), pp. 939-83.

412 *Sosa v. Alvarez-Machain,* 542 U.S. 692 (2004).

mental agencies abduct a defendant from a foreign land, courts of the offended nation may exercise personal jurisdiction over the abductee. The same is true if the kidnappers are merely at-will employees, contracted to do a job for the governmental agency. It is improbable that governmental agents will be extradited , to stand trial for what is undoubtedly a major offense; and it is unlikely that the contractors will ever be extradited to stand trial for kidnapping.[413]

Judicial Kidnapping Elsewhere

British courts have generally permitted the abduction of fleeing accused persons in foreign nations, even when the government agents or police were directly involved in the kidnapping.[414] It joins the United States in refusing to question the circumstances of extradition. [415] In 1865 an American police officer kidnapped an American national from England. In an opinion of the Law Officers of the Crown the justices suggested that the British government should not challenge this abduction, but should bring it to the attention of the United States government through diplomatic channels.[416] Likewise, the United Kingdom saw no problem with the American abduction of a British subject by his creditors. Perhaps, the court reasoned, a complaint might be issued for domestic assault, but ignoring the situation was the better policy.[417]

Before World War II, French courts had not allowed the abduction on foreign soil of persons wanted by the judicial system. In a case where French police had kidnapped a Belgian citizen in Belgium in order to prosecute him in French courts, the court ordered the defendant to be released.[418] The court ruled that an arrest in foreign terri-

---

413 Halberstam, Malvina, "In Defense of the Supreme Court Decision in Alvarez-Machain," American *Journal of International Law*, 86: 4 (1992), pp. 736-46; Wilske, Stephan and Schiller, Teresa (1998) "Jurisdiction over Persons Abducted in Violation of International Law in the Aftermath of United States v. Alvarez-Machain," *The University of Chicago Law School Roundtable*, 5: 1, (1998) Article 8, pp. 205-41.

414 Evans, "Acquisition of Custody over the International Fugitive Offender, Alternatives to Extradition: A Survey of United States Practice," *British Yearbook of International Law* (1966), 40: 77.

415 *Ex parte Elliott*, All E. R. 1: 373 (King's Bench, 1949).

416 *British Digest of International Law, 1860-1914* (1985), 5: 480-81

417 *British Digest of International Law, 1860-1914* (1965), 6: 482-83

418 *In re Joils*, (1933) in *Annotated Digest and Reports of Public International Law Cases, 1933-34*, p. 191.

tory had no legal effect. This position changed after World War II.

The most notorious example of kidnapping to bring a suspect to trial by state officials in France involved a would-be assassin, Antoine Argoud (1914 –2004). He was a French Army officer who specialized in counter-insurgency during the Algerian War of Independence (1954-1962). Argoud's opposition to Algerian independence from France impelled him to join the *Organisation armée secrète* (OAS) and support for its use of violence in opposition to this policy. He was twice placed on trial for attempting to assassinate French President Charles de Gaulle (1890-1970). He was convicted *in absentia* in the first trial. On February 25, 1963, when Argoud was hiding in Munich, following a failed assassination attempt on de Gaulle, he was kidnapped by French secret police (CRS) agents at the Eden-Wolff hotel. Smuggled to France, he he was interrogated, almost certainly with the use of intense torture. He eventually broke under questioning and provided information that led to the arrest the other would-be assassins. The French court ruled that such an abduction "although it engages the responsibility, even criminal responsibility, of those who committed it, is not of such a character as to involve nullifying prosecution."[419] Convicted of attempted murder/assassination in the second trial, he was sentenced to life imprisonment, but released as part of a general amnesty in 1968.[420]

One of the more bizarre cases of kidnapping from a foreign nation for the purpose of prosecution involved an Egyptian national, Mordecai Luk. Egypt attempted to smuggle him out of Italy in a trunk after kidnapping him. As a result, Italy expelled two Egyptian diplomats who were involved. Lu, reportedly a double agent, serving both Egypt and Israel, escaped to Israel, where he was arrested for desertion from the army.[421]

The Eichmann Case

Without a doubt, the most famous, perhaps notorious, case of abduction in order to prosecute a fleeing criminal is that of Adolf Eichmann in Israel.[422] It is absolutely not our position to discount

---

419 45 I. L. R. 97. See also "Antoine Argoud" in Wikipedia.

420 Cocastre-Zilgien, André *L'affaire Argoud. Considérations sur les arrestations internationalement irrégulières,* Pédone, 1965; I. L. R. 45: 90-98

421 *New York Times,* 18 November 1964; also in the *New York Times* on 19 November and 25 November 1964.

422 *Attorney General of Israel v Eichmann,* I. L. R. 36: 18 pp 78-079 (District

Eichmann's many crimes nor to minimize their effect. The sole question is the legality of his kidnapping and whether Israel had the legal right to prosecute after the abduction. It is a simple fact of law that many, perhaps most, litigants whose names are attached to prosecutions in the area of criminal law are most undesirable persons.

Most authorities agree that Israel had a right under the universality principle of international law to try Eichmann, even though Israel did not exist until 1948, at least three years after his acts had been committed. The universality principle allows for the assertion of jurisdiction in cases where the alleged crime may be prosecuted by all states, acts such as war crimes, crimes against the peace, crimes against humanity, slavery, and piracy. Universal jurisdiction authorizes all states and international organizations to claim criminal jurisdiction over an accused person regardless of where the alleged crime was committed, and irrespective of the accused's nationality, country of residence, or any other relation with the prosecuting entity. Crimes prosecuted under universal jurisdiction are considered crimes against all, too serious to tolerate jurisdictional arbitrage.

After fleeing from Germany, following the defeat of Nazism, Eichmann had emigrated to Argentina where he lived under an assumed name, but rather openly otherwise, having apparently acquired Argentine citizenship. Argentina had accepted many former Nazi officials and routinely rejected requests for their extradition. Once Mossad[423] operatives had identified Eichmann, Israel Prime Minister David Ben Gurion (1886-1973) personally approved the abduction. The Mossad team captured Eichmann on 11 May 1960 near his home in San Fernando, near Buenos Aires. A Mossad agent, Peter Malkin asked him in Spanish if he had a moment. Eichmann, suspecting something was amiss, became frightened and attempted to leave, but two more Mossad men appeared suddenly and the three wrestled Eichmann to the ground and, after a struggle, moved him to a car where they hid him on the floor under a blanket.[424]

Mossad took Eichmann to one of the safe houses that they had

Court of Jerusalem, 1961); affirmed, I. L. R. 36: 277 (Supreme Court of Israel, 1962).

423 Mossad, short for HaMossad leModi'in uleTafkidim Meyuḥadim meaning "Institute for Intelligence and Special Operations"), is the national intelligence agency of Israel.

424 "Attorney General v. Adolf Eichmann". International Crimes Database (2013). See also "Adolf Eichmann" in Wikipedia.

set up by the team, holding him there for nine day. During that time they confirmed Eichmann's identity and interrogated him concerning the location of other Nazis they believed were hiding in Argentina. Having learned what they could, and fearing discovery, about midnight on 20 May, and Israeli physician sedated Eichmann and dressed him as a flight attendant and smuggled him out of Argentina.[425]

Argentina immediately protested the illegal abduction of one of its citizens as well as violation of its national sovereignty. [426] It also expected better cooperation from the United Nations on the matter of kidnapping as a crime under international law.[427]

Following nine months of intensive interrogation, yielding 3500 pages of transcript, Eichmann was brought to trial before a special tribunal of the Jerusalem District Court, beginning on 11 April 1961. The legal basis of the charges against Eichmann was the 1950 Nazi and Nazi Collaborators (Punishment) Law. He was indicted on fifteen criminal charges, including crimes against humanity, war crimes, crimes against the Jewish people, and membership in a criminal organization. Israeli law had to be modified in order to allow Eichmann to retain a non-Israeli defense counsel. It took fifty-six days for the prosecution to present its case, which included testimony by 112 witnesses.

For his part, Eichmann argued that he was a non-decision maker who merely followed orders. Because he had sworn an oath of loyalty, he felt obliged to follow even those he found to be abhorrent. The orders, he asserted, could not be challenged, following under the rule of acts of state.[428]

The trial adjourned on 14 August, and the court rendered its verdict on 12 December. It convicted Eichmann of fifteen counts of crimes against humanity, war crimes, crimes against the Jewish people, and membership in a criminal organizations. Interestingly, it

---

425 Bascomb, Neal. *Hunting Eichmann: How a Band of Survivors and a Young Spy Agency Chased Down the World's Most Notorious Nazi*. Boston; New York: Houghton Mifflin Harcourt, 2009.

426 *New York Times,* 22 May 1960. Reported in most international newspapers of that date.

427 15 U. N. Sco, U. N. doc. S/4349

428 Knappmann, Edward W. "The Adolf Eichmann Trial, 1961," in *Great World Trials*. Detroit: Gale Research, 1997. See also Birn, Ruth Bettina (2011). "Fifty Years After: A Critical Look at the Eichmann Trial," *Case Western Reserve Journal of International Law.* 44 (2011), pp. 443–473

found not guilty of personally killing anyone and not guilty of over-seeing and controlling the activities of the *Einsatzgruppen*. He was found to be responsible for the inhumane conditions on board the deportation trains and for gathering up Jews to fill those trains. In addition to being found guilty of crimes against Jews, he was convicted for crimes against Poles, Slovenes and Gypsies. The judges concluded that Eichmann had not merely been following orders, but had been a key decision maker. It sentenced Eichmann to death by hanging, the sole application of capital punishment in the modern state of Israel.[429]

Was the trial of Adolf Eichmann legal, based, as it was, on abduction? Under the law of nations, he probably should have been released and returned to Argentina. Under the actual practice of nations, the answer is probably he could be so tried.[430] Perhaps the most intriguing perspective on the Eichmann prosecution came in a law journal which argued that, while Israel retained the right to prosecute him after the abduction, it should be made to pay reparations to Argentina for violating its sovereignty.[431]

In one subsequent incident that was noted internationally Israeli armed forces had kidnapped a group of suspects in Lebanon, including a Turkish citizen, Paik Bulut. Bulut and approximately ten others, all citizens of one or another Arab nations, were living in a Palestinian refugee camp in Lebanon about 100 miles from Israel. The charge was membership in, or support of, an organization whose purpose was to do harm to Israel. Counsel argued that none of those seized had actually committed any overt act against Israel. In July 1973 the Israeli military tribunal, not a regular civilian court, rejected defense counsel's argument, citing the Eichmann precedent.[432]

---

429 The literature on the capture, interrogation, trial, and execution of Adolf Eichmann is extensive. Among the better sources are the following: Arendt, Hannah. *Eichmann in Jerusalem: A Report on the Banality of Evil.* New York: Penguin, 1963; Lipstadt, Deborah E. *The Eichmann Trial.* New York: Random House., 2011; and Stangneth, Bettina. *Eichmann Before Jerusalem.* New York: Alfred A. Knopf, 2014.

430 Lippmann, Matthew. "The Trial of Adolf Eichmann and the Protection of Universal Human Rights under International Law," *Houston Journal of International Law,* 5: 1 (1982), pp. 1–34

431 Green, L. C. "The Eichmann Case," *Modern Law Review,* 23: 507 (1960).

432 *Jerusalem Post,* 14 August 1973; *Time* magazine, 20 August 1973; and *New York Times,* 24 July 1973.

Manuel Noreiga

Manuel Antonio Noriega Moreno (1934 – 2017) was a politician and military officer who was the de facto ruler of Panama from 1983 to 1989. Although he had longstanding ties to United States intelligence agencies, the United States was removed him from power by invasion of Panama

By the early 1970s, American law enforcement officials had reports of Noriega's possible involvement with narcotics trafficking, but undertook no formal criminal investigations, largely for political reasons. The U.S. was concluding a new Panama Canal treaty, the CIA saw him as a source of reliable intelligence from Panama, and Panama had generally supported U.S. foreign policy in the area of political unrest and instability.[433]

Noriega's involvement with drug smuggling continued to grow into the 1980s. It was reliably reported that Noriega frequently received large payments, sometimes as high as $100,000 per shipment, from drug smugglers who were under his protection.[434]

Meanwhile, Noreiga was having great political difficulties at home. One of the most effective opponents was Dr. Hugo Spadafora, a physician who had first begun opposing Noriega when they were both members of the earlier Torrijo's government. Although both men were allies of Torrijo's, the two men had become personal enemies for a long time. Spadafora began amassing evidence of Noreiga's corruption within the government. In September 1985 he accused Noriega of having connections to drug trafficking and announced that he intended to return from Costa Rica to Panama to oppose him. After crossing the border, the state secret police (PDF) removed Spadafora from the bus. Later, his decapitated body was found and it showed signs of brutal torture.[435]

Finally, the U.S. launched its invasion of Panama on December 20, 1989. Unfortunately, large number of civilians were killed in

433 Galván, Javier A. "Manuel Noreiga" in *Latin American Dictators of the 20th Century: The Lives and Regimes of Fifteen Rulers*. McFarland, 2012.

434 Scott, Peter Dale; and Marshall, Jonathan. *Cocaine Politics*. University of California Press, 1988.

435 Scranton, Margaret E. *The Noriega Years : U.S.-Panamanian Relations, 1981–1990*. Boulder, CO: L. Rienner, 1991. See also Dinges, John. *Our Man in Panama: How General Noriega Used the United States-And Made Millions in Drugs and Arms*. New York: Random House, 1990.

the invasion, with estimates as low as 200 and as high as 3000. [436] On the fifth day of the invasion, Noriega and four others took sanctuary in the Apostolic Nunciature, the Catholic Holy See's embassy in Panama. They surrendered most of their weapons, and requested sanctuary from the papal nuncio. Prevented by treaty from violating the sanctuary of that embassy, U.S. Soldiers surrounded it and cut off all outside communications. U.S. Forces turned to psychological warfare specialists and after ten days, Noriega surrendered.[437]

On 3 January 1990 U.S. military detained Noreiga as a prisoner of war, later moving him to the United States. The ensuing problem was: was Noreiga a prisoner of war or a captured drug lord who could be tried in court?[438] Eventually, he was arraigned on the ten charges which the Miami grand jury had returned two years earlier. The start of the trial was delayed until September 1991 due to complex legal maneuvering regarding his status. The trial ended in April 1992, when Noriega was convicted on eight of the ten charges of drug trafficking, racketeering, and money laundering. Conviction was sustained on appeal.[439] Despite his conviction, under Article 85 of the Third Geneva Convention, Noriega was considered a prisoner of war. This status brought Noriega a private prison cell, furnished with electronics and exercise equipment, nicknamed "the presidential suite".[440]

In the next act in the drama, the French government requested Noriega's extradition after he was convicted *in absentia* of money laundering in 1999. French law required a new trial after the subject of an *in absentia* sentence is apprehended. He faced up to 10 years in French prison if convicted. Noriega appealed his extradition because he claimed France would not honor his legal status as a prisoner of war. The Supreme Court refused to hear his case so he was extradited to France. The French court convicted Noriega, sentencing him to prison for seven years and confiscating approximately $3.6 million of

436 Kempe, Frederick. *Divorcing The Dictator America's America's Bungled Affair with Noreiga.* New York: Putnam's, 1990.

437 Gilboa, Eytan. "The Panama Invasion Revisited: Lessons for the Use of Force in the Post Cold War Era." *Political Science Quarterly*, 110.4 (1995), pp. 539–562.

438 *United States v Noreiga,* 746 F. Supp. 1506 (S.D.F., 1990).

439 *United States v Noreiga,* 117 F.3d 1206 (11th Cir. 1997)

440 Sherman, M. A. "An Inquiry Regarding The International and Domestic Legal Problems Presented in United States v. Noriega". *The University of Miami Inter-American Law Review,*. 20: 2 (1989), pp. 393–428.

his ill-gotten gains.[441]

In 1999, the Panamanian government also sought the extradition of Noriega to face murder charges in Panama because he had been found guilty *in absentia* in 1995 and sentenced to 20 years in prison. The French government notified France that it would not extradite Noreiga until he had served his sentence. On September 23, 2011, a French court ordered a conditional release for Noriega to be extradited to Panama to be incarcerated to serve time for crimes committed during his rule.[442] Noriega died on May 29, 2017, at the age of 83, still in Panamanian custody.

A South African Abduction Case

On 15 December 1986 Ebrahim Ismail Ebrahim was abducted from his home in Swaziland by two men and forcibly taken across the border between that country and South Africa where he was handed over to members of the South African National Intelligence Services. They took Ebrahim to Pretoria where he was arrested the following morning by the South African Police (SAP). Thereafter he was detained by the police for terrorist activities.[443] On 14 May 1987 he was charged with high treason. He appeared in the Pretoria magistrates' court on that charge and also other related charges. The police kept Ebrahim in custody until he was tried on those charges in a Transvaal circuit court on 3 August 1987.[444]

From the beginning, Ebrahim maintained that, because of his abduction, no South African court had jurisdiction to try him. Before he pleaded to the charges against him in the circuit court Ebrahim raised the plea of lack of jurisdiction. The court dismissed this argument. Here, at the trial, the South African courts upheld the abduction of Ebrahim, a person charged with a crime. had no court protection when being abducted. On February 1989, the trial court found guilty Ebrahim guilty of treason and sentenced to prison where he remained

---

441 "U.S. Court Rejects Noriega Appeal to Bar Extradition," Reuters World News, 25 January 2000. See also Richey, Warren, "Supreme Court Won't Halt Noreiga Extradition to France," *Christian Science Monitor,* 25 January 2000.

442 Blum, Vanessa, "Noriega is Cleared for Extradition," Los Angeles Times, 25 August 2007. *In re Extradition of Manuel Noreiga*, docket no. 07-21830 (S.D.F., 17 July 2007).

443 Violation of the Internal Security Act 74 of 1982.

444 *Ebrahim v Minister of Interior* (1977) 1 sa 665 a in

until 26 January 1991.[445] Basing its decision on traditional Dutch law, and also under even earlier Roman law, rather than international law, the trial court ruled that illegal abduction was not a legal consideration that could come before the courts. There was much negative discussion of the decision for it appeared to remove South Africa from emerging universally recognized international law.[446] In the Ebrhim case, officers from the South African constabulary, acting under official orders, had tracked and apprehended Ebrhim in Swaziland and returned him to South Africa. Thus, at that time, international law was not part of South African municipal law.[447]

On appeal this court found that the plea should have been upheld and set aside the respondent's conviction and sentence. However, on appeal, the higher court ruled that there could be delictual liability arising from the unlawful abduction. Delictual liability is concerned with damages suffered by a person resulting from a wrongful act, or omission of another, for which that person is entitled to compensation in terms of common law. The court found that the state was liable in respect of the abduction, arrest and detention until 14 May 1987 because the South African Police had "formed a common purpose with the National Intelligence Service (NIS) who were the abductors" and with the unlawful abduction and transportation of the plaintiff. As regards the detention from the date of the respondent's first appearance in the magistrate's court until his release from prison on 26 February 1991, the court found that that detention was a likely consequence of the original wrongs. Hence, the fact that the detention had been authorized by courts of law had no bearing on the award.[448]

---

445 State v Ebrahim [1991] ZASCA 3; 1991 (2) SA 553 (A). See also Orkin, Mark, "'Democracy Knows No Colour': Rationales for Guerrilla Involvement among Black South Africans," *Journal of Southern African Studies,* 18:3 (1992), pp. 642-69.

446 *State v Ebrahim,* South Africa 553 A (1991). See Booysen, H., "Jurisdiction to Tray Abducted Persons and the Application of International Law in South Africa," *South Africa Yearbook of International Law,* 16: 133-41.

447 *State v Ebrahim,* South Africa 553 A (1991). See Booysen, H., "Jurisdiction to Tray Abducted Persons and the Application of International Law in South Africa," *South Africa Yearbook of International Law,* 16: 133-41. See also *Ebrahim v Minister of Law and Order,* S. A. (T) (1993), pp. 563-64.

448 *Minister of Law and Order v Ebrahim,* November 1994, saflii.org/za/cases/ZA-SCA/1994/163. See also Barrell, Howard, "The Turn to the Masses: The African National Congress' Strategic Review of 1978-79," *Journal of South African Studies,* 18: 1 (1992), pp. 64-92.

The decision of the appellate court moved South Africa away from its Dutch municipal law roots and toward participation in international law as practiced among the members of the community of nations.[449]

Nduli Case in South Africa

Nduli and another were arrested in the Republic of South Africa and charged in South African court with crimes triable by it. Before he was apprehended he fled from South Africa to Namibia where he was apprehended by persons in that foreign state. The persons making the arrest were not authorized by South African State. The South African Court's jurisdiction was not ousted because of such apprehension under any rules of international law that had been incorporated in South African law. The court held that international law was an integral part of South African municipal law to the extent of its incorporation. The ultimate source of this proposition must be found in Roman-Dutch law, according to which public international law is based on the acceptance of territorial sovereignty of independent states.[450] Only such rules of customary international law are to be regarded as part of South African law as are either universally recognized or have received the assent of this country.[451]

Nduli and as many as 26 others were wanted in the Natal Provincial Division on a number of charges under the Terrorism Act, 83 of 1967, as amended, alternatively, under the Suppression of Communism Act, 1950, as amended. The charges under the Terrorism Act against all the accused included offenses committed in the Republic of South Africa and in Swaziland and a separate charge against the first appellant only related to military training in various countries, including Russia.[452]

---

449 Devine, Dermott J., "The Relationship between International Law and Municipal Law in the Light of the Interim South African Constitution 1993," *International and Comparative Law Quarterly,* 44: 1 (1005), pp. 1-18. See "South Africa: Supreme Court (Appelate Division) Opinion in *State v. Ebrahim* (Jurisdiction over Abducted Person)," *International Legal Materials,* 31: 4 (1992), pp. 888-99.

450 Stemmet, Andre, "The Influence of Recent Constitutional Developments in South Africa on the Relationship between International Law and Municipal Law," *The International Lawyer,* (Spring 1999), pp. 47-74

451 The decision in the Natal Provincial Division in Ndhlovu and Another v Minister of Justice and Others, 1976 (4) SA 250, confirmed.

452 https://lawblogsa.files.wordpress.com/2014/01/nduli-v-minister-of-justice.pdf

The central and important issue that was to be decided in his appeal was whether the fact that the appellants were before the Court with criminal charges pending, gave the Court jurisdiction to try them on those or any charges irrespective of whether they were kidnapped and forcibly and against their will brought from within the territory of another sovereign State or not. If that issue is decided in favor of respondents then *caedit quaestio* any dispute upon the facts as to whether they were so kidnapped or not. Assuming then, for this part of the argument, that appellants were kidnapped in Swaziland and forcibly removed therefrom by members of the H South African Police into the territory of the Republic of South Africa on the night of 25 March 1976, it is clear that at a point 20 kilometers within the South African borders a colonel in the South African Police arrested them and detained them until 14 May 1976 when they were brought before the Supreme Court in Pietermaritzburg.

Nduli and the other appellant averred that the Swaziland Government had raised with the South African Government the question of their having been kidnapped according to a report in the *Natal Mercury.* The Swaziland Government had protested against the violation of its territorial sovereignty and demanded the return of the two appellants. Both appellants had earlier been granted political asylum in that country. Swaziland, a sovereign independent State, had not waived its rights in respect of the two appellants, and had, in fact, protested the violation of its territorial sovereignty and has demanded the return to Swaziland of the two appellants.

The trial judge had found that the "Court has jurisdiction to try the appellants for the offences for which they were indicted even if they should have been taken into custody on Swaziland soil". On appeal the higher court found that such finding was wrong in the circumstances of this case and, failed to take into account the rights of the Swaziland government. It is not necessary for that Government to be a party to these proceedings and the Court will not, by their process, seize or retain property, or even some lesser interest which is that of the foreign sovereign. It is not necessary for a foreign state to prove its claim in the South African court. The right of the foreign sovereign to demand the return of persons arrested on its soil by another power, and the obligation to return such persons to the foreign sovereign, are well-established principles in international law as recognized by South African municipal law.[453]

The South African Court recognized that, in some countries, municipal courts have quite often insisted on their having jurisdiction to try criminal cases against persons brought before them. Those courts have rejected as irrelevant, objections to jurisdiction based on alleged illegalities in their apprehension in foreign sovereign States. None of the judgments binds the Courts in Britain or in the United States America to hold that where there has been a violation of the sovereignty of a State which had not waived its rights and which claims the return of the apprehended fugitives taken from their asylum, the circumstances are irrelevant and the criminal courts of the land must try the charges. This, however, was not the case in South Africa, and its courts were not bound by such decisions.[454]

The court chose to comment quite negatively on the Eichmann case and the Israeli kidnapping of that person.[455] The South African Court viewed that abduction as a major violation of international law. South Africa law made it quite clear that the Nduli appellants were before the Court "without due process of law". The kidnapping is not cured by a legal arrest under section 6 of the Terrorism Act nor by remand in Court. Stolen goods do not cease to be stolen because the police have taken them into custody or they have been made an exhibit of court. A remand in custody by a court does not render an illegal detention lawful.[456]

South Africa had enacted two major pieces of legislation, against communism in 1950, and against terrorism in 1976, in order to protect itself and its people. It was well known, the Court said, that terrorist took refuge in adjoining nations and engaged in terroristic activities in South Africa and then recrossed the borders. A state had a right to defend itself. Given the two conflicting values, honoring international law and protecting its citizens, South African courts sided

---

453 *State v Nduli and Others* (90/92, 398/92) [1993] ZASCA 120; [1993] 2 All SA 612 (A) (14 September 1993). Sanders, A. J. G. M., "The Applicability of Customary International Law in South African Law: the Appeal Court has Spoken," *Comparative and International Law Journal of Southern Africa,* 11: 2 (1978), pp. 198-207.

454 Schaffer, Rosalie P. "The Inter-Relationship between Public International Law and the Law of South Africa: An Overview," *International and Public Law Quarterly,* 32 (1983) pp. 277-83.

455 See Fawcett, J. E. S. "The Eichmann Case," in *The British Yearbook of International Law* (1962) at pp. 181 et seq.

456 Cf. *Re Geelat Khan* (1888) 9 N.L.R. at p. 51.

with national self-preservation.

In arriving at a decision regarding Nduli's arrest the Court then held that, assuming that the accused had been apprehended on foreign soil by non-operatives of the state, international law, as applied through South African municipal law, does not preclude his being tried in a South African court on charges otherwise within its jurisdiction. In the Nduli case, after being brought into South Africa by his abductors, he was lawfully arrested. His abductors had acted without the authority of the South African State. The Court left open the question whether the position would be different if they acted with State authority. [457]

Prosecutor v Nikolic

In 1994 Dragan "Jenki" Nikolic was a Bosnian Serb who was the first person indicted by the International Criminal Tribunal for the former Yugoslavia (ICTY). The prosecutor was to introduce several amended indictments, all of which essentially contained 80 or so counts of crimes against humanity, grave breaches of various Geneva Conventions, and violations of the laws and customs of war. Specifically, the case dealt with Nikolic's individual command responsibility for the infliction of a series of particularly brutal crimes committed in the Susica detention camp near the town of Vlasenica. There was no question that Dragan Nikolic was, at the time of the commission of various illegal acts, the commander in this internment camp, which Serb forces had established in June 1992.[458]

By 4 November 1994, the Tribunal had issued arrest warrants for Dragan Nikolic, but no authority was able to execute the warrants. On 20 October 1995, the Trial Chamber issued its decision which determined that there were reasonable grounds for believing that Dragan Nikolic had committed all the crimes in the indictment. The Bosnian Serb administration then in power declined to co-operate with ICTY, but he was apprehended in April 2000 in Bosnia and Herzegovina and immediately transferred to the Tribunal on 21 April 2000. Nikolic pleaded guilty on 4 September 2003 to the Third Amended Indictment

---

457 *Nduli and another v Minister of Justice,* 1 S A 893 (1978). See Devine, Dermott J., "The Relationship between International Law and Municipal Law in the Light of the Interim South African Constitution 1993," *International and Comparative Law Quarterly,* 44, No. 1 (1995), pp. 1-18. The Nduli case was the primary consideration.

458 https://www.icty.org/en/press/judgement-case-prosecutor-v-dragan-nikolic

which charged him with individual criminal responsibility for committing murder (Count 2), aiding and abetting rape (Count 3) and committing torture (Count 4), all internationally established as crimes against humanity.[459]

In May 2001 and again in October 2001, the Nikolic's defense filed motions challenging the jurisdiction of the Tribunal alleging that his arrest had been illegal. Unknown individuals carried out the abduction on the territory of what was at that time Yugoslavia, thereby barring the Tribunal from exercising its jurisdiction over the accused. He had been arrested in the territory of Bosnia and Herzegovina, but only after he had been illegally seized over by these unknown individuals. Defense argued that the illegal character of the apprehension leading to the arrest should in and of itself bar ICTY from exercising jurisdiction.[460]

The Trial Chamber of ICTY rejected defense counsel's assertion that there was a serious violation of state sovereignty and based its decision on three grounds: First, the Trial Chamber held that in the vertical relationship between the Tribunal and States, sovereignty cannot by definition play the same role as in the horizontal relationship between States. Second, the Trial Chamber recalled that no one acting for the ICTY Prosecution had at any time been involved in this transfer. Third, the Trial Chamber held that, in contrast to cases involving horizontal relationships between states, even if a violation of state sovereignty had occurred, the government of Yugoslavia would have been obliged to surrender the accused after his return to Yugoslavia.

Defense filed an interlocutory appeal against this decision on 24 January 2003, following certification of the appeal by the Trial Chamber. The Appeals Chamber rejected the defense argument in its decision of 5 June 2003. First, the Appeals Chamber held that, even if the conduct of the unknown individuals could be attributed to the prosecution, there was no basis upon which the ICTY should not exercise its jurisdiction in the present case. In reaching this conclusion, the Appeals Chamber weighed the legitimate expectation that those accused of universally condemned offenses will be brought to justice against the principle of State sovereignty and the fundamental human rights of the accused. Second, the Appeals Chamber held that certain

---

459 https://www.icty.org/en/case/nikolic
460 Simms, Marlise . "Serb at Hague Pleads Guilty To Brutalities" *New York Times*, 5 September 2003.

human rights violations are of such a serious nature that they require that the exercise of jurisdiction be declined. The Appeals Chamber concurred, however, with the Trial Chamber's evaluation and found that the rights of the accused were not egregiously violated in the process of his arrest. ICTY sentenced Nikolic to 23 years imprisonment.[461]

Extraordinary Extradition

Extraordinary extradition, also called extraordinary rendition, irregular rendition, or forced rendition, refers to the governmentally sponsored abduction and extrajudicial transfer of a person from one country to another with the purpose of circumventing the former country's laws on interrogation, detention, extradition and/or torture. Recent extraditions of this form have reportedly been carried out by the governments of the United States, Turkey and Communist China. Such extralegal abductions are usually designed to circumvent prevailing international law against torture. The Guardian's Defence and Security Editor charged that Great Britain was also participating in extraordinary rendition.[462]

The American Civil Liberties Union alleges that extraordinary rendition was developed during the Clinton administration. During the presidency of George W. Bush, the United States engaged in the practice known as *extraordinary rendition* which was used to apprehend and detain foreign nationals suspected of involvement in terrorism. An alleged suspect would be arrested and secretly transferred to prisons run by foreign intelligence agencies in foreign bases, often in countries known to employ torture, or to CIA-run so-called black sites. CIA director George Tenet testified before the 9/11 Commission that there were more than eighty cases of extraordinary renditions before September 11, 2001.[463]

Foreign nationals suspected of terrorism have been transported to detention and interrogation facilities in Jordan, Iraq, Egypt, Diego

---

461 *Prosecutor v Nikolic,* ICTY, IT-94-02-AE73 (2003)

462 Sabbagh, Dan, "Whitehall Held Secret Review into 15 Possible Cases of Torture or Rendition Court Proceedings Reveal Files Involving British Intelligence during 'War on Terror'," *The Guardian*, 9 June 2020.

463 Wikipedia has a long, detailed, and well documented entry on "extraordinary rendition." See also Horowitz, Jonathan and Stacy Cammarano,"20 Extraordinary Facts about CIA Extraordinary Rendition and Secret Detention," *Justice Initiative.org*, 5 February 2013.

Garcia, Afghanistan, Guantánamo (Cuba), and elsewhere. In the words of former CIA agent Robert Baer: "If you want a serious interrogation, you send a prisoner to Jordan. If you want them to be tortured, you send them to Syria. If you want someone to disappear -- never to see them again -- you send them to Egypt."[464]

The U. S. Congress has attempted to make it very clear, that "it is the policy of the United States not to: "expel, extradite, or otherwise effect the involuntary return of any person to a country in which there are substantial grounds for believing the person would be in danger of being subjected to torture, regardless of whether the person is physically present in the United States."[465] There was also an amendment to the Emergency Supplemental Appropriations Act for the Iraq War and Tsunami Relief, 2005[466] that it will not authorize the funding of any program that "subject[s] any person in the custody or under the physical control of the United States to torture or cruel, inhuman, or degrading treatment or punishment that is prohibited by the Constitution, laws, or treaties of the United States."[467]

In 2007, the American Civil Liberties Union[468] filed a lawsuit against Jeppesen DataPlan, Inc., a subsidiary of the Boeing Company, on behalf of five extraordinary extradition victims. The lawsuit charged that Jeppesen knowingly participated in these extraditions by providing critical flight planning and logistical support services to aircraft and crews used by the CIA to forcibly disappear these five men to torture, detention and interrogation. According to published reports, Jeppesen had real knowledge of the consequences of its activities. A former Jeppesen employee informed *The New Yorker* magazine that, at an internal corporate meeting, a senior Jeppesen official stated, "We do all of the extraordinary rendition flights - you know, the torture flights. Let's face it, some of these flights end up that way." Soon after the suit was filed, the federal government intervened and claimed the "state secrets privilege. It asserted that litigation would undermine national security interests, although at least some of the evidence that

---

464 Quoted in ACLU Fact Sheet on Extraordinary Rendition.
465 Foreign Affairs Reform and Restructuring Act of 1998, ("FARRA"), Pub. L.
   No. 105-277, § 2242, 112 Stat. 2681 (Oct. 21, 1998), reprinted in 8 U.S.C. §
   1231,
466 Public Law 109-13 (2005).
467 Public Law 109-13, § 1031 (2005).
468 See ACLU website, Extraordinary Rendition | American Civil Liberties Union
   (aclu.org)

would have been introduced in the case had previously become public knowledge.[469]

The federal courts have dramatically altered the scope and function of the state secrets privilege in extraordinary rendition cases, causing premature dismissal of well-pleaded complaints. This is especially true when the very subject matter of the suit is not a state secret and the parties' claims and defenses do not inevitably depend on privileged matter, as was *Jeppesen*. What is a common law evidentiary privilege has transformed into something more akin to an immunity doctrine. Rethinking the way courts handle invocations of the privilege could result in fewer dismissals on the pleadings in many types of cases while still maintaining the government's valid interest in not disclosing truly sensitive information. Reforming *Reynolds* could help clarify the courts' role in reviewing claims of state secrets and provide greater uniformity and fairness in judicial decision-making in this area.[470]

In 2003, CIA agents snatched an Egyptian Muslim cleric, Abu Omar, in Milan, Italy, and flew him to Cairo, where Egyptian security forces interrogated and tortured him. The Italian prosecutor stepped in and indicted twenty-six Americans involved in the daylight abduction. The Italian judge ruled against twenty-three of the defendants, sentencing them to as much as eight years in prison, although none will serve any prison time since they were tried *in absentia*. It was clear that the ruling was meant as a rebuke to the US government and its nearly 15-year-old extraordinary rendition policy. Reportedly, by 2009, the policy of transferring suspected terrorists to third countries had led to at least sixty-seven people being detained by American agents and then taken to one or more countries where they were tortured, imprisoned without trial, and/or killed. [471] A former CIA officer involved with extraordinary rendition in Italy is close to a deal that would let her take a lighter punishment instead of prison time. Sabrina

---

469 *Mohamed v. Jeppesen Dataplan, Inc.,* 579 F.3d 943 (9th Cir. 2009); *Mohamed v. Jeppesen Dataplan, Inc.*, 614 F.3d 1070 (9th. Cir. 2010, See also Turner, Alexander, " Extraordinary Results in Extraordinary Rendition," *Southern Methodist University Law Review,* 69: 2 (2016), pp. 559-82

470 *Mohamed v. Jeppesen Dataplan Inc.*, 614 F.3d 1070 (9th Cir. 2010); Turner, Alexander, "Comment, Extraordinary Results in Extraordinary Rendition," *Southern Methodist Law Review*, 69:2 (2016), pp. 558-82; Fuchs, Meredith, "Judging Secrets: The Role Courts Should Play in Preventing Unnecessary Secrecy," *Administrative Law Review*, 58 (2006), pp. 131-53.

471 *The Guardian*, 4 November 2009.

De Sousa was one of the twenty-six Americans tried and convicted *in absentia* for being connected to the kidnapping a Muslim cleric in 2003. She was arrested in Portugal and held for nine days on an Italian warrant in the case and then freed as she neared an agreement with Italian authorities.[472]

On December 13, 2012, the Grand Chamber of the European Court of Human Rights (ECHR) issued a final judgment in a case involving a German national of Lebanese origin, who was arrested by authorities of the Former Yugoslav Republic of Macedonia (FYROM) acting on suspicion of his having ties with terrorist organizations, under the so-called rendition program organized by the U. S. Central Intelligence Agency. Khaled El-Masri, the applicant, won the case and was awarded €60,000 (about US$79,000) for non-pecuniary damage. Additionally, the public prosecutor in Munich, Germany, issued criminal arrest warrants against several CIA agents for being involved in the detention and torture of El-Masri..[473]

---

472 *The Guardian,* 1 March 2017.

473 *El-Masri v. The Former Yugoslav Republic of Macedonia*, European Court of Human Rights (Dec. 13, 2012)

Evading Extradition

Extradition is a time-honored system to prevent criminals from escaping justice by escaping to another state or country, with legal precedents going back thousands of years. The ancient pharaohs of Egypt were known to negotiate the extradition of criminals from neighboring Hittite territories. There is a very old, but true, joke that one can get away with any crime if only he seeks refuge in a nation with which there is no treaty providing for extradition.

Extradition ordinarily is covered by an existing treaty or other agreement between two governments. However, even if no formal treaty exists, one nation may still request, and commonly be granted, extradition of an accused criminal from another country. Where there is a treaty, nations are bound by the interpretation and amplification of the treaty by the host nation's judiciary. Fleeing criminals sometimes avoid extradition because of some flaw or technicality in the extradition treaty.

One of the early cases involving flawed extradition treaty concerned an American forger who escaped to Canada. A certain Warner had created his own fifty cent so-called postage currency. The Union government created these notes, redeemable only for postage stamps, to fill a shortage of coins caused by inflation and hoarding during the Civil War. American authorities requested that Warner be returned under terms of the existing extradition treaty.[474] Warner's Canadian attorneys, intervened, claiming that the language of the extradition treaty did not cover the situation, that the matter was not such as was contemplated by the Act which speaks of persons who "being charged" with certain acts. In the case of Warner, however, the matter had already passed from a charge to a conviction. The sureties had been made to pay the forfeiture on their bond taken after such conviction and before Warner's escape to Canada. The court agreed that the acts referred to must have been made here before, not after, the trial. The court found that to escape from justice after conviction constituted a new and different crime, which was not specifically covered in the treaty, and thus Warner could not be delivered up for it.[475]

Even when two countries have an extradition treaty, the vagaries of law and public opinion can stand in the way of rendering up

---

474*New York Times,* 31 October 1864; See also *Toronto Leader,* 21 October 1864.
475Consolidated Statutes of Canada, cap. 89, and 24th Vic., cap. 6.

an accused criminal from one country to another. Many countries will refuse to extradite a person if they view the individual as a political prisoner, who will likely be tried for political or religious dissent rather than for an actual crime. Because of the international Convention against Torture[476] if there is reason to believe that the accused will face torture, the signatories of that international instrument are supposed to refuse extradition. Most members of the European Union, along with Australia, Canada and several other other nations, reserve the right to refuse extradition if the accused is likely to face the death penalty. These nations may require that a requesting nation which allows capital punishment give assurance that the accused will not be put to death if convicted.

The United States currently has no extradition treaty with China, North Korea, Iran, the Soviet Union and several other nations, according to the U.S. Department of State. As we have seen the United States and the Soviet Union have, at least occasionally, respected extradition requests. More frequently, the United States has granted asylum to Soviet citizens who have asked for such protection, ignoring Soviet requests for extradition. Technically there is still an extradition treaty with Cuba dating to 1926, but the suspension of relations between the two nations makes it unlikely that an extradition request would be respected. Any of these nations could become the refuge for an American looking to escape U.S. law enforcement. Of course, those seeking such protection from prosecution are under the authority of the host nation. Moreover, such American citizens could not expect any help whatsoever from the U. S. embassies or diplomatic personnel in case of problems.

Sheinbein Case: Nationality Principle

Samuel Sheinbein was an American-Israeli citizen who was convicted of murderer in Israel for the crime committed in Maryland.

476The Convention against Torture and Other Cruel, Inhuman or Degrading Treatment or Punishment (commonly known as the United Nations Convention against Torture (UNCAT). The text of the Convention was adopted by the United Nations General Assembly on 10 December 1984 and, following ratification by the 20th state party, it was said to have come into force on 26 June 1987. Since the convention's entry into force, the absolute prohibition against torture and other acts of cruel, inhuman, or degrading treatment or punishment has become accepted as a principle of customary international law. As of June 2018, the Convention has 164 state parties. From Wikipedia.

He was born on 25 July 1980. On 16 September 1997, Sheinbein, a 17-year-old senior at John F. Kennedy High School in Montgomery County, Maryland, and Aaron Benjamin Needle, a former classmate from the Charles E. Smith Jewish Day School, killed Alfredo "Freddy" Enrique Tello, Jr.

John McCarthy of Montgomery County, the Maryland Deputy State's Attorney, related the following regarding Sheinbein's background. .By the age of 17, Sheinbein had already decided to commit a murder. He informed a friend that he was willing to pay $5,000 for someone to kill the boyfriend of his intended girl friend or, alternately, pay $1,000 for someone to lure his rival into a vehicle so that he could kill that person. In the meanwhile, Sheinbein sought someone to murder just for practice so that he was properly prepared to kill his intended target. At the same time Sheinbein was planning to murder his rival, he became associated with Aaron Benjamin Needle. Needle knew and disliked Alfredo "Freddy" Enrique Tello Jr. Needle also came to know his Montgomery County classmate, Hannah Choi, and subsequently became romantically interested in her. Ms Choi was also a friend of Tello. In September 1997, Needle had gotten into an altercation with Tello who had punched Needle in front of Choi. Ms Choi told police that Needle appeared to be embarrassed and immediately called his friend Sam. According to McCarthy, this event led to Needle suggesting to Sheinbein that he made Tello his practice victim

Sheinbein and Needle killed Alfredo "Freddy" Enrique Tello, Jr. Investigators concluded that this murder was clearly premeditated. Sheinbein and Needle incapacitated Tello with a stun gun, and then choked and stabbed him, and finally beat him to death with a sawed-off shotgun. The autopsy report concluded that the cause of death of the victim was "a combination of blunt force injuries to the head, cutting wounds on the neck and chest, and ligature strangulation".

The young hoodlums stored Tello's body in Sheinbein's garage, where they dismembered the victim's limbs and burned the torso so that Tello could not be identified. Sheinbein arranged to dispose of what remained of the body in a vacant home previously owned by a classmate. Sheinbein told that classmate he wanted to use the vacant residence to be with a girl in private. Authorities concluded that Sheinbein and Needle transported the body to the residence in a garbage bag that they had placed in the back of Needle's Honda. They transported their tools in a wheelbarrow to the vacant home.

On 19 September 1997, a realtor was preparing the vacant home for a showing, but detected a strong odor coming from the garage. The realtor found Tello's mutilated torso wrapped in garbage bags.The realtor called the Montgomery County Police Department who responded. The body was so charred that witnesses believed it was a deer carcass. Investigators soon determined the contents of the garbage bags were human remains and ruled it as a homicide. Police also found the various tools, including a Makita electric circular saw, used to dismember the victim.

Initially, Montgomery County investigators were unable to determine the victim's identity. They began to interview neighbors who reported seeing the suspects. Using police canines, authorities discovered a trail of blood leading from the scene of the body to the garage of the Sheinbein residence. Eventually, investigation led authorities to determine that Sheinbein was the principal suspect. Based on physical evidence and eyewitness accounts, the detectives determined that Needle was a second suspect. Warrants for first degree murder and the arrest of Sheinbein and Needle were issued shortly thereafter. On 22 September 1997, Freddy Tello's mother reported that her son missing. Police investigation of the missing-persons report revealed that Tello had told friends that he would meet them at the Plaza del Mercado shopping center in Silver Spring along with Needle and Sheinbein, but never showed up. Detectives had to use dental records of to identify the victim's remains.[477]

Both Sheinbein and Needle were arrested. Needle committed suicide in a U.S. jail just before his trial was to start in April 1998. Sheinbein's accomplice, Aaron Needle, hanged himself in jail, while Sheinbein fled to Israel, where he claimed citizenship because his father was born in Palestine before the State of Israel was proclaimed, in 1944.

With the assistance of his father, Sol Sheinbein, the younger Sheinbein evaded apprehension by Maryland police by flying to Israel. Sol Sheinbein was an attorney with dual U.S.-Israeli citizenship. Sol reportedly brought Samuel a passport, purchased an airline ticket to Tel Aviv, and drove him to John F. Kennedy International Airport in order to escape the jurisdiction of the United States. Once Samuel

---

477 Most facts were recorded in Chaplin, Oren, "American Justice Across the Ocean? The Case of Samuel Sheinbein". *New England Law Review* (Summer 2001).

Sheinbein was in Israel, his brother Robert flew to Israel and met him in his hotel room, reportedly bringing him a bottle of wine and a prostitute. On September 25, 1997, Samuel took an overdose of sleeping pills along with the wine in a suicide attempt. Police found a suicide note addressed to his family. Israeli authorities then admitted Sheinbein to a psychiatric hospital. As the Israelis became aware of his crimes, they placed Sheinbein in custody and U.S. authorities were notified of his presence in Israel. In an attempt to avoid extradition, Sheinbein claimed and received Israeli citizenship as the son of an Israeli national through his father, who had been born in Mandatory Palestine and emigrated from Israel at age six.[478]

Samuel Sheinbein sparked an international extradition battle when he fled to Israel after Maryland authorities linked him to a dismemberment murder, may have escaped American justice The United States proceeded with the request to Israel to extradite Sheinbein as a fugitive who had been charged with a felony in Maryland. Israel rejected the request for extradition partially because Israel determined that Sheinbein had dual nationality, both U.S. and Israeli citizenship. Under Israeli domestic law as it was in force at that time, Israel could not extradite an Israeli national. Israel's refusal to extradite Sheinbein raised resentment and anger in the United States. The non-extradition of a brutal murderer to extradite an indicted felon to the U.S., a country which many considered to be Israel's closest ally, seemed difficult to comprehend not only to Americans, but also to the Israelis.[479]

The killing, and afterward Sheinbein's flight to Israel, became major issues among Maryland's Hispanic organizations and Latino community. These groups accused Maryland's prosecutors of negligence in allowing Sheinbein to escape. In Congress, several lawmakers threatened to introduce legislation designed to cut off American aid to Israel unless the teen-ager was returned to face charges. United States Representative Bob Livingston threatened to cut American foreign aid to Israel by $50 million if Israel did not extradite Sheinbein. Representative Sonny Callahan threatened to cut the entire $1.2 billion in aid. Indeed, a hold was placed on the interim payment of just over $75 million in October 1997. The incident also resulted in a peri-

---

478 Besser, James, "Israel rapped on Sheinbein," *Jewish Week*, 5 March 1999.
479 *State of Maryland v. Samuel Sheinbein*, Case No. 3D00051782, District Court of Maryland for Montgomery County; and *State of Maryland v. Samuel Sheinbein*, Case No. 81039C, Circuit Court for Montgomery County.

od of frosty relations with then-Secretary of State Madeleine Albright.

Israel claimed that it could not extradite Sheinbein because of prevailing national law. An amendment in 1978 to Israel's Extradition Law that prohibited the extradition of Israeli nationals but subjected them to Israeli adjudication. This was the work of former prime minister Menachem Begin. Begin accused foreign nations of anti-Israeli prejudices, thus denying these accused Jews their full legal rights. Specifically, Begin claimed there was antisemitism in most foreign courts. In agreeing with Begin's amendment, the Israeli high court noted that "[c]elebrated cases such as the Dreyfus affair and the anti-Zionist show trials in the Communist bloc undermined Israeli trust in the fairness of foreign judicial systems toward Jewish defendants" The 1978 amendment, though, clearly achieved the most undesirable results in the case of Sheinbein.

Having considered the U.S. extradition request in the Sheinbein case in view of the 1978 Amendment, Israel Supreme Court, in a split vote, held that Sheinbein was not extraditable. The Opinion, by Justice Or, with Justice Matsa and Justice Ilan concurring, held that the language of the 1978 amendment was clear regarding non-extradition of Israeli nationals. The question whether there was any logical justification for the protection of nationals who did not reside in Israel and had no real linkage to the State could be relevant, according to Justice Or, in determining the preferred law, but not for interpretation of the clear language of the existing law. He therefore rejected the minority opinion that called for interpreting the term "Israeli national" in the Extradition Law as a national who maintains a real linkage with the State of Israel, a condition that did not apply to Sheinbein.[480]

Maryland State's Attorney Douglas Gansler commented on Israel's high court ruling that Sheinbein could not be extradited to the U.S. because of a law which stated that Israeli citizens must be tried in Israeli courts, even for crimes committed in other countries. "It is an insult to justice that Mr. Sheinbein will be free to walk the streets of Israel under the most likely scenario when he is 33 years of age."

Nearly two years after he fled the U.S., the 19-year-old fugitive admitted that he murdered Alfredo Tello Jr. His lawyers arranged a plea bargain under which arrangement Sheinbein was to serve a 24-

---

480 Abramovsky, A. and J. Edelstein, "The Sheinbein Case and the Israeli-American Extradition Experience: A Need for Compromise," 32 *Vanderbilt Journal of Transnational Law* 305 (1999).

year jail sentence. The plea bargain was subject to approval by the court which accepted it. Of that sentence, he was required to serve at least 16 years in prison.[481].

At one point, a judge read a clause in the charge sheet that accused Sheinbein of having strangled Tello. The judge asked if he admitted to this. Sheinbein answered yes in Hebrew. The proceedings were held in Hebrew, but translated into English for the defendant. The plea bargain came as a surprise. Sheinbein had fought to be tried in Israel, where he fled after he was linked to the killing of Tello, also 19.[482]

After the plea bargain was announced, Maryland State's Attorney Douglas Gansler speculated that Sheinbein had changed his plea because of a "mountain of evidence" against him. "We have a bevy of eyewitnesses," Gansler told CBS News. "There is also a recipe for murder which he actually in his handwriting transcribed describing how he was going to commit this murder right down to the very make of the circular saw that he used to dismember the body. . . . They picked Mr. Tello because he disrespected Mr. Needle in front of one of Mr. Needle's girlfriends and they said, 'let's go ahead and do our practice murder on him,'" Gansler said. "They dismembered him and torched the body beyond recognition."

Tello's family has blasted the plea bargain. "The Tello family feels that justice has not been achieved in this case, that Mr. Sheinbein and his family have continually manipulated the judicial systems of both Israel and the United States," a family statement said.[483]

Israeli authorities said this would be the heaviest sentence ever imposed on a minor and were angry with the American attorneys for revealing the plea bargain before the trial court accepted it.

Sheinbein's own attorney, former Justice Minister David Libai, said he took the case to underscore the need to change the law that prevents Israelis from being extradited. Ironically, once the law was changed, the alteration was not made retroactive. Following the termination of proceedings in the Israeli courts, the Israeli legislature, the Knesset passed two amendments in 1999. It proposed one bill prior

---

481 Kraft, Dina, "Samuel Sheinbein Sentenced to 24 Years", *Washington Post,* 24 October 1999; Matthews, Mark. "Sheinbein sentenced to 24 years from Israeli court", *Baltimore Sun*, 25 October 1999.

482 "Israel Sentences Maryland Man In U.S. Murder", *New York Times,* 25 October 1999.

483 CBS News Staff, "Sheinbein Admits Murder" 24 August 1999, 3:05 PM.

and unrelated to the Sheinbein affair. In 2001 it broadened the criteria for the extradition of Israeli nationals. Accordingly, where the requested suspect possesses both Israeli nationality and domicile at the time of the offense, the extradition will be conditioned upon a guarantee that, if convicted, the Israeli national would be permitted to serve the sentence in Israel. According to the Israeli Report to the United Nations Committee on Counter-terrorism, delivered on 27 December 2001, "[s]uch guarantees are provided in the framework of treaties such as the European Treaty on the Transfer of Sentenced Persons, bilateral agreements or via ad-hoc arrangements to which Israel is a Party," as well as in the Protocol Between the Government of the United States and the Government of the State of Israel Amending the Convention on Extradition signed on December 10, 1962. The Protocol between Israel and the U.S. was signed in Jerusalem on July 6, 2005. The Protocol provides for reciprocal extradition of persons charged with or convicted of an offense, including an attempt or conspiracy to commit an offense, which is punishable under the laws in both Parties by deprivation of liberty for a period of one year or by more severe penalty. The Protocol further amends Article IV of the original 1962 text that provided that the Parties could not decline to extradite a person sought because he was a national of the requested Party. Among additional provisions the Protocol prohibits extradition in cases of double jeopardy and where the statute of limitations in the requested Party's jurisdiction has lapsed.[484]

For his role in assisting his son to flee to a "safe harbor from justice" in Israel, Sheinbein's father, who is now living in Israel, will be prosecuted for obstruction of justice if he ever returns to the United States, Gansler has said. After Samuel fled to Israel, his parents, Sol and Victoria, moved to Israel, where Sol found work as a patent law consultant. Shortly after Samuel's arrest, Sol Sheinbein and his son Robert, who was also present in Israel, were arrested by Israeli police for hampering an investigation and had their passports seized, but were released shortly afterward.[485]

Sheinbein proved to be anything but a model prisoner. He became a prolific complainer against Israeli prison authorities. Although

---

484 https://blogs.loc.gov/law/2014/03/the-sheinbein-saga-and-the-evolution-of-israels-extradition-law/

485 *Attorney Grievance Commission of Maryland v. Sheinbein*, Court of Appeals of Maryland, Court of Appeals of Maryland, Misc. AG No. 37, Sept. Term 2001.

he knew little Hebrew when he fled to Israel he soon became quite proficient if only so that he could complain. His complaints extended from lack of access in jail to TV American movie channels in English, to criticizing the credentials of a newly appointed prison superintendent. The waste of courts' time reviewing his multiple complaints, not to mention his extensive furlough privileges, were disturbing to many Israelis. Many Israelis expressed dismay that Israeli taxpayers would have to fund Sheinbein's incarceration for a crime that had nothing to do with Israel, especially considering that the perpetrator was an American with very few ties to Israel except for being born to a father who held Israeli nationality in addition to his American citizenship.[486]

On 6 February 2014, Sheinbein received a furlough from jail. Although such vacations are usually offered to Israelis in jail, his furloughs had previously been suspended for cause. However, his attorney pleaded his case and the furloughs were restored. On this occasion he proceeded to go to the city of Ramla, where he attempted to obtain a gun from a man he had met online. Before the furlough Sheinbein had arranged a meeting with his internet correspondent to buy the gun. On their way to obtain ammunition, while in a car, Sheinbein stole the gun and fled from the seller with the gun. However, the seller caught and held him until the police arrived and arrested him. Sheinbein was returned to prison. He was confined to his cell over the weekend while an indictment was filed against him because of the incident. The Israel Prison Service decided to move him to another facility

On 23 February 2014, Sheinbein called his attorney, Orit Hayoun, thanked her for her many good efforts, and told her goodbye, but added that she would hear of him shortly. Fearing that he was about to commit suicide, the lawyer called prison authorities and the district attorney's office, urging them to take action. The authorities dismissed her concerns out of hand. Soon after, while being transferred to a different prison, Sheinbein requested that they make a rest-room stop. He immediately pulled out a handgun, and shot three guards, seriously injuring two of them, and then barricaded himself in the rest-room. As a standoff developed, police and other authorities attempted to ne-

486 Levush, Ruth "The Sheinbein Saga and the Evolution of Israel's Extradition Law" Library of Congress, March 20, 20114. https://blogs.loc.gov/law/2014/03/the-sheinbein-saga-and-the-evolution-of-israels-extradition-law/

gotiate with him. The negotiations proved to be fruitless. Tiring of this game, Sheinbein began shooting at police and guards. They returned fire, seriously wounding him. During the gun battle, Sheinbein wounded six officials and one prisoner. The shooting occurred one year before Sheinbein would have been eligible to apply for parole. The Israeli police reported the shooting to CBS News:

> SHARON PRISON, Israel - Israeli special forces raided a prison in central Israel on Sunday, killing one of the country's most notorious inmates after he seized a guard's weapon, shot three guards and barricaded himself inside the compound. Police identified the inmate as Samuel Sheinbein, an American who fled to Israel after committing a gruesome murder in Maryland in 1997 and whose case sparked a high-profile row between the two allies. Police special forces rushed to this prison in central Israel after Sheinbein stole the weapon and shot three guards, wounding two of them seriously. A standoff ensued, with counter-terrorism units dispatched to the scene. The inmate then opened fire again before the forces killed him, police spokesman Micky Rosenfeld said.[487]

The Israeli Prison Service immediately investigated, trying to learn how Sheinbein had acquired the gun, which they believed had to have been smuggled into the prison. Police traced the gun to a resident of central Israel whose gun had been stolen a year before, but never were able to trace the movements thereafter. It was reportedly "the first known case in Israel of an inmate opening fire inside a secured compound". [488] A writer for *Tablet Magazine*,[489] in a wonderful case of gross understatement, called the fact that Sheinbein was able to acquire a gun "the latest of several major IPS screw-ups".[490]

Presently, and despite the changes in Israeli law, should a case similar to the one involving Sheinbein occur, extradition would still be a major problem. In accordance with section 16 of Israel's Extradition Law, Israel cannot extradite a person to a state where that person could face penalty of death, except where Israeli law itself provides

---

487 CBS News, 23 February 2014, 1:03 PM
488 CBS News, 24 February 2014, 12:07 PM
489 Hartman, Ben. "American Murderer Killed in Israeli Prison". *Tablet Magazine*, 24 February 2014.
490 Hartman, Ben, "American-Israeli murderer gunned down in prison after opening fire on officers", Jerusalem Post, 23 February 2014; "U.S.-born killer shoots guards, is slain in Israeli prison", *Los Angeles Times*, February 23, 2014 ; Associated Press, "Samuel Sheinbein killing: American had smuggled gun, Israeli police say", CBS News, February 24, 2014.

for such a penalty, or upon receipt of assurance from the Requesting Party that the person whose extradition is requested will not be executed. The death penalty is authorized under Israeli law only in extremely rare cases, such as in genocide. To date Israel has executed only one person, Adolf Eichmann, for his role in the genocide of Jews in Europe. The 1962 Convention on Extradition between Israel and the U.S. provides, accordingly, that [w]hen the offense for which the extradition is requested is punishable by death under the laws of the requesting Party and the laws of the requested Party do not permit such punishment for that offense, extradition may be refused unless the requesting Party provides such assurances as the requested Party considers sufficient that the death penalty shall not be imposed, or, if imposed, shall not be executed.[491]

Now at at the age of 33, Samuel Sheinbein is dead in what Montgomery County State's Attorney John McCarthy called "death by cop." The last chapter in a bizarre and disturbing crime appears to have been written. But no one can find comfort in that ending. "At the end of the day," says McCarthy, who was originally assigned to the case, "three young men are dead." So also were Israeli guards.[492]

Legal analysts generally speculate that had the Sheinbein affair taken place in 2014, with his not being domiciled in Israel at the time he committed the offense, Samuel Sheinbein would probably have been extradited to the United States. Once brought to America he would most likely have been tried for first degree premeditated murder with aggravating circumstances. Evidence was so overwhelming that he would almost certainly been convicted and then sentenced to life imprisonment without the possibility of parole. And unlike his tine in Israeli jail, he would not have been given furloughs and coddled in his preference for television watching.

Bobby Vesco Found Safe Haven

Bobby Vesco was born in Detroit, Michigan, the son of a Detroit autoworker. He quit engineering school during his early twenties and went to work for an investment company. After a brief period he made an independent $800 stake matching buyers and sellers in the aluminum market, until he eventually acquired a portion of the profits of a floundering aluminum plant. By 1965, he could borrow enough

---

491 Section 2A(1) of Israel's Extradition Law, 5714-1954, as amended,
492 Meyer, Eugene L. "The Killer Next Door," *Bethesda Magazine*, 12 May 2014.

money to acquire International Controls Corporation (ICC). Through aggressively hostile expansions and debt-financed takeovers of other businesses he increased ICC quickly. By 1968 the company owned an airline and several manufacturing plants, and Vesco had shares totaling US$50 million. [493]

During 1970, Vesco began a successful takeover bid for Investors Overseas Service, Ltd. (IOS), a mutual fund investment company with holdings of $1.5 billion. The company was managed by financier Bernard Cornfeld, who trouble with the U. S. Securities and Exchange Commission. When IOS began to experience financial difficulty, and no outside capitalist was willing to get involved, Vesco saw his chance to assume control of the company. Vesco's maneuvers were opposed by Cornfeld and others. While Cornfeld was jailed in Switzerland and Vesco reportedly looted IOS of hundreds of millions of dollars. Many prominent figures in global business, finance. Among the accusations against Vesco were that he parked funds belonging to IOS investors in a series of dummy corporations, one of which had an Amsterdam address that was later associated with Prince Bernhard of the Netherlands. There were allegations that Vesco broke into a Swiss bank vault to obtain shares. These allegations are unproven, as Vesco fled the country and spent the next fifteen years relocating between countries that lacked extradition treaties with the United States.[494]

In February 1973 Vesco used the IOS corporate jet to flee to Costa Rica along with about $200 million worth of IOS's investments. He fled because the U. S. Securities and Exchange Commission opened an investigation into his company, International Controls Corporation. Federal authorities wanted Vesco for securities fraud, drug trafficking and political bribery, according to *The New York Times*. Vesco waged a major legal battle from Costa Rica and the Bahamas in an attempt to maintain control of his ICC stock. With five outstanding indictments for securities fraud awaiting him, Vesco could not return to the United States. It was a hard-fought battle because it was not until 1981 that ICC became free of Vesco's control. Still, ICC payed him nearly $12 million.

Estimates vary widely as to exactly how much financier Bob-

493 https://en.wikipedia.org/wiki/Robert_Vesco
494 Herzog, Arthur, III, *Vesco: From Wall Street to Castro's Cuba The Rise, Fall, and Exile of the King of White Collar Crime*. iUniverse, 2003.

by Vesco was able to steal. Estimates run to more than $224 million, or about $1 billion today, the British newspaper *Guardian* guessed that his take was about $224 million. In any event it was the biggest financial fraud in history at the time. Vesco's legend continued to grow after he left the United States. Vesco managed to evade extradition to the United States for 35 years by choosing to flee to nations that had no extradition treaty with the United States. Reportedly, he also placed bribes in all the right places. In Costa Rica, he poured some $60 million into the country's economy. According to *The New York Times,* then Costa Rican President Jose Figueres was quoted as saying, "I wish more Vescos would come to Costa Rica — we need them."[495]

Eventually Figueres forced Vesco to leave, but only after Vesco made plans to set up a machine gun factory. According to the British news magazine the Economist, on an amazing display of chutzpah he tried to buy half of the island of Barbuda in order to create his own Principality of the Sovereign Order of New Aragon. He had his own airplane, the Silver Phyllis, which featured an on-board sauna and discotheque.

Vesco eventually ended up in Cuba, where he outsmarted himself. Convicted of defrauding investors on that communist island, Vesco spent 13 years in prison for defrauding investors to whom he sold shares in his drug called TX, a supposed cure for AIDS and cancer.[496] Supposedly, Vesco died November 23, 2007, one year before the international community heard the news. Although he was reportedly buried at Colon Cemetery, Havana, there is at least one report that he fled to, and is still living in, the African nation of Sierra Leone.[497]

Illness: Lori Love and His Computer

Lauri Love was born on 14 December 1984, in Stradisall, Suffolk, United Kingdom, a son of Alexander Love, a prison chaplain, and Sirkka-Liisa Love, a Finnish citizen, who also works at the prison. Lauri thus has dual citizenship, British and Finnish. Love ap-

495 Terpil, Frank, "How a CIA spy went rogue to court the world's worst dictators". *The Observer,* 6 March 2016

496 Rohter, R. "Robert Vesco, the Fugitive Financier, Goes on Trial in Cuba on Fraud Charges", *The New York Times.* 2 August 1996

497 Lacey, M. and Kandell, J. "A Last Vanishing Act for Robert Vesco, Fugitive", *New York Times.* May 3, 2008

plied for a Finnish passport, served in the Finnish Army for six months, became a conscientious objector, and finished his obligation to Finland in alternative civilian service. He started college but dropped out three times, citing physical and mental problems. Despite the physical exhaustion he joined Hetherington House Occupation, a left-wing student protest at Glasgow University in 2011.

He is a British activist charged with stealing data from United States government computers including the United States Army, Missile Defense Agency, and NASA via computer intrusion. Specifically, the United States indicted Love in 2013 in the District Court of New Jersey, 2014 in Southern District of New York, and also in Eastern District of Virginia, for allegedly "breaching thousands of computer systems in the United States and elsewhere – including the computer networks of federal agencies – to steal massive quantities of confidential data." He was involved in #OpLastResort, which was a series of online protests against alleged American militarism. On that basis the United States attempted to extradite him from the U. K. to answer these charges.[498]

British authorities held an extradition hearing in June 2016 at the Westminster Magistrates' Court in London. At that time, his father testified that his son is a victim of Asperger syndrome and thus should not be extradited. A psychologist also testified that Love should not be extradited because of his various established disorders, which also include eczema, psychosis, and depression. Further, the psychologist stated that Love told him that he would commit suicide if extradited. The mental health specialist diagnosed Love with Asperger syndrome in 2012 when Love was in his late 20s. Love's father testified that his son was autistic, a condition not identified until he was an adult serving in the Finnish Army.[499] Lauri himself testified concerning his mental and physical health issue.[500]

The crown, for its part, strongly suspect that Love and his attorney had crafted the health issues to avoid extradition. With the encouragement of support groups like the Courage Foundation, Love was able to attract considerable public support for his challenge to ex-

498 https://en.wikipedia.org/wiki/Lauri_Love
499 "Autistic man accused of computer hacking could kill himself if extradited, court is warned" *Daily Telegraph*, 28 June 2016.
500 McGoogan, Cara. "The full story of Lauri Love's fight against extradition". *Daily Telegraph,* 27 June 2016.

tradition.[501]

On 16 September 2016, at Westminster Magistrates' Court a judge ruled that Love could be extradited to the United States. Love's solicitor appealed that ruling, and on 5 February 2018, Lord Chief Justice Lord Burnett and Mr Justice Ouseley, at the High Court, upheld his appeal against extradition. However, the two justices also ruled that it would "not be oppressive [to] prosecute Mr Love in England for the offences."[502]

Working on the advice of the high court the British National Crime Agency (NCA) arrested Love in 2013. He was arrested on 28 October 2013 for alleged offenses under the British Computer Misuse Act. NCA seized Lauri's computers and tried to force him to turn over his encryption keys, but Lauri refused to cooperate and was ultimately released on bail. Nine months later, Lauri's police bail was allowed to expire and the British investigation against him appeared to be closed, although the NCA refused to return six devices that they could not decrypt.[503] For his part, Love took legal action seeking the return of computers seized by the NCA when he was arrested. In May 2016, the Westminster Magistrates' Court ruled that Love did not have to tell the NCA what his passwords, or encryption keys, were. Following dismissal of the case against him, Lauri has become increasingly recognized as an expert on hacking, surveillance and privacy issues and is viewed as a cult hero by the Left, which has dedicated an internet site to him.[504]

Double Jeopardy

The United States had sought to prosecute Adem Yilmaz for giving advice and instructions on military-type training to a man involved in a 2008 suicide bombing in Afghanistan that killed two American soldiers and injured at least 11 others. In addition it charged Yilmaz with participating in Islamic State terroristic attacks on the Afghanistan-Pakistan border. The indictment against Yilmaz, brought in the Southern District of New York and unsealed earlier this week,

---

501 O'Cleirigh, Fiona and Goodwin, Bill, "Lauri Love may be faking mental illness claims lawyer for US". *Computer Weekly*, 29 June 2016.

502 "Hacking suspect wins extradition appeal". *BBC News Online*, 5 February 2018.

503 https://www.computerweekly.com/opinion/Lauri-Love-escaped-extradition-to-the-US-what-does-that-mean-for-future-cases

504 https://freelauri.com/

includes charges of providing material support to a terrorism organization and aiding and abetting military-style training.

Acting in the name of the radical Islamic Jihad Union, he and three others had stockpiled what they thought was highly concentrated hydrogen peroxide, purchased from a chemical supplier, and planned to mix it with other substances to make explosives equivalent to 1,200 pounds of dynamite. German authorities, acting partly on U.S. Army intelligence, had been watching them and covertly replaced the hydrogen peroxide with a diluted substitute that could not have been used to produce a bomb. Germany tried and convicted him for the planned attack. He had been in prison in Germany until October 2018 after his conviction for involvement in a foiled 2007 plot to attack American citizens and facilities in the country, including the U.S. Air Force's Ramstein base.[505]

Germany rejected an American request for the extradition of Adem Yilmaz, a Turkish citizens wanted in the United States on terrorism charges, arguing that there was no other option under German law. Adem Yilmaz, who was indicted under seal in the U.S. in 2015 on charges of participating nearly ten years earlier in attacks on U.S. military forces along the border between Afghanistan and Pakistan. He was convicted of membership in a terrorist organization in Germany in 2010.

The German government argued that to extradite him to face trial in the U.S. on terrorism charges would constitute double jeopardy under German law according to the Frankfurt state court. It might allow extradition if the United States would restrict the charges to crimes not already punished.

Following the Frankfurt court's rejection of the American request last week, Hesse state officials deported Yilmaz to his native Turkey. There was nothing unusual about the deportation of a foreign national who had violated German laws, but the decision angered American officials.

American diplomats filed additional assurances, attempting to address the Frankfurt court's objections to extradition, but the deportation was carried out before those arguments could be considered.

---

505 https://en.wikipedia.org/wiki/2007_bomb_plot_in_Germany; "Communications Intercept Led To Bomb-Plot Arrests". *Los Angeles Times*, 7 September 2007; Purvis, Andrew. "German Plot Signals al-Qaeda Revival". *Time*, 5 September 2007.

Deputy U.S. Secretary of State John Sullivan called a meeting with German Foreign Minister Heiko Maas, who was in Washington to take part in meetings of the coalition fighting against the Islamic State group, to express American displeasure. The Secretary filed a formal complaint in the matter of the deportation, of Adem Yilmaz to Turkey, rather than his extradition to the United States to face justice for his complicity in the murder of two American servicemen.

As it was, upon his arrival back in Turkey, anti-terrorism authorities at Istanbul's Ataturk Airport, detained him on charges relating to incidents there. It was not immediately clear whether he would face charges in Turkey.[506]

Parental Kidnapping

One of the common reasons for which another country requests extradition involves cases of international parental kidnapping. A relatively new crime, parental kidnapping has become more common across international lines. Within a few hours, a parent can take their child away to another country, without the other parent finding out until after the plane has already landed. These cases involve more than a simple custody battle, they may involve cases of international diplomacy.

Parents may take their children out of the country for religious reasons, safety reasons, fear of the other parent or their family, or because they were denied custody. However, even if the parent has a good reason for taking their own child away, they may still be charged with parental kidnapping. It is a federal crime to remove or attempt to remove a child from the United States, or retain a child outside the United States with intent to obstruct another parent's custodial rights.[507]

Some extradition treaties between the U.S. and other countries do not specify parental kidnapping as an extraditable offense. However, the Extradition Treaties Interpretation Act of 1998 authorizes the interpretation of the term kidnapping to include parental abduction. In the past, extradition treaties listed one of the extraditable crimes to be kidnapping, but parental abduction was never considered kidnapping. Today, most extradition treaties include dual criminality provisions which provide for extradition when both parties consider an offense a

---

506 https://www.apnews.com/4c2b098d12084201b83d3825710f0d8e
507 18 U.S.C. § 1204

felony. As a result, the United States included parental abduction in the treaty if the foreign country did so. In response to these findings, the Extradition Treaties Interpretation Act was passed. [508] By authorizing the interpretation of the term "kidnapping" to include parental kidnapping, Congress allowed for a clearer interpretation of extradition law. The Act aimed to rectify extradition law to protect the interests of American children and their parents.[509]

Colin Bower lost his two sons when his ex-wife, Mirvat el Nady, kidnapped the boys and removed them to her native Egypt. That country has never ratified the Hague Convention on the Civil Aspects of Child Abduction, so his remedies have been diplomatic, not legalistic. Bower and Nady were divorced in Massachusetts in 2008, with sole custody being granted to Bower. When he took them to visit their mother, she immediately flew them to Egypt, using forged passports for the boys. Elnady was charged with two counts of kidnapping of a minor and international parental kidnapping. Technically, she is a fugitive from international justice, because she was charged in the United States with kidnapping. Interpol has issued a warrant for her arrest. Egyptian officials apparently know where Nady and the boys are, but refuse to assist because parental abduction is not a crime in Egypt.[510]

In 2000 in Frankfort, Kentucky, Gerardo Serrano's ex-wife kidnapped their son and removed him to her native Poland. A judge in Illinois issued an order that he have custody, but a Polish court issued a competing order in favor of the mother, including a demand that he pay his ex-wife substantial child support. When that order was sent to the Illinois Division of Child Support Services, it was treated like any other order of child support. Since the state determined that Serrano was not paying the the child support to the woman who had kidnapped his child, the state garnished his bank account. Serrano said the state acted hastily in trying to enforce a foreign court's order, which was in conflict with the Cook County judge's ruling, without knowing the details of his case and that his child was kidnapped.[511]

---

508 McKeon, Merritt L. "International Parental Kidnapping: A New Law, a New Solution" *Family Law Quarterly,* 30: 1 (Spring 1996), pp. 235-244.
509 Pub. L. 105-323, title II, Oct. 30, 1998, 112 Stat. 3033 (18 U.S.C. 3181 note)
510   https://www.nationalparentsorganization.org/blog/9682-two-more-tragic-case. See also Szaniszlo, Marie "Whitey Tactics Used in Kidnap Case" *Boston Herald*, 2 December 2011; https://letsfindthem.wordpress.com/tag/mirvat-el-nady/
511 *Southtown Star,* 26 August 2010.

`Bibliography

Abramovsky, A. and J. Edelstein, "The Sheinbein Case and the Israeli-American Extradition Experience: A Need for Compromise," 32 *Vanderbilt Journal of Transnational Law* 305 (1999).

Allain, Jean. 2001, "The jus cogens Nature of Non-refoulement", *International Journal of Refugee Law*, 13: 4 (2001), pp. 533-558.

Arendt, Hannah. *Eichmann in Jerusalem: A Report on the Banality of Evil.* New York: Penguin, 1963.

Assange, Julian and O'Hagan, Andrew. Julian Assange: *The Unauthorised Autobiography.* Canongate, 2011.

Bascomb, Neal. *Hunting Eichmann: How a Band of Survivors and a Young Spy Agency Chased Down the World's Most Notorious Nazi.* Boston; New York: Houghton Mifflin Harcourt, 2009.

Bassiouni, M. Cherif, *International Extradition and World Public Order.* Dobbs Ferry: Oceana, 1974

Beith, Malcolm. *The Last Narco: Inside the Hunt for El Chapo, the World's Most Wanted Drug Lord.* Grove Press, 2010.

Birn, Ruth Bettina (2011). "Fifty Years After: A Critical Look at the Eichmann Trial," *Case Western Reserve Journal of International Law.* 44 (2011), pp. 443–473.

Black, Forrest Revere," Interstate Rendition as Applied to a Person Brought Involuntarily into the Surrendering State," 29 *American Institute of Criminal Law & Criminology* 309 (1938-1939).

Blakesley, Christopher L. "The Evisceration of the Political Offense Exception to Extradition". *Denver Journal of International Law and Policy* (1987).

Bruin, Rene and Wouters, Kees (2003). "Terrorism and the Non-derogability of Non-refoulement". *International Journal of Refugee Law.* 15.1 (2003), pp. 5–29.

Cantrell, Charles L. "The Political Offense Exemption in International Extradition: A Comparison of the United States, Great Britain and the Republic of Ireland". *Marquette Law Review.* 60: 3 (Spring 1977).

Carlisle, Jeffrey J. "Extradition of Government Agents as a Municipal Law

Remedy for State Sponsored Kidnappers," *California Law Review*, 81 (1993), 1541-86.

Chaplin, Oren, "American Justice Across the Ocean? The Case of Samuel Sheinbein". *New England Law Review* (Summer 2001).

Cocastre-Zilgien, André *L'affaire Argoud. Considérations sur les arrestations internationalement irrégulières,* Pédone, 1965; I. L. R. 45: 90-98.

D'Angelo, Ellen F. "Non-Refoulement: The Search for a Consistent Interpretation of Article 33" *Vanderbilt Journal of Transnational Law.* 42: 1 (2009).

Dinges, John. *Our Man in Panama: How General Noriega Used the United States-And Made Millions in Drugs and Arms*. New York: Random House,1990.

Fawcett, J. E. S. "The Eichmann Case," in *The British Yearbook of International Law* (1962) at pp. 181 et seq.

Forde, Michael and Kelly, Kieran. *Extradition Law and Transnational Criminal Procedure*. Roundhall, 4th ed., 2011.

Garcia-Mora, Manuel R. (1957) "Criminal Jurisdiction of a State Over Fugitives Brought From a Foreign Country By Force or Fraud: A Comparative Study," *Indiana Law Journal,* 32 : 4 (1957), Article 1.

Gilboa, Eytan. "The Panama Invasion Revisited: Lessons for the Use of Force in the Post Cold War Era." *Political Science Quarterly*, 110.4 (1995), pp. 539–562.

Goldstein, Shelley. "Extradition and Double Jeopardy" *North Carolina Journal of International Law,* 6:1 (2016).

Gonzalez, Guadalupe and Tienda, Marta, eds. *The Drug Connection in U.S.-Mexican Relations*. San Diego: Bilateral Commission on the Future of U.S.-Mexican Relations, 1989.

Goodwin-Gill, Guy S. "The International Law of Refugee Protection". *The Oxford Handbook of Refugee and Forced Migration Studies*. Oxford University Press, 2014.

Greig, Charlotte. *Evil Serial Killers: In the Minds of Monsters*. New York: Barnes & Noble, 2005.

Haynes, John Earl, and Harvey Klehr. *Venona: Decoding Soviet Espionage in America,* Yale University Press, 1999.

_____. *Early Cold War Spies: The Espionage Trials that Shaped American Politics,* Cambridge University Press, 2006.

Herzog, Arthur, III, *Vesco: From Wall Street to Castro's Cuba The Rise, Fall, and Exile of the King of White Collar Crime.* IUniverse, 2003.

Iraola, Roberto. "The Doctrine of Specialty and Federal Criminal Prosecutions," 43 *Valpariso University Law Review.* 43: 89 (2008). Available at: http://scholar.-valpo.edu/vulr/vol43/iss1/2

Kempe, Frederick. *Divorcing The Dictator America's America's Bungled Affair with Noreiga.* New York: Putnam's, 1990.

Kelly, Michael J. "Cheating Justice by Cheating Death: The Doctrinal Collision for Prosecuting Foreign Terrorists—Passage of *Aut Dedere Aut Judicare* into Customary Law & Refusal to Extradite Based on the Death Penalty". *Arizona Journal of International and Comparative Law,* 20: 491 (2003).

Kumar, Megha. "History and Gender in Savarkar's Nationalist Writings". *Social Scientist.* 34: 11/12 (2006), pp. 33–50.

Legge, Jerome S.,Jr. (2010). "The Karl Linnas Deportation Case, the Office of Special Investigations, and American Ethnic Politics". *Holocaust and Genocide Studies.* Spring. 24 (1): 26–55 (2010).

Levush, Ruth "The Sheinbein Saga and the Evolution of Israel's Extradition-Law" Library of Congress, March 20, 20114.

Lippmann, Matthew. "The Trial of Adolf Eichmann and the Protection of Universal Human Rights under International Law," *Houston Journal of International Law,* 5: 1 (1982), pp. 1–34

Lipstadt, Deborah E. *The Eichmann Trial.* New York: Random House., 2011.

Lowe, A. V. and Warbrick, Colin. "Extraterritorial Jurisdiction and Extradition " *International and Comparative Law Quarterly,* 36: 2 (1987) 398-410.

Lowenfeld, Andreas F. "Kidnapping by Government Order," *American Journal of International Law,* 84: 3 (1990).

_____. "Still More on Kidnapping," *American Journal of International Law,* 85: 4 (1991).

Martinelli, Patricia A. *True Crime Pennsylvania: The State's Most Notorious*

Criminal Cases. Harrisburg: Stackpole Books, 2008.

McKeon, Merritt L. "International Parental Kidnapping: A New Law, a New Solution" *Family Law Quarterly,* 30: 1 (Spring 1996), pp. 235-244.

Mitchell, Greg and Gosztola, Kevin. *Truth and Consequences: The U.S. vs. Bradley Manning*. Sinclair Books, 2012.

Nadelmann, Ethan E. "The DEA in Latin America: Dealing with Institutionalized Corruption," *Journal of Interamerican Studies and World Affairs*, 29: 4 (1987-1988), pp. 1-39.

O'Higgins, Paul, "Disguised Extradition: The Soblen Case," *Modern Law Review,* 27: 521 (1964).

Owens, Gregg, *No Kill, No Thrill: The Shocking True Story of Charles Ng - One of North America's Most Horrific Serial Killers*. Red Deer Press, 2001.

Padmanabhan, , Vijay. "To Transfer or not to Transfer: Identifying and Protecting Relevant Human Rights Interests in Non-Refoulement". *Fordham Law Review,* 80 (2011), pp. 73–123.

Parry, John T. "International Extradition, the Rule of Non-Inquiry, and the Problem of Sovereignty," *Boston University Law Review,* 90 (1973-74), pp. 1973-2073.

"Pirates and Smugglers: Analysis of the Use of Abductions to Bring Drug Traffickers to Trial," *Virginia Journal of International Law*, 32: 233 (1991).

Preuss, Lawrence, "Settlement of the Jacob Kidnapping Case, Switzerland v Germany" *American Journal of International Law,* 30: 1 (1936), pp. 123-24.

_____, "Kidnapping of Fugitives from Justice on Foreign Territory," *American Journal of International Law*, 29: 502 (1935).

Quigley, John, "The Rule of Non-inquiry and the Impact of Human Rights on Extradition Law," *North Carolina Journal of International Law and Commercial Regulation*, 15: 3 (1990), pp. 401-39.

Reid, Herbert O., "Interstate Rendition and Illegal Return of Fugitives". *Howard Law Journal* 2: 76 (1956).

Rubenstein, Alvin Z., George Ginsburgs, and Oles M. Smolansky. *Russia and America : From Rivalry to Reconciliation*. Routledge, 1993.

Schaffer, Rosalie P. "The Inter-Relationship between Public International Law and the Law of South Africa: An Overview," *International and Public Law Quarterly,* 32 (1983) pp. 277-83.

Scott, Austin W., Jr. "Criminal Jurisdiction of a State over a Defendant Based upon Presence Secured by Force or Fraud". *Minnesota Law Review.* 37: 91. (1953).

Scott, James Alexander *The law of interstate rendition erroneously referred to as interstate extradition; a treatise on the arrest and surrender of fugitives from the justice of one state to another; the removal of federal prisoners from one district to another; and the exemption of persons from service of civil process; with an appendix of the statutes of the states and territories on fugitives from justice.* (1917). Reprint by Hardpress, 2013.

Scott, Peter Dale; and Marshall, Jonathan. *Cocaine Politics.* University of California Press, 1988.

Scranton, Margaret E. *The Noriega Years: U.S.-Panamanian Relations, 1981–1990.* Boulder, CO: L. Rienner, 1991.

Selleck, Kathryn, "Jurisdiction after International Kidnapping" A Comparative Study," *Boston College International and Comparative Law Review,* 8: 1 (1985), article 9.

Semmelman, Jacques, "Federal Courts, the Constitution, and the Rule of Non-inquiry in International Extradition Proceedings," *Cornell Law Review,* 76: 6 (1991), pp. 199-1241.

Sharma, Jyotirmaya, "Vinayak Damodar Savarkar" in *Hindutva: Exploring the Idea of Hindu Nationalism.* Penguin Books India; third ed., 2011.

Sherman, M. A. "An Inquiry Regarding The International and Domestic Legal Problems Presented in United States v. Noriega". *The University of Miami Inter-American Law Review,.* 20: 2 (1989), pp. 393–428.

Stangneth, Bettina. *Eichmann Before Jerusalem.* New York: Knopf, 2014.

Stemmet, Andre, "The Influence of Recent Constitutional Developments in South Africa on the Relationship between International Law and Municipal Law," *The International Lawyer,* (Spring 1999), pp. 47-74.

Stefanovska, Vesna, "Right to Life vs. Capital Punishment in Extradition Proceedings: a Legal Aspect" *International Journal of Scientific & Engineering Research,* 7: 1 (January 2016).

Stigall, Dan E. "Ungoverned Spaces, Transnational Crime, and the Prohibition on Extraterritorial Enforcement Jurisdiction in International Law". *Notre Dame Journal of International & Comparative Law* 3: 1 (February 2013).

Sullivan, David B. "Abandoning the Rule of Non-inquiry in International Extradition," *Hastings International and Comparative Law Review,* 15: 1 (1991).

Vang, Jerry, "Limitations of the Customary International Principle of Non-refoulement on Non-party States: Thailand Repatriates the Remaining Hmong-Lao Regardless of International Norms". *Wisconsin International Law Journal.* 32:2 (2014), pp. 355–383.

Wedgwood, Ruth, "The Argument against International Abduction of Criminal Defendants," *American University International Law Review,* 6: 4 (2011), pp 537-69;

Wharton, Francis, *A Treatise on the Conflict of Laws, or Private International Law,* § 941, at 597-98 (Philadelphia 1872) .

Zieck, Marjoleine. *UNHCR and Voluntary Repatriation of Refugees: A Legal Analysis.* The Hague: Martinus Nijhoff Publishers, 1997.